Quiet Water

MASSACHUSETTS, CONNECTICUT, & RHODE ISLAND

Canoe & Kayak Guide

2nd Edition

Alex Wilson & John Hayes

APPALACHIAN MOUNTAIN CLUB BOOKS
BOSTON, MASSACHUSETTS

Front cover photograph: © Nancie Battaglia Photography
Back cover hotographs (l-r): *Angler* and *Man with Child* © David Brownell
                             Kayaker © Diane Meyer,
                             www.dianemeyerphoto.com

Cover Design: Mac & Dent
Book Design: Amy Winchester
Map Design: 2nd Edition—Vanessa Gray; 1st Edition—Nadav Malin
All interior photographs by the authors unless otherwise noted.
Illustrations: © 1993, 2003 Gordon Morrison. All rights reserved.

Quiet Water Massachusetts, Connecticut, & Rhode Island:
Canoe & Kayak Guide, 2nd Edition
© 1993, 2004 Alex Wilson & John Hayes. All rights reserved.

Distributed by The Globe Pequot Press, Inc., Guilford, CT.

Library of Congress Cataloging-in-Publication Data
Wilson, Alex, 1955-
Quiet water Massachusetts, Rhode Island, and Connecticut : canoe and kayak
guide : best paddling lakes, ponds, and rivers for all ages / Alex Wilson and John
Hayes.— 2nd ed.
p. cm.
Rev. ed. of: Appalachian Mountain Club quiet water canoe guide,
Massachusetts, Connecticut, Rhode Island. c1993.
Includes bibliographical references and index.
ISBN 1-929173-49-0 (alk. paper)
1. Canoes and canoeing—Massachusetts—Guidebooks. 2. Canoes and
canoeing—Rhode Island—Guidebooks. 3. Massachusetts—Guidebooks.
5. Rhode Island—Guidebooks. 6. Connecticut—Guidebooks. I. Hayes, John.
II. Wilson, Alex, 1955- Appalachian Mountain Club quiet water canoe guide,
Massachusetts, Connecticut, Rhode Island.
GV776.M4W55 2004
797.1'22'09744—dc22   2003027970

The paper used in this publication meets the minimum requirements of the
American National Standard for Information Science—Permanence of Paper
for Printed Library Materials, ANSI Z39.48—1984. ∞

**Due to changes in conditions,
use of the information in this book
is at the sole risk of the user.**

Printed on recycled paper using soy-based inks.
Printed in the United States of America.

10 9 8 7 6 5 4 3 2   06 07 08

Contents

Locator Maps

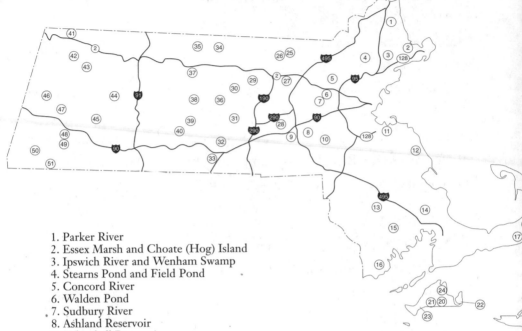

1. Parker River
2. Essex Marsh and Choate (Hog) Island
3. Ipswich River and Wenham Swamp
4. Stearns Pond and Field Pond
5. Concord River
6. Walden Pond
7. Sudbury River
8. Ashland Reservoir
9. Whitehall Reservoir
10. Charles River
11. Weymouth Back River
12. North River
13. Lake Rico and Big Bearhole Pond
14. East Head Pond
15. New Bedford Reservoir
16. Slocums River
17. Herring River and West Reservoir
18. Cliff Pond, Flax Pond, and
    Little Cliff Pond
19. Nauset Marsh and Salt Pond Bay
20. Edgartown Great Pond
21. Tisbury Great Pond
22. Pocha Pond
23. Menemsha Pond and Quitsa Pond
24. Sengekontacket Pond
25. Nashua River
26. Squannacook River
27. Nashua River and the Oxbow National
    Wildlife Refuge
28. Assabet Reservoir
29. Paradise Pond
30. Moosehorn Pond
31. Eames Pond
32. Quaboag Pond, Quaboag River, and
    East Brookfield River

33. East Brimfield Lake, Quinebaug River,
    Holland Pond, and Long Pond
34. Millers River, Otter River, and
    Lake Denison
35. Tully Lake and East Branch Tully River
36. Ware River and East Branch
    Ware River
37. Lake Rohunta
38. Pottapoag Pond and Quabbin
    Reservoir, North End
39. Muddy Brook and Hardwick Pond
40. Swift River
41. Mauserts Pond
42. Bog Pond and Burnett Pond
43. Plainfield Pond
44. Upper Highland Lake
45. Littleville Lake
46. Housatonic River and East Branch
    Housatonic River
47. Buckley Dunton Lake
48. West Branch Farmington River
49. Upper Spectacle Pond
50. Threemile Pond
51. Thousand Acre Swamp and East
    Indies Pond

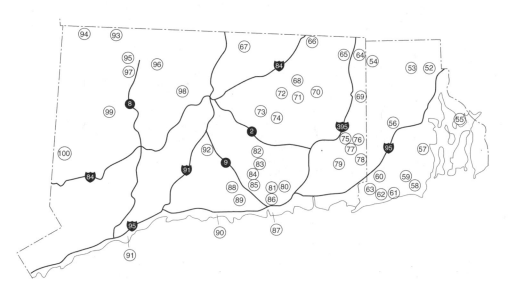

52. Olney Pond
53. Stillwater Reservoir
54. Bowdish Reservoir
55. Brickyard Pond
56. Big River
57. Belleville Pond
58. Tucker Pond
59. Worden Pond and Great Swamp
60. Wood River and Alton Pond
61. Ninigret Pond
62. Watchaug Pond
63. Pawcatuck River
64. Quaddick Reservoir and Stump Pond
65. West Thompson Lake and
    Quinebaug River
66. Mashapaug Lake and Bigelow Pond
67. Somersville Mill Pond and Scantic River
68. Knowlton Pond
69. Ross Marsh Pond
70. Pine Acres Lake
71. Mansfield Hollow Lake
72. Eagleville Pond and Willimantic River
73. Bishop Swamp
74. Mono Pond
75. Hopeville Pond and Pachaug River
76. Pachaug River and Beachdale Pond
77. Glasgo Pond
78. Green Falls Pond

79. Lake of Isles
80. Powers Lake
81. Uncas Pond
82. Babcock Pond
83. Moodus Reservoir
84. Salmon River
85. Selden Creek and Whalebone Creek
86. Lord Cove
87. Great Island Estuary and Wildlife
    Management Area
88. Pattaconk Reservoir
89. Messerschmidt Pond
90. East River
91. Housatonic River and the Charles E.
    Wheeler Wildlife Management Area
92. Mattabesset River, Coginchaug
    River, and the Cromwell Meadows
    Wildlife Management Area
93. Wood Creek Pond
94. Housatonic River
95. Lake Winchester
96. Lake McDonough
97. Burr Pond
98. Farmington River and Pequabuck River
99. Bantam River, Bantam Lake, and
    Little Pond
100. Squantz Pond

Map Legend

⌒	Tents
▲	Lean-to
⊼	Picnic area
Ⓐ	State or federal campground
⚑	Private campground
⌣	Boat access
P	Parking area
⸺	Marsh
☼	Hill

State highway	———	
Paved road	▪-▪-▪-▪	
Graded dirt road	═══	
Rough dirt road	═ ═ ═ ═	
Footpath	········	
River	⇒	arrow indicates direction of flow
Stream	→	

Preface to the Second Edition

The first edition of the *Quiet Water Canoe Guide: Massachusetts, Connecticut, and Rhode Island*, written by Alex Wilson and published in 1993, was the second in a series that now includes guides to New Hampshire/Vermont, Maine, New York, and New Jersey. John Hayes, coauthor with Alex of the New Hampshire/Vermont, Maine, and New York guides, coauthored this second edition.

The first edition enjoyed great success, but lake and pond descriptions inevitably go out of date, necessitating a new edition. Also, we took this opportunity to add new material, nearly doubling the amount of water covered. The first edition contained sixty-four entries covering ninety-three bodies of water; for the second edition, we dropped seven of those entries: Aaron River Reservoir, Long Cove, and Squibnocket Pond because of limited access; Otis Reservoir, Benedict Pond, and Lake Waramaug because of overuse; and Holbrook Pond because its most interesting feature, bryozoan colonies, has been crowded out by invasive exotic weeds.

We added forty-three new entries covering fifty-nine bodies of water. Of the 145 bodies of water in the 100 entries in this second edition, new bodies of water comprise 41 percent of the total. We also added sections to the Quaboag River, Pachaug River, and Wood River entries.

We rechecked all original bodies of water to ensure that new housing developments had not crowded the shores, and we revised directions to reflect new road names. When possible, we tried to avoid bodies of water with substantial development, but for the most part we worried more about the effect of personal watercraft and high-speed boating on safety, the quietwater experience, and the environment. Through publication of this expanded guide, we hope to draw attention to the need to preserve these wonderful places. All quietwater paddlers should work together at local and state levels to bring added protection to these precious resources.

Introduction

If you seek the adrenaline rush of paddling cascading rivers, there are plenty of excellent resources to guide you in that pursuit—but this is not one of them. This guide will help you find peaceful and quiet places. It will lead you to wood ducks swimming through early-morning mists, to old-growth white pine towering above crystal-clear ponds where you can imagine what our forests looked like centuries ago, to the Canada goose's plaintive wail wafting off the water as afternoon settles into dusk.

With quietwater paddling, you can focus on *being* there instead of *getting* there. You don't need a lot of fancy high-tech gear—though a light canoe or kayak makes portaging over or around beaver dams a lot easier. Binoculars and field guides to fauna and flora make up our most important gear.

This guide will not only lead you to a body of water but also describe why you might want to paddle it. Generally, we tried to include places that have abundant wildlife or extensive marshlands or beautiful scenery; many entries have all three. We hope that our research will allow you to spend your valuable time paddling, instead of driving around for hours trying to find elusive accesses. We designed the *AMC Quiet Water Guides* for paddlers of all experience levels, to help you better enjoy our wonderful water resources.

Natural History

Diverse wetlands—among the richest, most readily accessible ecosystems—provide wonderful opportunities to learn about nature. You can visit saltwater tidal marshes; deep, crystal-clear mountain ponds; and unique bog habitats. You can observe hundreds of species of birds; dozens of species of mammals, insects, turtles, and snakes; and literally thousands of plants. Some quite rare species—such as a delicate bog orchid or a family of otters—provide a real treat when you observe them. But even ordinary plants and animals lead to exciting discoveries and can provide hours of enjoyable observation.

We have described a few interesting plants and animals that you might encounter. We interspersed these descriptions—and accompanying pen-and-ink illustrations by Gordon Morrison—throughout. By learning a little more about these species, you will find them all the more fun to observe.

The Selection Process

This guide includes only a small percentage of the lakes, ponds, estuaries, and slow-flowing rivers in Massachusetts, Rhode Island, and Connecticut. In our selection process, we looked for nice scenery; limited development; not too many motorboats and personal watercraft; a varied shoreline with lots of coves and inlets to explore; and interesting plants, animals, and geologic formations.

We include a variety of water types: big lakes and rivers for longer excursions and small, protected ponds and marshes for when you have limited time or when weather conditions preclude paddling big lakes.

The book contains a wide geographic spread of small and large bodies of water from the tristate region. We found these by asking people about the best places to paddle, by consulting DeLorme's *Massachusetts Atlas and Gazetteer* and *Connecticut and Rhode Island Atlas and Gazetteer*, and by systematically searching the U.S. Geological Survey (USGS) 7.5-minute topographic maps of the states. In all, we found 145 suitable bodies of water for inclusion among the 100 entries.

Though we tried hard to include the very best places to paddle, we may have missed some really good locations. If you have suggestions of other lakes and ponds to include, please let us know (Alex Wilson or John Hayes, c/o AMC Books, 5 Joy Street, Boston, MA 02108). Also, please bring to our attention inaccuracies and suggestions for improvements to make future editions better.

Do We Really Want to Tell People about the Best Places? Many people have asked us how we could, in good conscience, tell others about the more remote, pristine places, still unspoiled by too many people. After all, increased visitation would make these places less idyllic. We spent many an hour grappling with this difficult issue as we paddled along.

We believe that by getting more people out enjoying these places—people who value wild, remote areas—support will build for greater protection of these waters. We hope you will help protect some of our most treasured water resources. Policymakers need to hear from low-impact users. Currently, users and manufacturers of motorized watercraft—people who often have the greatest negative impact on these delicate environments—are often the most vocal.

We had hoped that we could report that many of these waters have more protection now than they did when the first edition was published in 1993, and there are some wonderful successes. For example, the town of Charlestown banned personal watercraft on Watchaug Pond—one of the largest bodies of water in Rhode Island. While The Nature Conservancy and land trusts continue to protect more of the shoreline along a few key ponds and lakes, however, most bodies of water suffer from continued development and more high-speed boating. When we next update this guide, we hope to report a lot more progress in protecting these lakes and ponds.

Safety First

We all long for the idyllic paddle on mist-filled, mirror-smooth surfaces of quiet ponds at daybreak. But you can also encounter some quite dangerous conditions. Strong winds can arise quickly, whipping up 2- to 3-foot waves in no time—waves big enough to swamp an open boat. If you capsize in cold water far from shore, hypothermia—a cooling of the body's core that can lead to mental and physical collapse—can set in quickly. If you have just driven a long way to reach a particular lake and find it dangerously windy, choose a more protected body of water, or go hiking instead.

All New England states require each boater to carry a U.S. Coast Guard–approved personal flotation device, or PFD. We recommend that everyone wear PFDs at all times on the water; all three states require children to wear PFDs. With children in the boat, you should wear your PFD so that if the boat capsizes you can help the children better. A foam- or kapok-filled PFD will also keep you warmer in cold water. If you do not normally paddle wearing a PFD, at least don it in windy conditions, when crossing large lakes, or when you may encounter substantial motorboat wakes. It could save your life.

Avoid shallow, marshy waters during waterfowl-hunting season, especially if you see blinds and decoys in the water. For hunting-season dates, check the appropriate fish and game department website:

Massachusetts: www.state.ma.us/dfwele/dfw/dfwrec.htm
Rhode Island: www.state.ri.us/dem/pubs/regs/index.htm#FandW
Connecticut: dep.state.ct.us/burnatr/wildlife/fguide/fgindex.htm

Other safety guidelines include:

- Carry a first-aid kit and know how to use it.
- Get off the water when lightning is occurring. Lightning almost always strikes the highest object in the vicinity, which would be you in a boat out on a lake.
- Stay dry to avoid hypothermia.
- Know what to do if you capsize, and have experience doing it.
- Avoid dehydration by drinking plenty of liquids.
- Avoid areas with a lot of high-speed boating.
- Check the weather forecast before going out.

Paddling with Kids

When canoeing with kids, try to make it fun. If you keep calm, your kids will do better, and you will have a better time. Even though you may be plenty warm from paddling, children can get cold while sitting in the bottom of the boat. Remember that everyone should have PFDs on at all times, and PFDs will help keep children warm. They also need protection from sun and biting insects. Watch for signs of discomfort. On long paddling excursions, set up a cozy place where young children can sleep. After the initial excitement of paddling fades, the gently rolling canoe often puts children to sleep, especially near the end of a long day. Also, for those longer excursions, make sure to bring dry clothes for everyone in a waterproof stuff sack.

Equipment

For quietwater paddling, almost any canoe or sea kayak will do, but avoid high-performance racing or tippy whitewater models. Borrow a boat before buying; selection will be easier with a little experience.

Whether canoe or kayak, look for a model with good initial and good secondary stability. A boat with good initial stability and poor secondary stability will tip slowly, but once it starts it may keep going. The best canoes for lakes and ponds have a keel or shallow-V hull and fairly flat keel line to help track in a straight line, even in a breeze. Kayaks perform extremely well in rough water, particularly if equipped with a foot-operated rudder. To keep from taking on water in rough water, they require a sprayskirt.

If you like out-of-the-way paddling requiring portages, get a Kevlar boat if you can afford it. Kevlar is a strong carbon fiber, somewhat like fiberglass, but much lighter. We paddle a rugged, high-capacity 18-foot,

4-inch Mad River Lamoille canoe that weighs just 60 pounds, a 15-foot, 9-inch Mad River Independence solo canoe that weighs less than 40 pounds, a 14-foot Wenonah Wigeon kayak that weighs 38 pounds, and a 14-foot Wilderness Systems Chaika kayak that weighs 32 pounds. If you plan to go by yourself, consider a sea kayak or a solo canoe, in which you sit (or kneel) close to the center of the boat. You will find paddling a well-designed solo canoe far easier than a two-seater used solo. The touring or sea kayak—with its long, narrow design, low profile to the wind, and two-bladed paddling style—is faster and more efficient to paddle than canoes.

A padded portage yoke in place of the center thwart on a canoe is essential if you plan on much carrying. With unpadded yokes, wear a life vest with padded shoulders. Attach a rope—called a "painter"—to the bow so that you can secure the boat when you stop for lunch, line it up or down a stream, and—if the need ever arises—grab onto it in an emergency. We both have embarrassing stories about not using a painter to secure the boat—wind can cause Kevlar boats to disappear very quickly!

Choose light and comfortable paddles. For canoeing, we use a relatively short (50-inch), bent-shaft paddle handmade in West Danby, New York (Hilltop Paddles). Laminated from various woods, the paddle has a special synthetic tip to protect the blade. Bent-shaft paddles allow more efficient paddling, because the downward force converts more directly into forward thrust. However, straight-shaft paddles also work well. Always carry at least one spare paddle per group, particularly on longer trips, in case a porcupine gets a hold of one.

As mentioned above, the law requires PFDs for everyone in the boat. The best life preserver is U.S. Coast Guard–approved Type I, II, or III. A floating cushion (Type IV) is less effective than a life vest that you wear. A good PFD keeps a person's face above water, even if he or she loses consciousness. Children must wear their PFDs, and they must be the right size so that they will not slip off; adult PFDs are not acceptable for children. Although the law does not require adults to wear PFDs, we strongly recommend that you do so, especially when paddling with children.

You should also bring along a waterproof first-aid kit. The best kit is one that you assemble yourself; make sure that it has bandages or moleskin for blisters, an antihistamine for allergic reactions, sunscreen, an extra hat, a pain reliever, and any special medications that you might require.

On a rainy-day paddle, usually you see more wildlife and fewer boaters.

As for clothing, plan for the unexpected. Even with a sunny-day forecast, a shower can appear by afternoon. On trips of more than a few hours, we bring along rain gear. On longer trips, we also carry extra dry clothes in a waterproof stuff sack. Along with rain coming up unexpectedly, temperatures can drop quickly, especially in spring or fall, making conditions ripe for hypothermia. Lightweight nylon or polypropylene clothing dries more quickly than cotton, and wool still retards heat loss when wet. Remember that heads lose heat faster than torsos—bring a hat.

Paddling Technique

On a quiet pond, does it matter if you use the proper J-stroke, the sweep stroke, the draw, or the reverse J? No. Learning some of these strokes, however, can make a day of paddling more relaxing and enjoyable. We watch lots of novices zigzagging along, frantically switching sides while shouting orders fore and aft. People have told us about marriage counseling sessions devoted to paddling technique.

If you are new to the sport and want to learn canoeing or kayaking techniques, buy a book or participate in a paddling workshop, such as those offered by the Appalachian Mountain Club, equipment retailers, and boat manufacturers. Books we recommend on canoeing are *Basic Essentials Canoeing*, second edition, by Cliff Jacobson (Globe Pequot Press, 1999), and *Basic Essentials Canoe Paddling*, second edition, by Roberts and Salins (Globe Pequot Press, 2000). For kayaking, good books include *The Essential Sea Kayaker*, second edition, by David Seidman (International Marine Publishers, 2000); *Basic Book of Sea Kayaking* by Derek Hutchinson (Globe Pequot Press, 1999); and *Complete Book of Sea Kayaking*, fourth edition, by Derek Hutchinson (Globe Pequot Press, 1995).

Start out on small ponds. Practice paddling into, with, and across the wind. On a warm day close to shore, with your PFD on and others to help out if you encounter difficulties, you might want to practice capsizing. Intentionally tipping your canoe or kayak will give you an idea of how easily it can tip over. Try to get back into the boat when you are away from shore. Getting the water out of a kayak while treading water is impossible without a hand pump; you can have one mounted permanently on your boat, or you can carry a portable one. You should be able to right a canoe with two people, getting most of the water out (keep a bailer fastened to a thwart). Getting back in is another story . . . Good luck!

Public Access

With a few exceptions, we have listed only public access locations; however, private property bounds most bodies of water. Never launch your boat from private land without getting permission first. Do not get out onto or picnic or camp on posted land.

Respect for the Environment

Wetlands are extremely important ecosystems and home to many rare and endangered species. Even low-impact use such as canoeing or kayaking can substantially affect fragile marsh habitat. An unaware paddler can disturb nesting osprey and eagles, rare turtles, and fragile bog orchids. And even a canoe or kayak can carry invasive weeds and zebra mussels from one body of water to another—use care to clean off your boat before you visit other water bodies.

Heavy infestations of the introduced Eurasian water-milfoil have choked many lakes and ponds in the Northeast. Biologists have had limited success controlling the plant with a milfoil-eating insect, but we know of no case where the plant has been eradicated from a body of water. Currently, physical removal costs up to $2,000 per acre. Clearly, trailered boats cause most infestations, as we have noted few infestations in bodies of water that require a hand launch, whereas almost every body of water that we have visited that has a boat ramp has an infestation.

You can go even farther than the old adage, "Take only photographs, leave only footprints." Carry along a trash bag and pick up the leavings of less thoughtful individuals. If each of us does the same, we will enjoy more attractive places to paddle. While motorboaters tend to have a bad reputation when it comes to leaving trash, paddlers should have the opposite reputation—which could come in handy when seeking restrictions on high-impact resource use.

For information on low-impact camping and other uses of fragile habitats, see *Soft Paths: How to Enjoy the Wilderness without Harming It* by Hampton and Cole (Stackpole Books, 1995) or *Ultimate Guide to Backcountry Travel* by Michael Lanza (AMC Books, 1999). Also, visit Leave No Trace—an organization dedicated to teaching people how to have minimal impact on areas they visit—at www.LNT.org, and see page 346 in this book.

Besides reducing our impact on the environment, we can actively work to protect it. Fragile bald eagle, osprey, otter, and other wildlife populations need protection. If we care about preserving these species and their habitats for future generations, we will demand that elected and appointed officials make wildlife preservation and ecosystem protection a higher priority. We can also join conservation organizations—such as the AMC, the Sierra Club, The Nature Conservancy, and many others— so that when these groups speak about preserving the environment, their voices carry the weight of tens of thousands of like-minded members.

How to Use This Book

For each body of water included in this book, we have provided a short description, a map, information on wildlife and habitat, and other useful information.

Maps. We designed the maps and access descriptions in this guide to accompany road maps. If unfamiliar with your destination, you should use a good highway map or the DeLorme Mapping Company's *Massachusetts Atlas and Gazetteer* or *Connecticut and Rhode Island Atlas and Gazetteer*; www.delorme.com. We key each lake to these atlases, which divide each state into 10-inch by 15-inch maps. These detailed, 1:80,000-scale maps for Massachusetts and 1:65,000-scale maps for Connecticut and Rhode Island include most—but not all—boat access locations, road names, campgrounds, parks, and other pertinent information. For more detail and information on topography, marsh areas, and so forth, refer to the 7.5-minute, 1:24,000-scale USGS topographic maps that we list at the beginning of each section.

Area and River Length. We include areas of lakes and ponds and river lengths to allow you to plan your trips better. Choose larger bodies of water and longer rivers when you have a day or more to spend and the weather forecast is good. Under windy conditions, choose smaller bodies of water or small rivers to paddle.

Camping. All three states maintain a network of public campgrounds that charge modest fees. For most entries, we include contact information for nearby public camping areas; sixteen of the 100 entries have on-site public camping facilities. For information on private campgrounds, see the extensive lists in the DeLorme atlases.

Habitat Type. This section describes the type of environment that you will encounter. Most entries include substantial shallow-water marshlands. Some include coastal estuaries. A few include deep, clear-water lakes.

Expect to See. Here we describe the predominant animals and the type of vegetation that you should see.

Take Note. This section mentions whether there is development and whether motors are allowed, as well as whether there are hazards to be avoided.

Getting There. We give directions from the nearest city or major highway to the access site. We provide distances between points, with the cumulative distance given in parentheses.

Happy paddling!

Eastern Massachusetts

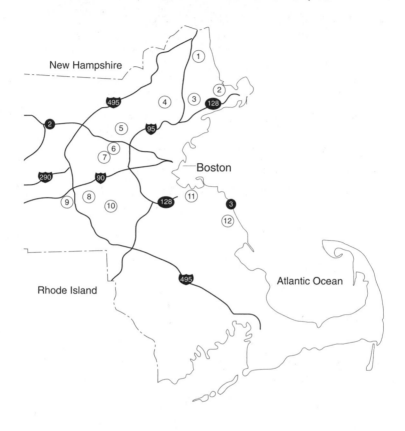

Parker River
Newbury and Rowley, MA

MAPS: Massachusetts Atlas, Map 19
 USGS Quadrangles, Newburyport East and Newburyport West
LENGTH: 8 miles
CAMPING: Salisbury Beach State Reservation, 978-462-4481;
 reservations: 877-422-6762 or www.ReserveAmerica.com
INFORMATION: tide charts, www.maineharbors.com
HABITAT TYPE: tidal estuary, broad marshland, few trees
EXPECT TO SEE: snowy egret, waterfowl, marsh wren, marsh birds
TAKE NOTE: little development; motors allowed

GETTING THERE

Route 1. Access is at the bridge, about 3.0 miles south of the junction of Routes 1 and 1A in Newburyport. We prefer the quieter access on Middle Road.

 Middle Road. From the Parker River bridge on Route 1, go south for 0.9 mile (0.9 mile), and turn right onto Elm Street. Turn right in 0.2 mile (1.1 miles) onto Middle Road; proceed through Governor Dummer Academy to the access on the right in 0.5 mile (1.6 miles).

The Parker River, tidal in this entire stretch, flows through broad, mostly treeless marshland. The 2,000-acre William Forward Wildlife Management Area protects much of the drainage. Upstream of the WMA, near the end of this section, a few houses and a high school loom over the marsh. Though salt marshes have very high biological productivity, they harbor fewer species than many other habitats. We felt fortunate to see red-tailed hawks soar overhead while great blue and green herons and snowy egrets stalked the shallows. Occasional gulls flew over, tail-bobbing spotted sandpipers fled before us, swamp sparrows occasionally flitted into view, and male red-winged blackbirds serenaded us from streamside perches.

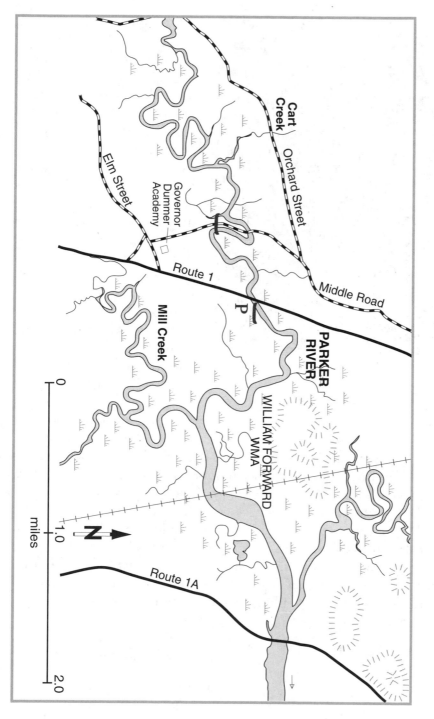

Cart
Creek

Orchard Street

Elm Street

Governor
Dummer
Academy

Route 1

Middle Road

P

Mill Creek

PARKER
RIVER

WILLIAM FORWARD
WMA

Route 1A

0

miles

N

1.0

2.0

Parker River

A marsh wren nest woven from narrow-leaved cattails.

Singing marsh wrens, *Cistothorus palustris*, provided a real treat for us. They prefer nesting in narrow-leaved cattails, which abound upstream of the Middle Road bridge. Males weave several elliptical nests to attract females and use false nests for roosting. Densities of territorial males can reach one per acre. The denser the vegetation, the more successful the rearing of young. Males destroy eggs and nests of other marsh wrens and, indeed, of other bird species. Listen for metallic trilling; with patience and binoculars, you should be able to spot singing males.

We saw large stands of grasses and bulrush. Along with the more common salt marsh grasses *(Spartina alterniflora* and *S. patens)*, we saw the less common *S. pectinata* and *S. cynosuroides*—the latter a quite dramatic species in fall. We also saw salt marsh bulrush *(Scirpus robustus)* and some large stands of wild rice *(Zizania aquatica)*. Beyond the sea of grasses lie stands of red and scarlet oaks, hickory, and white pine.

While in this area, visit Parker River National Wildlife Refuge on Plum Island. Because so many bird-watchers flock to this area, rare species get reported regularly. Over the years we have seen little egret, black swan, king eider, tufted duck, Ross's gull, ivory gull, and yellow-headed blackbird, along with many more common species.

Essex Marsh and Choate (Hog) Island
Essex and Ipswich, MA

MAPS: Massachusetts Atlas, Map 30
   USGS Quadrangles, Ipswich and Rockport
AREA: 3,000 acres
CAMPING: Salisbury Beach State Reservation, 978-462-4481;
   reservations: 877-422-6762 or www.ReserveAmerica.com
INFORMATION: Crane Wildlife Refuge: The Trustees of Reserva-
   tions, 978-356-4351 or www.thetrustees.org; excellent descrip-
   tion in *Nature Walks along the Seacoast* (Appalachian Mountain
   Club Books, 2003); tide charts, www.maineharbors.com
HABITAT TYPE: salt marsh estuary; island hiking; dunes
EXPECT TO SEE: osprey, marsh birds
TAKE NOTE: some development; lots of main-channel boat traffic in summer; watch out for wind, waves, and tides, especially
   near Route 133 bridge and in Castle Neck River; this trip is
   not recommended to novice paddlers

GETTING THERE

From Route 128, Exit 14, go west on Route 133 for 3.3 miles to the access in
Essex, on the right, across from Woodman's Restaurant. After unloading your
boat, park at a small roadside park behind the restaurant.

Essex Marsh and Choate Island, just an hour's drive north of Boston,
offer splendid paddling and hiking. Spend a few hours or an entire day
exploring this interesting area. The Essex and Castle Rivers and several
thousand acres of tidal creek and salt marsh comprise the Essex Marsh.
Castle Neck's sand dunes and beach plum and bayberry highlands protect the marsh from open ocean. In the middle of the marsh, Choate
Island (also known as Hog Island), a rather dramatic drumlin—a glacial
deposit formed by a receding glacier—dominates the local topography.

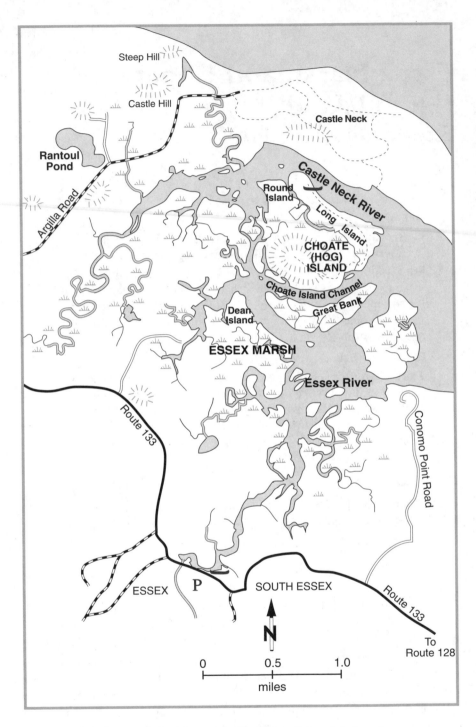

Essex Marsh and Choate (Hog) Island

Rising steeply on the western side to 177 feet, it then slopes gradually east. The Trustees of Reservations owns 697 acres that include Choate Island, Long Island, and three smaller islands, maintaining them as the Crane Wildlife Refuge.

We love paddling here, especially during the week when there's less boat traffic in the main channels. With an 8-foot tide differential and extensive mudflats at low tide, try to avoid paddling at low tide.

Paddling to the left on the Essex River will shortly take you to the Route 133 bridge. While the salt marsh on the inland side of the bridge offers enjoyable exploration, the tidal current under the bridge, where the channel constricts, causes very fast and tricky currents. Use caution!

We prefer paddling to the right to Choate Island, following the widening channel, rounding successive curves, and heading generally north. Look back periodically, noting landmarks that will guide your return. As water levels change, the area can look quite different. We recommend taking along a compass and a photocopy of the map in this book.

To hike on the islands, through the Crane Wildlife Refuge, head for the boat landing on the north side of Long Island. Aim initially for the steeper, western end of Hog Island. As you get near, head off into Choate Island Channel right in front of the island, following it to the right and then around the island, or—if the tide is high enough—continue around the island's west side. The more direct western route suffers from exposed tidal flats on either side of low tide. You can land your boat at Long Island between 8 A.M. and sunset year-round.

You can explore a little way into Lee's Creek between Choate Island and Round Island, but much of this area is protected as bird nesting habitat. The water around Hog Island seemed exceptionally clear, with white sand visible even 10 or 15 feet down. Paddling across to Castle Neck, you can explore the sand dunes and Crane's Beach, also owned by The Trustees of Reservations. If you pull your boat up on Castle Neck, watch for rising tide, and be careful not to damage the fragile dune ecosystem.

You could also explore Castle Neck River and the inlet creeks and channels that reach into the salt marsh, an extremely interesting ecosystem dominated by saltwater cordgrass (*Spartina alterniflora*) and salt-meadow grass (*S. patens*). At high tide you can explore deeply into the little side creeks and look out over thousands of acres of *Spartina*. At low tide you will see mussels clinging to the sod banks, fiddler crabs, perhaps horseshoe crabs, and clumps of seaweed clinging to rocks. On the mudflats, keep an eye out for various sandpipers and gulls. You should also see osprey and many other bird species here, especially during migration.

From the south, Choate (Hog) Island's distinct profile rises above the salt marsh.

Wind, blowing across a fairly broad expanse of water and low salt marsh, can present even more of a problem than tidal currents, generating sizable waves. Wear your PFD when paddling here; novice paddlers should avoid this area.

Choate Island. A wonderful trail extends southeast from the Long Island dock, then across to Choate Island. Maintained by The Trustees of Reservations, the trail takes you past a large barn on Long Island, a newer Cape-style cottage, and the original Choate House on the main island. Thomas Choate built the house, a beautiful example of early-eighteenth-century architecture, between 1725 and 1740. From Choate House, the trail extends uphill to the island's peak, passing through the oddly out-of-place 95-acre spruce forest planted in the 1930s by Richard Crane, the Chicago plumbing magnate, who purchased the island and much of the surrounding land in the early 1900s.

Until recently the Crane Wildlife Refuge hosted a large deer population, typically numbering from fifty to seventy-five. With no hunting and native predators long gone, the deer became quite tame. Since the mid-1980s, however, Lyme disease, borne by deer ticks, has become a major problem on isolated islands such as this. To reduce the deer population in an effort to control deer ticks, the refuge has permitted limited hunting in recent years; numbers have decreased, and deer have become much more wary of humans.

～3～

Ipswich River and Wenham Swamp

Hamilton, Topsfield, and Wenham, MA

MAPS: Massachusetts Atlas, Maps 29 and 30
  USGS Quadrangles, Ipswich and Salem
LENGTH: 7 miles
CAMPING: Perkins Island, accessible only by boat; reservations:
  Massachusetts Audubon Society, 978-887-9264
HABITAT TYPE: slow, meandering river through vast marshland;
  some islands; overhanging trees and vines
EXPECT TO SEE: muskrat, great egret, waterfowl, marsh birds,
  aquatic vegetation, varied shrubs and trees
TAKE NOTE: no development; no motors

GETTING THERE

Route 97. From the junction of Routes 1 and 97 in Topsfield, go south on Route 97 for 0.8 mile to the access on the right.

Asbury Street. From the junction of Route 1 and Ipswich Road, go east on Ipswich Road for 1.2 miles (1.2 miles), and turn right onto Asbury Street. Access is by the bridge in 0.2 mile (1.4 miles). We do not recommend this access because of limited parking and because you can't get your car off the road completely.

Ipswich Road. From the junction of Asbury Street and Ipswich Road, take Ipswich Road east for 0.4 mile to the access on the right. This and the Asbury Street access are part of Bradley Palmer State Park.

We love paddling here, following the Ipswich River's narrow twists and turns as it meanders through vast, tree-filled Wenham Swamp. Silver maple dominates the shoreline, interspersed with large swamp white oak, willow, red maple, cherry, and white pine. Trees reach out over the water, lending a closed-in, protected feeling. The section included here courses for 7 miles, which could easily require a full day to paddle,

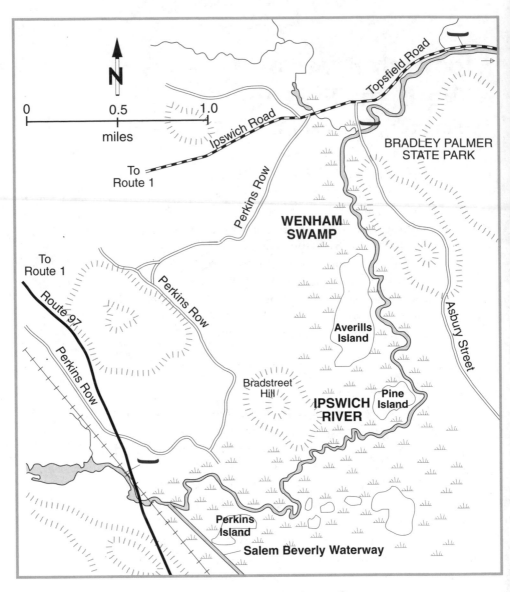

Ipswich River and Wenham Swamp

A great egret stalks the shallows.

especially if you explore side channels and hidden coves and stop for a picnic lunch.

We especially enjoyed Perkins Island—where you can camp with Mass Audubon permission—with its huge straight-trunked trees. Its relatively clear understory stands in stark contrast to the brushy banks and encroaching vegetation along most of the streambed. Prominent shrubs and vines include dogwood, wild grape, arrowwood, and poison ivy. Royal and sensitive fern share the banks with cardinal flower, while patches of water celery and pondweed undulate in the gentle current.

Damselflies and painted turtles sunned on the many deadfalls, and the constant presence of flitting songbirds held our attention for much of the way. We paddled right up to a rather unconcerned great egret and found a couple of cormorants fishing in one of the more open areas. Paddling back to the Route 97 access, retracing our steps, we saw the swamp from a new perspective and continued to glimpse new things. We hated to leave this wonderful spot and vowed to return soon . . . and often.

~4~
Stearns Pond and Field Pond
Andover and North Andover, MA

MAPS: Massachusetts Atlas, Map 29
 USGS Quadrangle, Reading
AREA: Stearns Pond, 41 acres;
 Field Pond, 59 acres
CAMPING: Harold Parker State Forest, 978-686-3391;
 reservations: 877-422-6762 or www.ReserveAmerica.com
HABITAT TYPE: shallow, marshy ponds; hiking trails
EXPECT TO SEE: Canada goose, ducks, typical marsh birds
TAKE NOTE: no development; no motors

GETTING THERE

From the North. From Lawrence, take Route 114 south. When Routes 114 and 125 split, continue on Route 114 south for 3.8 miles (3.8 miles) to the marked entrance to Harold Parker State Forest on the right. Stearns Pond access is on the left in 0.8 mile (4.6 miles). To get to Field Pond, continue on for 0.3 mile (4.9 miles) to the T at Middleton Road, turn right, and go 1.1 miles (6.0 miles) to the stop sign at Jenkins Road. Turn left onto Jenkins Road, go 0.8 mile (6.8 miles), and turn right onto Harold Parker Road. The access is on the left in 1.2 miles (8.0 miles).

From the South. From I-93, Exit 41, go north on Route 125 for 2.6 miles (2.6 miles) to Gould Road and the state forest entrance. Take a shallow right onto Harold Parker Road (a hard right leads to Gould Road). Field Pond is on the right in 0.6 mile (3.2 miles). To get to Stearns Pond, continue on Harold Parker Road for 1.2 miles (4.4 miles) to the stop sign, and turn left onto Jenkins Road. Go 0.8 mile (5.2 miles) on Jenkins Road, turn right onto Middleton Road, go 1.1 miles (6.3 miles), and turn left onto Harold Parker Road. Access is on the right in 0.3 mile (6.6 miles).

From Salem. Go north on Route 114 for 3.4 miles past the intersection with Route 62 in Middleton to the state forest entrance on the left, and follow directions for From the North.

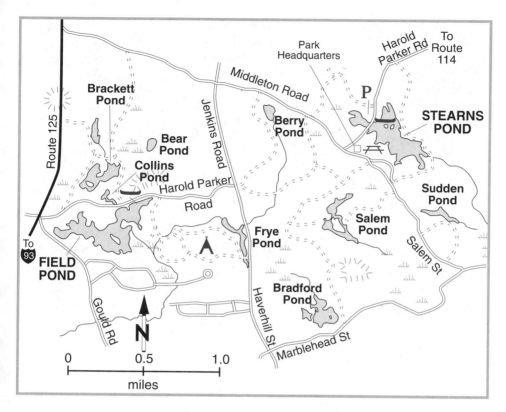

Stearns Pond and Field Pond

A collection of small ponds in Harold Parker State Forest, half an hour north of Boston, provides opportunity for very relaxing quietwater paddling. Of the eleven ponds in the forest, we include the two largest, Stearns Pond and Field Pond.

Both ponds have highly varied shorelines—full of coves, inlets, and islands—so despite their small sizes, you can do a surprising amount of exploration. White pine, red and sugar maples, red, white, and scarlet oaks, and gray birch cloak the hillsides. Sweet pepperbush, highbush blueberry, winterberry, sheep laurel, and other shrubs form a dense tangle for most of the shoreline, but intermittent patches of needle-carpeted forest floor allow you to stretch your legs or enjoy a picnic lunch.

Floating pond vegetation dominates the surface, particularly on Stearns Pond, and bur-reed, purple loosestrife, and cattail occur in the

Puffy, ball-like flowers dot the buttonbush, a shrub that can withstand root immersion for short periods of time.

marshy spots. Bladderwort and other submerged plants provide hiding places for largemouth bass. Mossy hillocks of tree stumps remain from years ago when dams raised water levels. Look for small, carnivorous sundews amid the sphagnum moss on these stumps. Along the shallow, sandy shores, look for freshwater mussel shells left behind by the area's industrious raccoons. The forest's vernal pools also provide habitat for rare blue-spotted salamanders *(Ambystoma laterale)*.

The 3,500-acre state forest provides plenty of opportunity for exploring, especially if you don't mind a small portage. You can paddle any of the ponds as long as you park off the pavement. You can put in across the road from Field Pond into Collins Pond, for example, paddle to the north end, and then carry over to Brackett Pond. Getting to Salem Pond, the most remote, requires a considerable carry. To explore these areas, use the Harold Parker State Forest Trail Map, which shows the forest's network of trails and unpaved roads, most closed to vehicles.

5

Concord River
Bedford, Billerica, Carlisle, and Concord, MA

MAPS: Massachusetts Atlas, Maps 28 and 40
  USGS Quadrangles, Billerica and Maynard

LENGTH: 6.5 miles

CAMPING: Harold Parker State Forest, 978-686-3391;
  reservations: 877-422-6762 or www.ReserveAmerica.com

INFORMATION: *The Concord, Sudbury and Assabet Rivers* by Ron
  McAdow (Bliss Publishing, 1990); Great Meadows National
  Wildlife Refuge, 978-443-4661

HABITAT TYPE: slow-flowing river through wildlife refuge;
  shrubby marshlands

EXPECT TO SEE: waterfowl, marsh birds, aquatic vegetation
  including American lotus, varied shrubs

TAKE NOTE: limited development; motors allowed,
  10 MPH speed limit

___

GETTING THERE

From Route 62 in Concord, go north on Lowell Road for 0.4 mile to the
access on the southeast side of the bridge.

From the junction of Routes 4, 62, and 225, go northwest on Route 225
for 1.4 miles to the access on the northeast side of the bridge.

___

The Concord River flows generally north with imperceptible current
from the confluence of the Assabet and Sudbury Rivers in Concord
until it reaches Lowell and the Merrimack River. We include here a
6.5-mile section that flows through the Great Meadows National
Wildlife Refuge. Thoreau wrote about his travels on the Concord in
1839 in *A Week on the Concord and Merrimack Rivers*. This historic area
includes the Old North Bridge, about which Emerson penned:

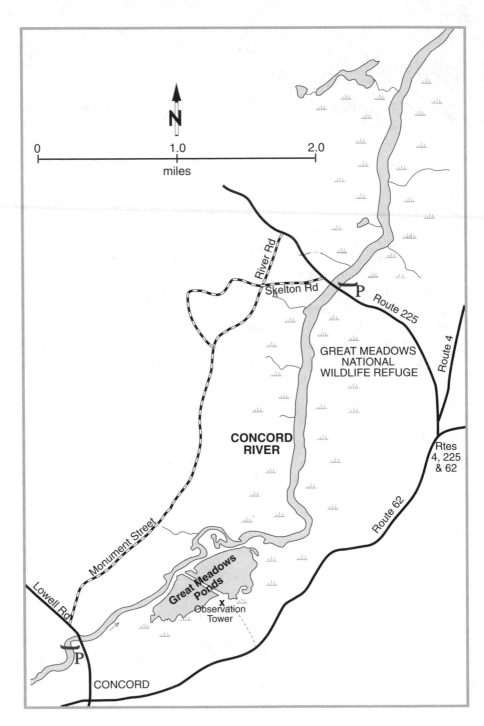

Concord River

By the rude bridge that arched the flood,
Their flag to April's breeze unfurled,
Here once the embattled farmers stood,
And fired the shot heard round the world.

Motorboats ply this section of the river but must comply with a 10-mile-per-hour speed limit. Paddling here on a June weekend, we saw more canoes and kayaks than motorboats. Because of the narrowness of the wildlife refuge on the river's west side, you will see a few large houses perched on large lots above the riverbank, but they do not impinge much on this mostly undeveloped section of river.

High plant diversity characterizes this area, including American lotus *(Nelumbo lutea)*, with its enormous yellow flowers, found in impoundments within the wildlife refuge. This unusual waterlily is found only in a few New England locations. Dominant plants along the shrubby shoreline include buttonbush, smartweed, silver maple, pickerelweed, and invasive purple loosestrife. We also noticed patches of Eurasian water-milfoil and water chestnut. Towering oaks and white pine occur on higher ground. Common yellowthroats, white-throated sparrows, eastern kingbirds, grackles, and yellow warblers called from the underbrush, while crows, red-eyed vireos, chickadees, and robins called from the treetops. Tree swallows fed their nearly fully fledged young on a bare branch overhanging the river.

6

Walden Pond
Concord, MA

MAPS: Massachusetts Atlas, Map 40
USGS Quadrangle, Maynard
AREA: 61 acres
INFORMATION: Walden Pond State Reservation, 978-369-3254
HABITAT TYPE: historic, glacial, kettle-hole pond; hiking trails
EXPECT TO SEE: many hikers, swimmers, boaters
TAKE NOTE: recreation area development only; no motors

GETTING THERE

From the West. Take Route 2 east for 3.5 miles (3.5 miles) past the rotary in Concord, and turn right (south) onto Route 126 at the stoplight. Access is on the right in 0.5 mile (4.0 miles).

From the East. Take Route 2 west for about 4.5 miles past I-95 (Route 128), and turn left onto Route 126 at the stoplight. Access is on the right 0.5 mile past the stoplight.

Walden Pond has come a long way since the first edition of this book. In the intervening ten years, a major revegetation effort has added tens of thousands of new native plants, restoring the shoreline and nearby trails to a condition not seen in seventy-five years.

We include the pond primarily for its historical significance. Simply paddling the same water that Thoreau and Emerson (two of the founders of the environmental movement) knew so well can give you—well, we have to say it—a transcendental experience. Henry David Thoreau lived at Walden Pond, on land owned by Ralph Waldo Emerson, from July 4, 1845, until September 1847, and he later reflected on the experience in *Walden*, published in 1854.

At the time Thoreau lived here, Walden Pond's woods were among the last in the Concord area not cleared for farming. He built a small one-room cabin near the pond's northern tip and spent his days

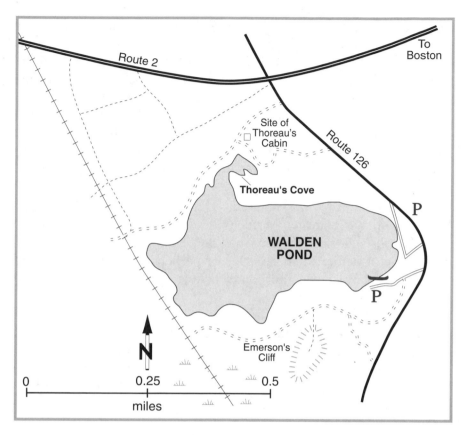

Walden Pond

studying natural history, gardening, reading, writing, and entertaining guests. His writing career began here, penning *A Week on the Concord and Merrimack Rivers*.

Society's destruction of forests deeply affected Thoreau: "When I first paddled a boat on Walden it was completely surrounded by thick and lofty pine and oak woods . . . but since I left those shores, the woodcutters have still further laid them waste." To compensate, Thoreau planted 400 white pine, but the great hurricane of 1938 knocked them down; look for the few remaining stumps above the house site.

When Thoreau lived here, loons occasionally visited the pond, but they disappeared, pushed away by encroaching civilization and a lack of fish. (Today, loons nest on only four bodies of water in Massachusetts, all public water supplies and off-limits to boating.) In the twentieth century Walden became far more crowded than Thoreau could have imagined, in part from the fame he himself had given to the pond. In the early 1900s as many as 2,000 tourists visited the pond per day. By the summer of 1935, after an 80-acre parcel of land around the pond had been granted to the commonwealth as a public park, as many as 485,000 people visited the pond each summer, with up to 25,000 visitors on a single Sunday. Today visitors number 600,000 annually, with folks turned away on warm summer afternoons when the park reaches capacity.

Since 1975, the Massachusetts Department of Environmental Management has managed Walden Pond and worked to restore its eroded banks and trails. If your schedule permits, come midweek after Labor Day or before Memorial Day or perhaps on a drizzly day that will help you reflect on the pond's historic past as you paddle the deserted shores.

Walden Pond, a "kettle hole," formed 12,000 years ago when receding glaciers left behind a large chunk of ice buried in glacial till. Melting ice created a 100-foot-deep, sandy-bottomed pond, which provides superb swimming. The absence of any major inlet streams keeps Walden Pond relatively sterile, though; without stocking, it would provide little in the way of fishing.

7

Sudbury River
Concord, Lincoln, Sudbury, and Wayland, MA

MAPS: Massachusetts Atlas, Map 40
    USGS Quadrangles, Framingham and Maynard

LENGTH: 10.6 miles

INFORMATION: *The Concord, Sudbury and Assabet Rivers* by Ron McAdow (Bliss Publishing, 1990)

HABITAT TYPE: slow-flowing river through wildlife refuge; broad, shrubby marshlands

EXPECT TO SEE: osprey, waterfowl, marsh birds, aquatic vegetation, varied shrubs

TAKE NOTE: some development; motors allowed, 10 MPH speed limit

---

GETTING THERE

Access points are given in order, starting upstream (south end).

Pelham Island Road. From the junction of Routes 20, 27, and 126 in Wayland, take Route 20 west. Take an immediate diagonal left onto Pelham Island Road. Go 0.4 mile; park along the bridge; launch from the northwest side.

Route 20 (Boston Post Road). From the junction of Routes 20, 27, and 126, take Route 20 west for 0.7 mile; access is on the right just before the bridge.

River Road. From the junction of Routes 20, 27, and 126, take Route 27 north for 1.3 miles; turn left onto River Road just after the bridge; access is immediately on the left.

Route 27 (Old Sudbury Road). From the junction of Routes 20, 27, and 126, take Route 27 north for 1.3 miles; access is on the right before the bridge.

Sherman Bridge. From the junction of Routes 117 and 126 in Lincoln, take Route 126 south for 1.5 miles (1.5 miles); turn right onto Sherman Bridge Road; access is on either side in 0.7 mile (2.2 miles).

Route 117 (South Great Road). From the junction of Routes 117 and 126, take Route 117 west for 1.1 miles; access is on the right before the bridge.

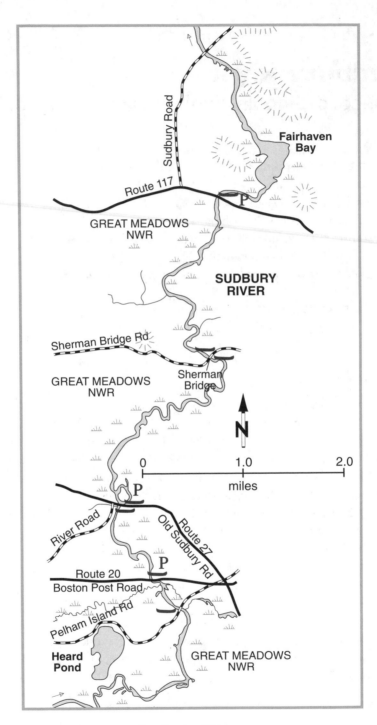

Sudbury River

A mechanical harvester prepares to unload a few thousand pounds of water chestnuts, a very destructive invasive plant.

This section of the Sudbury River from Heard Pond downstream to Sudbury Road offers wonderful paddling through broad expanses of the Great Meadows National Wildlife Refuge. In another 2.4 miles downstream, the Sudbury joins the Assabet to form the Concord River. Like the Concord, which also flows through Great Meadows NWR, you can paddle the Sudbury both directions through the lazy current. The Sudbury lacks the breadth of the Concord but has broader surrounding meadows, filled with low-growing grasses and other marsh plants.

At times of high water, you can paddle up the Heard Pond outlet and explore the prime birding habitat of this small pond and the surrounding marshes and woods (part conservation lands, part Great Meadows NWR). At the other end of this section of the Sudbury, in Fairhaven Bay, look for osprey fishing alongside the human anglers. In between, you can spend hours paddling along, enjoying the surrounding marshlands with their abundant birdlife.

Look for buttonbush, with its spherical white flowers and seedheads, growing along the banks and in the water. Purple loosestrife, an introduced species, grows on slightly higher ground. We found small patches of water clover—aptly named *Marsilea quadrifolia*—an aquatic fern introduced into New England from Europe, along with larger patches of water chestnut, *Trapa natans*, another alien and far more destructive species. When we paddled here, the towns of Lincoln and Concord were harvesting truckloads of water chestnut from Fairhaven Bay, using a huge floating harvesting machine.

The birds, however, impressed us most as they called from their streamside perches. Bobolink, white-throated and song sparrows, barn and tree swallows, wood duck, eastern kingbird, red-winged blackbird, grackle, tufted titmouse, common yellowthroat, yellow warbler, chickadee, cedar waxwing, mourning dove, killdeer, catbird, and cardinal all made appearances.

— 8 —

Ashland Reservoir
Ashland, MA

MAPS: Massachusetts Atlas, Map 51
　USGS Quadrangle, Medfield
AREA: 157 acres
INFORMATION: Ashland State Park, 508-435-4303
HABITAT TYPE: deep reservoir; wooded shoreline
EXPECT TO SEE: mallards, mixed deciduous-conifer shoreline
TAKE NOTE: little development; motors allowed up to 10 HP

GETTING THERE

From I-495, Exit 21A, take West Main Street/Hopkinton Road northeast, joining Route 135. From the junction of Routes 85 and 135, continue northeast on Route 135 for 3.8 miles (3.8 miles) to the stoplight at Main Street. Turn right onto Main Street, go 0.7 mile (4.5 miles), and veer right onto Chestnut Street at the stoplight. Go south on Chestnut Street for 1.3 miles (5.8 miles), and just past the Western Conference Center of Northeastern University, turn right onto South Street (unmarked). Go 0.4 mile (6.2 miles) on South Street, and turn right onto the access road.

Ashland Reservoir, popular with canoers and kayakers, provides a great spot for a quiet morning or afternoon paddle. With a largely undeveloped shoreline, a 10-mile-per-hour limit for motors, and attractive woods surrounding the reservoir, Ashland offers some of the best paddling within the I-495 loop. A little more than 1 mile long and about 0.25 mile wide, the reservoir seems quite deep, with little aquatic vegetation. Ashland State Park, located at the north end off Route 135, offers picnic and swim areas, hiking trails, and a boat launch (open seasonally).

　　Paddling north from the south-end access, the reservoir quickly opens up, with some deep coves on the west shore. The west shore—with more variation and no development—provides more interesting

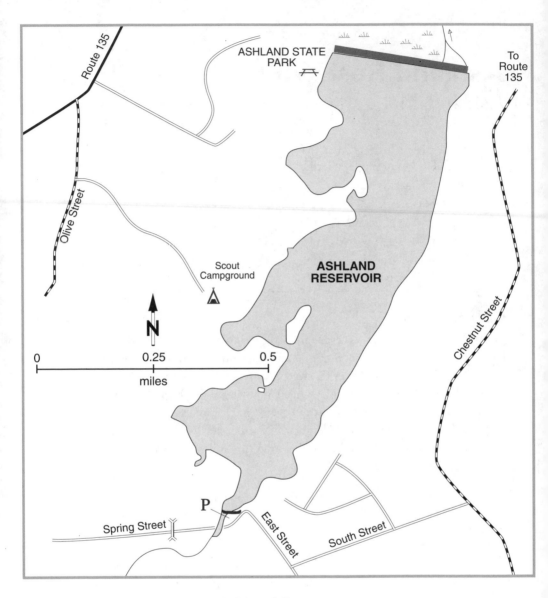

Ashland Reservoir

Mallards, a frequent sight on Ashland Reservoir, take a break from feeding along the shoreline.

paddling than the east shore. Red oak and white pine dominate the heavily wooded shoreline, but you will also see red maple, American chestnut, scarlet and white oaks, gray and black birches, sassafras, black gum, and pitch pine. Shrubs—sweet pepperbush, alder, blueberry, and winterberry—grow densely along the shore. During a mid-September paddle, we found some edible grapes overhanging the water along the east shore.

In places you will see numerous shallow depressions in the sand a foot or two in diameter. Spawning sunfish keep these locations free of debris and organic matter. During summer, adult males valiantly guard these depressions, fanning the eggs that their mates deposited to provide good aeration. Along with lots of sunfish, Ashland Reservoir harbors healthy populations of largemouth bass, yellow perch, and stocked rainbow trout.

9

Whitehall Reservoir
Hopkinton, MA

MAPS: Massachusetts Atlas, Map 51
USGS Quadrangle, Milford
AREA: 601 acres
HABITAT TYPE: reservoir; many islands and protected bays
EXPECT TO SEE: mixed deciduous-conifer shorelines; some
islands with Atlantic white cedar, spruce, tamarack
TAKE NOTE: little development; motors allowed,
12 MPH limit

GETTING THERE

From I-495, Exit 21, take West Main Street/Hopkinton Road northeast for
about a mile to the stoplight at the junction with Route 135 (Wood Street).
Turn left, and go 2.7 miles to the access on the left.

Whitehall Reservoir at one time served as a water supply for areas west
of Boston, but with Quabbin Reservoir's creation in 1939, drinking
water from Whitehall was no longer needed, and the area eventually
was turned into a state park. Its years of restricted access mean great
boating today. The park encompasses the reservoir's entire shoreline
but allows homeowners to erect small docks. From the water, the reservoir feels undeveloped and wild.

The highly varied shoreline includes numerous deep coves and
dozens of wonderful islands to explore. A few marshy areas occur
along the mainly heavily wooded shoreline. The open and inviting
woods invite picnicking. Mixed deciduous trees and conifers, typical of
southern Massachusetts, along with mountain laurel and highbush
blueberry, grow along the shore. Near the center of the reservoir on
the west side, a fantastic grouping of islands sports far different vegetation, however, including Atlantic white cedar, tamarack, and black
spruce—trees you would expect to see much farther north. On a quiet

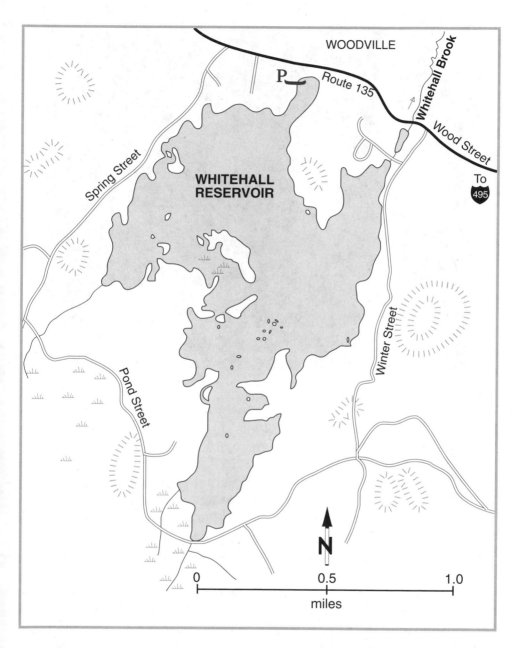

WOODVILLE

P

Route 135

Whitehall Brook

Wood Street

To 495

WHITEHALL RESERVOIR

Spring Street

Winter Street

Pond Street

N

0   0.5   1.0
miles

Whitehall Reservoir

Mountain laurel blooms in profusion in mid-June.

weekday morning, weaving in and out of these almost magical islands and the channels that cut through them, the rest of the world can seem pretty far away.

While the wetness of the islands near the reservoir's center preclude exploration on foot, the higher islands on the reservoir's north end present a perfect place for a picnic or blueberry-picking excursion. Also, near the dam at the northeastern tip, some gorgeous open woodlands—tall white pine with a thick carpet of pine needles underfoot—invite exploration.

While Whitehall Reservoir's 575 acres offer some great paddling for a half day or more, we would avoid it on busy summer weekends. Motorboats that routinely ignore the 12-mile-per-hour speed limit can make paddling unpleasant at times; water-skiing and personal watercraft are prohibited.

10

Charles River

Dover, Medford, Millis, Natick, and Sherborn, MA

MAPS: Massachusetts Atlas, Maps 40 and 52
  USGS Quadrangles, Framingham and Medfield
LENGTH: 13.4 miles
INFORMATION: *The Charles River* by Ron McAdow (Bliss
  Publishing, 1992); The Trustees of Reservations, 508-785-0339
  or www.thetrustees.org; Massachusetts Audubon Society,
  508-655-2296 or www.massaudubon.org
HABITAT TYPE: meandering, slow-flowing river through mostly
  preserved land; marshlands
EXPECT TO SEE: red-tailed hawk, great horned owl, waterfowl,
  marsh birds, warblers, muskrat, swamp rose, varied shrubs
  and trees
TAKE NOTE: limited development; too shallow for motors

GETTING THERE

Access points are given in order, starting upstream (south end).

Route 115. Use only for a one-way trip downstream. From the junction of Routes 109 and 115 in Millis, go south on Route 115 for 1.8 miles. Access is just over the bridge on the left.

Forest Road. From the junction of Routes 109 and 115, go east on Route 109 for 0.7 mile (0.7 mile), and turn right onto Village Street. Take the first left onto Birch Street, followed by a left onto Forest Road (1.5 miles). Park on either side of the bridge in 0.7 mile (2.2 miles).

Dwight Street. From the junction of Routes 109 and 115, go east on Route 109 for 1.8 miles (1.8 miles), and turn right onto Dwight Street. Access is on the right in 0.3 mile (2.1 miles).

West Street. From the junction of Routes 109 and 115, go east on Route 109 for 1.1 miles (1.1 miles), and turn left onto Dover Road (which turns into West Street). Turn left in 1.1 miles (2.2 miles), just after crossing the bridge, at the sign for the waste treatment plant; access is immediately on the left.

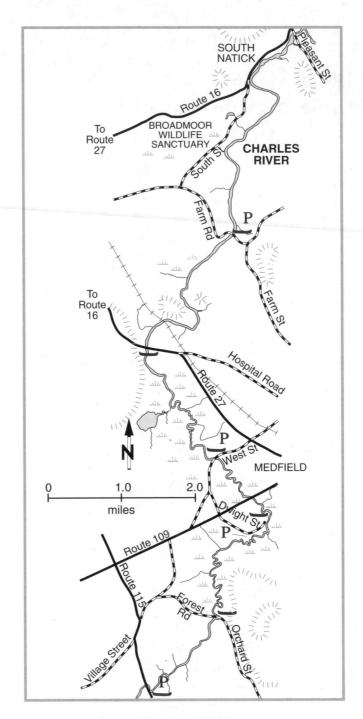

SOUTH
NATICK

Pleasant St

Route 16

To
Route
27

BROADMOOR
WILDLIFE
SANCTUARY

South St

**CHARLES
RIVER**

Farm Rd

P

Farm St

To
Route
16

Hospital Road

Route 27

N

P

West St

MEDFIELD

0   1.0   2.0
miles

Dwight St

P

Route 109

Route 115

P

Forest
Rd

Village Street

Orchard St

Charles River

Route 27. From the junction of Routes 27 and 115, go south on Route 27 for 0.3 mile to the access on the right.

Farm Road. From Sherborn, go south on Routes 16 and 27, bear left onto Route 27 at the Y, and turn left in 0.2 mile (0.2 mile) onto Farm Road. Access is on the left, just across the bridge, in 2.5 miles (2.7 miles).

Broadmoor Wildlife Sanctuary. From the junction of Routes 16 and 27 in Sherborn, go northeast on Route 16 for 1.6 miles to the visitor center on the right.

If you think of boating on the Charles as sailing or rowing through Cambridge, then try the upper Charles, one of the finest paddling destinations in the Northeast. When we paddled here in late June, wild grapes clung to the streamside vegetation, swamp rose bloomed in profusion, and the sweet scent of swamp azalea wafted along on the slightest breeze. Red maples dominate the shores in marshy sections, but you may also spot some stately elms and swamp white oaks, along with a variety of other trees.

In the Charles' north-flowing upper reaches, we watched the boat compass needle swing back and forth endlessly as the river meandered through low-lying red maple swamps and wet meadows. As a muskrat swam before us, towing a clump of grass, and a great horned owl eyed us from an overhead perch, we marveled at this truly wild place that lies a stone's throw from Boston suburbs. Two very large snapping turtles dove for cover in deeper water as we glided by, and we watched a green heron and a great blue heron stalk the shallows for fish and other prey. A red-tailed hawk wheeled overhead while myriad songbirds sang from hidden perches. We listened to beautiful, flutelike notes of a hermit thrush—normally a deep-woods resident—and thought of the similarities to northern New England. We strained to hear road noise but heard none.

Medfield State Forest, Sherborn Town Forest, The Trustees of Reservations, Massachusetts Audubon Society, and private landowners protect much of the land in this section from development. The Forest Road access marks the beginning of a river section navigable even during periods of low water. We recommend paddling upstream to start, especially in spring, and letting the light current help carry you back down. Our favorite paddle starts at Dwight Street and heads upstream (south) to Route 115, a round-trip distance of 7.5 miles through the most pristine areas.

A kingfisher watches us warily from its streamside perch.

Hiking trails abound. About a mile downstream from Farm Road, The Trustees of Reservations maintains a landing on the left bank. From there, you can hike uphill for nearly a mile to King Philip's Lookout in the contiguous Sherborn Town Forest. Foot trails meander through Peters Reservation on the right bank, just downstream from Farm Road. Also, visit the Broadmoor Wildlife Sanctuary (owned by Mass Audubon; see above for directions) with its elevated boardwalk and 9 miles of trails.

～ 11 ～

Weymouth Back River
Hingham and Weymouth, MA

Maps: Massachusetts Atlas, Map 53
   USGS Quadrangles, Hull and Weymouth
Length: 3.6 miles
Camping: Wompatuck State Park, 781-749-7161;
   reservations: 877-422-6762 or www.ReserveAmerica.com
Information: tide charts, www.maineharbors.com
Habitat Type: tidal estuary; wooded shores
Expect to See: gulls, osprey, herons, and egrets
Take Note: no water-skiing or personal watercraft south of Route
   3A bridge; no development; visit at or near high tide—exposed
   mud banks at low tide reduce the paddling area dramatically

---

Getting There

From Boston, go south on I-93/Route 1, and take Exit 12 onto Route 3A.
Go southeast for 6.8 miles (follow signs carefully, because Route 3A takes a
few turns) to the stoplight at the junction of Route 3A (Bridge Street) with
Green Street (right/south) and Neck Street (left/north). Directions to the
three access points given from this junction.

Abigail Adams Park. From the junction, continue east on Route 3A for
0.3 mile, and turn right in order to cross Route 3A to get into the park, just
before the bridge.

Weymouth Public Launch. From the junction, go north on Neck Street for
0.6 mile to the access on the right. Launch fee in 2003 was $5.

Great Esker Park. From the junction, go south on Green Street for 1.1 miles
(1.1 miles), and turn left onto East Street at the stoplight. Go 0.8 mile (1.9 miles),
and turn left onto Puritan Road. Go 0.5 mile (2.4 miles) to the end, and park by
the gate.

Abigail Adams Park is the preferred access; carry over the bank to the
water. Weymouth Public Launch is the easiest access but is not free. Great
Esker Park does not have a developed boat launch but is a good place to launch
when it's windy. It's very muddy at low tide.

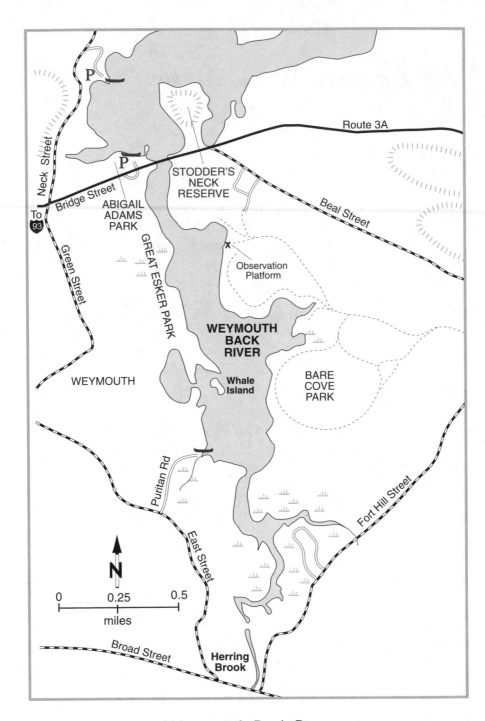

Route 3A

Neck Street

P

P

STODDER'S
NECK
RESERVE

Bridge Street

Beal Street

To 93

ABIGAIL
ADAMS
PARK

Green Street

GREAT ESKER PARK

x
Observation
Platform

WEYMOUTH
BACK
RIVER

WEYMOUTH

Whale
Island

BARE
COVE
PARK

Puritan Rd

Fort Hill Street

N

East Street

0   0.25   0.5
miles

Broad Street

Herring
Brook

Weymouth Back River

Bounded by wildlife preserves, Weymouth Back River presents an outstanding paddling resource within the Greater Boston Metropolitan Area. Harbormasters from Hingham and Weymouth established the river as a no-wake zone, with no water-skiing and no personal watercraft allowed south of the Route 3A bridge. The wooded shores—the longest in the Boston Harbor area—enclose modest areas of salt marsh, standing in stark contrast to the seas of *Spartina* encountered in other estuaries.

Three active osprey nests fledged eight young in 2002. The 469 acres of Bare Cove Park harbor many species of plants, including bear oak and pitch pine growing on tree-covered dunes. Look for coyote, fox, and deer here; an observation platform provides views of the river and the surrounding woods. Hiking trails course through the park and also through 1.5-mile-long, 237-acre Great Esker Park across the way. The esker, which reaches 90 feet in height, appears as a long, winding, snakelike ridge of stratified sand and gravel, formed during the last glacial epoch about 12,000 years ago. Subglacial streams laid the deposits as they tunneled beneath the melting glacier. Also in this area, valuable archaeological finds dating back as far as 9,000 years indicate a long Native American presence along the river.

Alewives, locally known as herring, make a famous annual pilgrimage here, up the river to Whitman's Pond. From eggs laid in spring, young fish grow up to 4 inches by fall when they return to the sea. As adults, the fish return the following spring, now a silvery 12 inches long, to begin the cycle anew. As Henry Beston said in his book *The Outermost House:*

Somewhere in the depths of the ocean each Weymouth-born fish remembers Whitman's Pond, and comes to it through the directionless leagues of the sea. What stirs in each cold brain? What call quivers, as the new sun strikes down into the river of ocean? How do the creatures find their way? Whatever the reason, the herring are "in" at Weymouth, breasting the brook's overflow to the ancestral pond.

~ 12 ~

North River
Hanover, Marshfield, Norwell, and Scituate, MA

> **MAPS:** Massachusetts Atlas, Map 54
> USGS Quadrangles, Hanover and Weymouth
>
> **LENGTH:** 8 miles
>
> **CAMPING:** Wompatuck State Park, 781-749-7161; Myles Standish State Forest, 508-866-2526; reservations: 877-422-6762 or www.ReserveAmerica.com
>
> **INFORMATION:** tide charts, www.maineharbors.com
>
> **HABITAT TYPE:** tidal river; undeveloped marshlands
>
> **EXPECT TO SEE:** marsh and riverine birds, marsh wrens
>
> **TAKE NOTE:** motors allowed, 6 MPH speed limit; treacherous tides around bridges and river bends—wear your PFD; novice paddlers should avoid this area

---

GETTING THERE

Bridge Street. From Route 3, Exit 13, go north on Route 53 for 0.5 mile (0.5 mile); turn right onto Route 123. Go east for 4.0 miles (4.5 miles), and turn right onto Bridge Street. Access at the Marshfield Conservation Area is in 0.4 mile (4.9 miles) on the right, just over the bridge.

From the junction of Routes 3A and 123, go west on Route 123 for 1.8 miles (1.8 miles), and turn left onto Bridge Street. Access is in 0.4 mile (2.2 miles) on the right.

Indian Head Drive. From Route 3, Exit 13, go south on Route 53. After Route 139 joins, continue south for 0.3 mile (0.3 mile), and turn right onto Broadway. Go 0.3 mile (0.6 mile), and veer left onto Elm Street. After another 0.4 mile (1.0 mile), stay on Elm Street as it veers left again. In another 0.2 mile (1.2 miles), turn left onto Indian Head Drive at the cartop access sign.

From Route 3, Exit 12, go west on Route 139 for 2.0 miles (2.0 miles), then veer right onto Routes 53/139. Go 0.7 mile (2.7 miles), turn left onto Broadway, and continue as above (left onto Elm at 3.0 miles; veer left at 3.4 miles; left onto Indian Head drive at 3.6 miles).

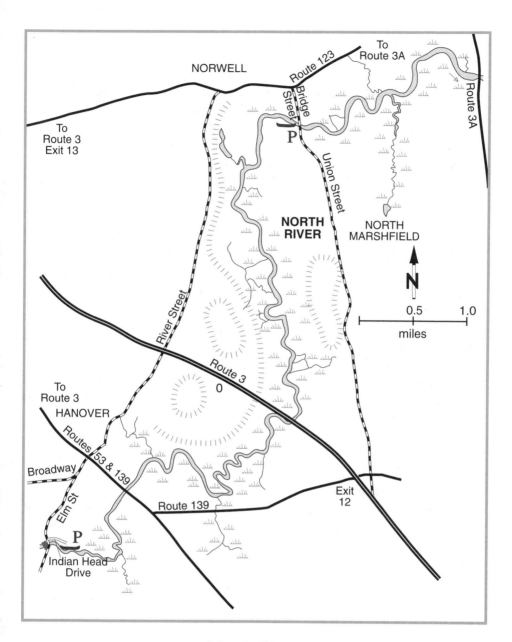

North River

This North River section forms part of the Wampanoag Commemorative Canoe Passage that ends at the mouth of the Taunton River. Though we did not see much species diversity, we did get a lot of exercise paddling against the tide. If we had timed it better, we could have paddled upstream on an incoming tide and returned on an outgoing tide. Another possibility, with two vehicles, would be to make this a one-way trip on an outgoing tide, putting in at the Indian Head Drive access and taking out at Bridge Street. Though you could paddle up to the Indian Head access on an incoming tide if you had enough time, you could not paddle there against an outgoing tide. A warning: tidal flow around bridges and river bends can lead to treacherous conditions; always wear your PFD, and do not take novice paddlers here.

Though we had to work hard, we did enjoy the scenery. A number of marsh wrens called from the narrow-leaved cattails along the river's upper stretches. Where the surrounding forests reach the shores, we saw many bird species. While the river traverses mostly undeveloped swampland, and thereby provides a wonderful paddling resource, Route 3 road noise does impinge in one short stretch.

The North River meanders inland until it reaches a dam in Hanover, where it becomes the Indian Head River. Along the way, we noticed several historical markers for shipyards, among them the Rogers, Wanton, Chittenden, and Block House Shipyards that operated variously for nearly 200 years, from 1678 to 1871, producing more than 1,000 ships that ranged from 20 to 470 tons. The vessel from which the Columbia River received its name was built here, along with one of the ships involved in the Boston Tea Party.

Southeastern Massachusetts and Cape Cod

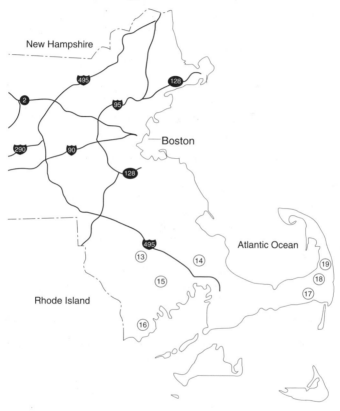

New Hampshire

New Bedford

Boston

Atlantic Ocean

Rhode Island

Lake Rico and Big Bearhole Pond
Taunton, MA

MAPS: Massachusetts Atlas, Map 57
   USGS Quadrangles, Assawompset Pond, Bridgewater,
   Somerset, and Taunton
AREA: Lake Rico, 250 acres;.
   Big Bearhole Pond, 37 acres
CAMPING: Massasoit State Park, 508-822-7405;
   reservations: 877-422-6762 or www.ReserveAmerica.com
HABITAT TYPE: wooded reservoir in a state park
EXPECT TO SEE: mute swan, various ducks, great blue heron,
   deep woodlands
TAKE NOTE: no motors; limited development

GETTING THERE

From I-495, Exit 5, go south on Route 18 for 0.4 mile (0.4 mile), and turn
right onto Taunton Street/Middleboro Avenue, following signs to Massasoit
State Park. Pass by the park entrance in 2.2 miles (2.6 miles); Lake Rico
access is on the left in 0.4 mile (3.0 miles). To reach Big Bearhole Pond, turn
into the state park and follow signs to the access; it can also be accessed off
Turner Street.

Lake Rico and the other small ponds in Massasoit State Park provide
superb quietwater paddling—some of the best in this part of the state.
Though some maps show six bodies of water (Lake Rico, Kings Pond,
Furnace Pond, Middle Pond, and Little and Big Bearhole Ponds), Lake
Rico, Kings Pond, and Furnace Pond are connected. Formerly used by
cranberry growers, these separate ponds merged when the state raised
the water level after acquiring the property. Some development
intrudes on the western side of Furnace Pond and Lake Rico and on the
eastern end of Big Bearhole Pond, but the rest of these ponds lie fully
within 1,500-acre Massasoit State Park, so only recreational development occurs there.

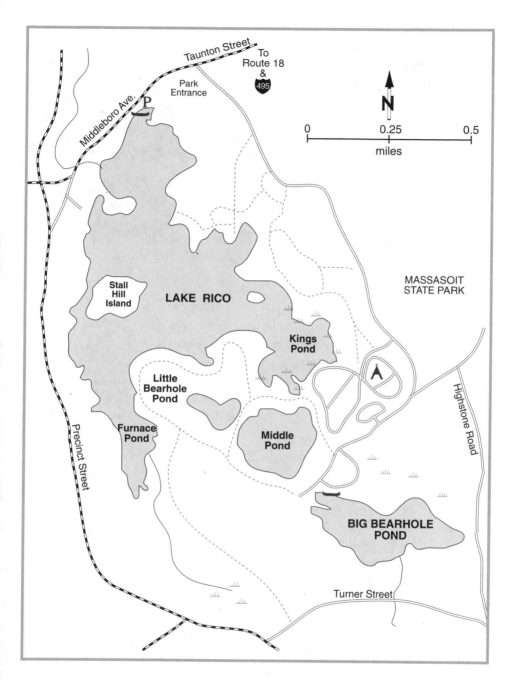

Lake Rico and Big Bearhole Pond

In the early-morning light, mist rising off still waters makes Lake Rico seem almost mystical.

Lake Rico offers several miles of shoreline, enough to provide enjoyable paddling for half a day. From the access on Middleboro Avenue, you can see only Lake Rico's northern cove. Paddling to the south, you leave the road noise, passing some large stands of white pine with open forest floor—quite accessible if you want to get out for a picnic lunch or a short walk. Marshy Kings Pond presents a challenge, but you can pick your way through the abundant vegetation, paddling carefully around the bulrushes, pickerelweed, stands of cattail, and waterlilies. Near the tip of this cove, listen for the small waterfall inlet from Middle Pond (you can carry into Middle Pond). Watch for great blue heron, green heron, wood duck, teal, and pied-billed grebe in here.

We saw two pairs of mute swan, each with two cygnets, on the more open sections of the lake. While much open water remains, Eurasian water-milfoil and fanwort seemed to be crowding out the bladderwort, pondweed, and other native aquatic vegetation when we paddled here in 2002. Other invasive plants—purple loosestrife and *Phragmites*—also seemed to be taking hold.

Big Bearhole Pond, a lot smaller than Lake Rico and with some houses on the eastern tip, still rates a visit. White pine dominates the shoreline vegetation, mixed with red maple, black gum, scarlet oak, gray birch, sweet pepperbush, blueberry, winterberry, and alder. Patches of swamp loosestrife grow along the shore, and some shallow coves sport patches of yellow pondlily and fragrant waterlily. Underwater vegetation includes fanwort and bladderwort.

~ 14 ~

East Head Pond
Carver and Plymouth, MA

MAPS: Massachusetts Atlas, Map 58
    USGS Quadrangle, Wareham
AREA: 92 acres
CAMPING: Myles Standish State Forest, 508-866-2526;
    reservations: 877-422-6762 or www.ReserveAmerica.com
HABITAT TYPE: glaciated kettle hole surrounded by sand barrens
EXPECT TO SEE: pine and prairie warblers (seen only with
    persistence), eastern towhee, pitch pine, bear oak, bracken
    fern, blueberries
TAKE NOTE: no gasoline motors; no development

GETTING THERE

From I-495, Exit 2, go north on Route 58 toward South Carver. In 2.4 miles (2.4 miles), when Route 58 goes left, continue straight on Tremont Street. In 0.8 mile (3.2 miles), turn right onto Cranberry Road, and follow it for 2.7 miles (5.9 miles) to the Myles Standish State Forest. At the yield sign, go right 0.1 mile (6.0 miles) to the visitor center. Park in the visitor center lot and carry your boat about 100 yards, crossing the bridge over the outlet, to the access on the left.

Myles Standish State Forest—one of the largest publicly owned tracts of land in Massachusetts at 14,635 acres—harbors many rare and endangered plants and animals and contains many ecologically rich kettle-hole ponds. When the glaciers receded 12,000 years ago, they left a few large chunks of glacial ice behind, usually buried in debris. As these ice blocks melted, they left depressions in the surrounding sand that formed ponds.

    Compared with most of New England, a quite different species set surrounds East Head Pond and the other, smaller ponds of the state forest. Dominant species include pitch pine (*Pinus rigida*) and bear or

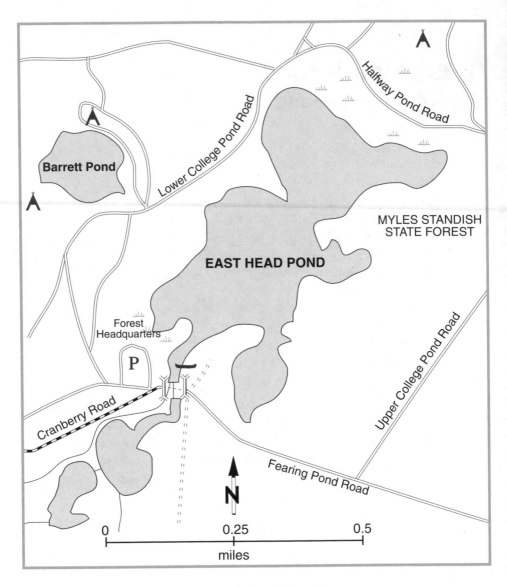

East Head Pond

scrub oak *(Quercus ilicifolia)* in a pine-barrens ecosystem. This forest community develops on acidic, sandy soil and requires frequent fires for pitch pine seed release.

Along with the dominant species—pitch pine and bear oak—red maple, gray birch, white pine, black gum, scarlet oak, and big-tooth aspen grow along the shores of East Head Pond. A rich diversity of shrubs also lines the shore: two species of blueberries (highbush and black highbush), sweet pepperbush, leatherleaf, sweetgale, mountain laurel, wild raisin or witherod *(Viburnum cassinoides)*, and inkberry *(Ilex glabra)*. Pond vegetation includes water shield, fragrant waterlily, and bladderwort. Freshwater mussels inhabit the sandy bottom. Anglers fish for largemouth bass, pickerel, and yellow perch, and you may be lucky enough to see an osprey join the human anglers, as we did on an early-September morning. If you are extraordinarily lucky, you might see one of the approximately 300 remaining endangered Plymouth redbelly turtles *(Pseudemys rubriventris bangsi)* in one of these coastal ponds.

With no gasoline-powered motors, East Head Pond provides a great spot for a morning or evening of relaxed paddling. The extremely popular campground (reservations required) provides a base for hiking on one of the many trails of the state forest. In all, the state forest boasts 90 miles of hiking, horse, and bicycle trails that crisscross the pine barrens.

Myles Standish State Forest and surrounding areas contain the largest pitch pine–scrub oak community remaining in New England and, along with those on Long Island and New Jersey, one of only three major pine-barrens ecosystems remaining. Unfortunately, more economically valuable white and red pines have replaced much of the pitch pine; agriculture and development have pared away the surrounding barrens; and destructive off-road vehicles have threatened other rare and endangered plants of the community. During the eighteenth century, settlers mined this area for bog iron, contained in thin strata under the ponds. After this industry petered out, cranberry production took over; many commercial cranberry bogs still dot the area. Amid great controversy, ATVs have been banned because of past degradation of this fragile ecosystem. Not surprisingly, a strong movement to let them back in has surfaced, backed by the contention that doing so will greatly reduce the even more destructive illegal use that occurs now.

15

New Bedford Reservoir
Acushnet, MA

MAPS: Massachusetts Atlas, Map 64
   USGS Quadrangles, Assawompset Pond and New
   Bedford North
AREA: 219 acres
CAMPING: Massasoit State Park, 508-822-7405; Myles Standish
   State Forest, 508-866-2526; Horseneck Beach State Reserva-
   tion, 508-636-8816; reservations: 877-422-6762 or
   www.ReserveAmerica.com
HABITAT TYPE: swampy, weed-choked reservoir
EXPECT TO SEE: mute swan, Canada goose, wood duck, mallard,
   great blue heron, green heron
TAKE NOTE: motors limited by aquatic vegetation; limited
   development

GETTING THERE

From Route 140, Exit 7, just north of New Bedford, go left (east) for 0.4 mile (0.4 mile), and turn left (north) onto Acushnet Avenue (Route 18). Turn right in 0.4 mile (0.8 mile) onto Peckham Road. Go 1.7 miles (2.5 miles), and turn left onto Lake Street. The access is on the left in 0.6 mile (3.1 miles).

A huge flock of Canada geese greeted us at the access when we revisited New Bedford Reservoir, and many small groups of wood ducks fled before us as we paddled up the channel. In spring, nesting songbirds fill the surrounding area. In July, swamp azalea and swamp rose bloom in profusion along the wooded shore, where green and great blue herons stalk fish and amphibian prey and mute swans eat their fill of abundant aquatic vegetation. In mid-September, early-migrating blue-winged teal join the resident waterfowl. A highly varied shoreline and many marshy coves provide a haven for all sorts of waterfowl and wetland plants. Don't expect easy paddling, though.

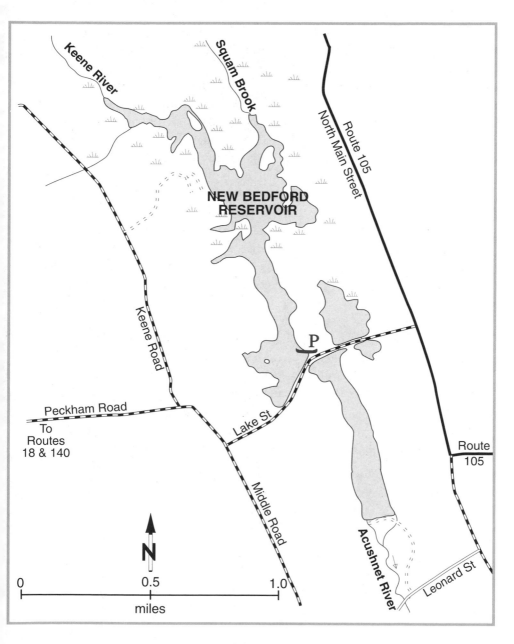

New Bedford Reservoir

When we paddled here in 1992, Eurasian water-milfoil had already started to take over; by 2002 it had choked the bays and side channels, crowding out bladderwort, coontail, and other native vegetation. Paddling into the bays and side channels presented a real challenge, even in early July. Small motorboats belonging to a few cabins keep a central passageway open. As we paddled out into the weed-choked bays and side channels, we joked that if we did not pay attention we might find ourselves poling through an upland meadow, not having noticed the gradual transition from open water. If you want easier paddling, visit in spring.

On a sunny day, expect to see painted turtles sunning on logs or floating vegetation, and you might see a snapping turtle. Large numbers of this reclusive turtle inhabit marshy bodies of water. Look for the triangular tip of its nose extending above water for air, though in late spring or early summer you may see one on land looking for new habitat or laying eggs. We also see this turtle underwater, often hanging lazily just below the surface, scanning the depths for prey.

A small group of houses cluster along the western shore midway up, and paddling north you eventually reach a few houses and cranberry operations at the upper end. Some much less weedy canals connect with and run basically parallel to the main reservoir. Growers use water from these shaded canals to flood their cranberry bogs periodically. These canals have a very different, almost eerie feel, with a dark canopy of overhanging maples and grapevines closing in from both sides.

16

Slocums River
Dartmouth, MA

MAPS: Massachusetts Atlas, Map 63
USGS Quadrangles, New Bedford South and Westport
LENGTH: 4 miles
CAMPING: Horseneck Beach State Reservation, 508-636-8816;
reservations: 877-422-6762 or www.ReserveAmerica.com
INFORMATION: Demarest Lloyd State Park, 508-636-8816;
The Lloyd Center, 508-990-0505; tide charts,
www.maineharbors.com
HABITAT TYPE: tidal estuary, salt marsh
EXPECT TO SEE: herons and egrets, black duck, cardinal, fiddler
crab, oaks, salt marsh plants
TAKE NOTE: little development; motors allowed

GETTING THERE

Slocums River. From Fall River, take I-195 east to Exit 10 south to Route 6 east. At the junction with Route 177, take Beeden Road south for 1.3 miles (1.3 miles). Jog right for one and a half blocks (1.4 miles), and turn left onto Fisher Road. Go south for 4.5 miles (5.9 miles) to Russells Mills Road (at the stop sign, stay left where Gidley Road goes right; stay right where Woodcock Road goes left). Go south on Russells Mills Road for 0.1 mile (6.0 miles) to the junction with Slades and Horseneck Roads. Go straight across onto Horseneck Road; access is in 0.2 mile (6.2 miles) on the left at Russells Mills Town Park.

Demarest-Lloyd State Park. To reach the state park, continue south on Horseneck Road. Turn left onto Barneys Joy Road, and follow it to the park.

Lloyd Center. To reach the center by car, from the junction of Horseneck Road and Russells Mills Road, go southeast onto Rock O'Dundee and Potomska Roads for 2.5 miles to the entrance on the right.

Slocums River represents one of the best tidal rivers in New England for quiet paddling, birds, and salt marsh plants. You could easily spend a day

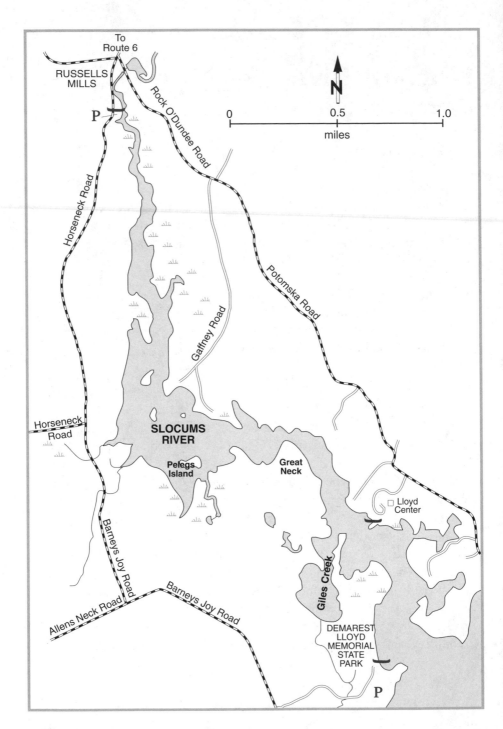

Slocums River

Labels within the map image:

To Route 6

RUSSELLS MILLS

P

N

0   0.5   1.0
miles

Rock O'Dundee Road

Horseneck Road

Gaffney Road

Potomska Road

Horseneck Road

SLOCUMS RIVER

Pelegs Island

Great Neck

Lloyd Center

Giles Creek

Barneys Joy Road

Allens Neck Road

Barneys Joy Road

DEMAREST LLOYD MEMORIAL STATE PARK

P

Slocums River, one of New England's most beautiful tidal estuaries, provides wonderful wildlife watching opportunities.

or two exploring the river, getting to know its different personalities at high and low tide. The few houses along the river do not detract from the peace and quiet. The Slocum family originally settled this isolated corner of Dartmouth township. Joshua Slocum, a distant relative, sailed a small ketch out of nearby Fairhaven and around the world in the early 1900s in the first solo circumnavigation of the earth in a small craft. The feat perhaps epitomizes the rigor and determination of the early Slocums: Anthony, who first cleared the land, and Giles, who founded the Society of Friends Apponeagonsett Meeting in 1638, still active not far from Russells Mills.

Launch your boat at the town park in Russells Mills at the north end of Slocums River. The 8-mile round-trip distance from the park to the Demarest-Lloyd State Park at the entrance to Buzzards Bay can be paddled in half a day, but we recommend that you spend more time and explore the islands, inlets, and coves. We particularly enjoyed paddling up Giles Creek and the various inlets near Pelegs Island.

Giles Creek often fills with egrets, herons, and gulls that feed amid the salt marsh grass (*Spartina spp.*). At low tide, you may see only the egrets' heads extending above the grasses. An unnamed creek off to the west of Pelegs Island offers a superb spot to learn about the salt marsh ecosystem. Paddling up this creek in early September at just about low tide, we saw literally thousands of fiddler crabs along the banks (one claw grows much larger than the other, making the critter look as if it's holding a fiddle). The exposed mud flats seemed to move as we paddled close, and the startled crabs scurried to safety—with the *clickety-clack* of thousands of tiny legs on the pebbles and mud.

When we paddled here in early July, some large patches of very fragrant swamp azalea diverted our attention from the legions of fiddler crabs. We also imagine that many migrating waterfowl join the resident black ducks in the fall. Out on Buzzards Bay, watch for interesting gulls and terns. Though the bay has swells, barrier islands usually keep the water fairly calm.

While here, you may want to visit the Lloyd Center for Environmental Studies, across the mouth of the river from Demarest-Lloyd State Park. This highly regarded nature center, on 55 acres, offers exhibits and a wide range of educational programs, nature walks, lecture programs, and canoe trips. You can reach the center either by boat or by car.

17

Herring River and West Reservoir

Harwich, MA

Maps: Massachusetts Atlas, Map 67
 USGS Quadrangle, Harwich
Area/Length: West Reservoir, 47 acres;
 Herring River, 4.5 miles
Camping: Nickerson State Park, 508-896-3491;
 reservations: 877-422-6762 or www.ReserveAmerica.com
Information: tide charts, www.maineharbors.com
Habitat Type: fresh- and saltwater estuary; wooded reservoir
Expect to See: turtles, herons, and egrets
Take Note: limited development; motors allowed

GETTING THERE

Herring River. From the junction of Routes 28 and 134, go east on Route 28 for 2.2 miles to the access on the right, just over the bridge. From the junction of Routes 28 and 39, go west on Route 28 for 0.9 mile to the access on the left, just before the bridge.

West Reservoir. From the Route 28 bridge over the Herring River, go 0.4 mile (0.4 mile) west on Route 28 and turn right onto Depot Road. Go 0.9 mile (1.3 miles), and bear right onto Depot Street. Go 0.2 mile (1.5 miles), and turn right onto an unmarked dirt road. In 0.2 mile (1.7 miles) you will reach the reservoir parking area by the Harwich Conservation Lands sign.

Well away from usual Cape Cod recreation destinations, the Herring River provides superb quietwater paddling through bird-filled saltwater and freshwater marshes. The best paddling occurs from Route 28 up to West Reservoir. You can also paddle south to Nantucket Sound, but houses interrupt the solitude below Route 28.

Paddling upriver from the Route 28 bridge, you will quickly leave the few houses behind and wind through a wild, broad salt marsh, a

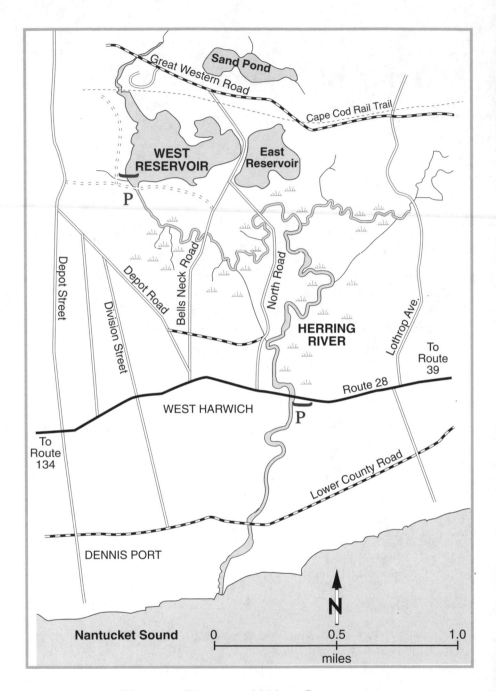

Herring River and West Reservoir

tremendous spot for birding. You might see gulls, snowy egrets, great blue and green herons, yellowlegs, Canada geese, cormorants, mallards, black ducks, mute swans, red-winged blackbirds, and various hawks as you paddle along. The salt marsh environment grows thick with grasses and cattails that provide nesting habitat for species of birds that you hear but rarely see: marsh wren, swamp sparrow, Virginia rail, and least bittern. Trees along the marsh's edge contain many woodland species, including northern parula, a warbler that uses the beard moss found hanging from many trees here to make its nest.

The Herring River, though tidal for its entire length, has an increasing saltwater gradient as it flows downstream. Heading upriver on an incoming tide makes for easier paddling, though the river flows gently enough that wind—a common Cape companion—usually presents a bigger obstacle than current. Near high tide you can explore numerous little canals and inlets along the river. At the West Reservoir outlet, carry up over the dike on the left by the fish ladder to get onto the reservoir. During the herring (alewife) spawning season, you can watch the fish swimming up the fish ladder.

West Reservoir provides a great location for studying freshwater aquatic plants, birds, and other wildlife. We saw a dozen black-crowned night-herons, but the turtle life excited us even more, including literally hundreds of painted turtles sunning on logs. We also saw a good-sized snapper and two far less common stinkpot turtles. This latter species sports a steeply humped carapace that seems undersized, a pointed "beak," and a musky smell you will probably notice if you pick one up (a defensive musky secretion released from glands on both sides of the body). The smell that emanates from the stinkpot (*Sternotherus odoratus*) and other musk turtles gives them their names. Generally, you see these turtles underwater, but on occasion they sun on protruding logs or rocks, even in trees—and unlike painted turtles, you can often quietly paddle right up to them for close observation.

Groves of black and white oaks and pitch pine surround this fairly deep reservoir. Black gum or tupelo—with brilliant crimson fall foliage—grows by water's edge. The Town of Harwich Conservation Lands protect much of the land surrounding the reservoir and Herring River. A nice trail and several dirt roads begin at the reservoir. Also, the Cape Cod Rail Trail passes the reservoir's north end. This wonderful biking and hiking trail extends for 25 miles along an abandoned railway bed through the towns of Dennis, Harwich, Brewster, Orleans, and Eastham.

18

Cliff Pond, Flax Pond, and Little Cliff Pond
Brewster, MA

MAPS: Massachusetts Atlas, Map 61
USGS Quadrangles, Harwich and Orleans
AREA: Cliff Pond, 204 acres
CAMPING: Nickerson State Park, 508-896-3491;
reservations: 877-422-6762 or www.ReserveAmerica.com
HABITAT TYPE: shallow kettle ponds
EXPECT TO SEE: woodland bird and flower species,
recreation enthusiasts
TAKE NOTE: no motors on Flax Pond; 10 HP motors allowed
on Cliff and Little Cliff Ponds; development limited to
recreational facilities

GETTING THERE

From Route 6, Exit 12, go west on Route 6A for 1.6 miles, following signs for Nickerson State Park. Pick up a map at park headquarters and follow it or signs to the launches. Canoe rentals are available on Flax Pond.

Nickerson State Park—one of the largest state parks in Massachusetts, with more than 1,900 acres and 420 campsites—draws many hikers, bikers, and paddlers. If you avoid the peak summer season, you'll find very pleasant paddling and about the best camping on the Cape. The park's dozen or so shallow kettle ponds formed approximately 12,000 years ago when large chunks of buried ice melted as glaciers receded. Because significant streams do not feed most kettle ponds, their levels fluctuate seasonally.

Three of these ponds—Cliff, Little Cliff, and Flax—provide the best paddling. Cliff Pond, the largest, has launch sites on two sides, west (primary launch point) and east. The typical wide, shallow, sandy shoreline—such as between Cliff and Little Cliff Ponds—requires you

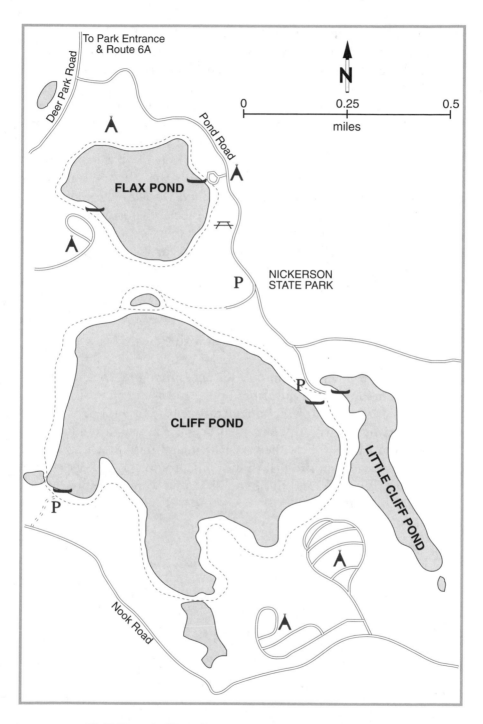

Cliff Pond, Flax Pond, and Little Cliff Pond

to go out a few hundred feet until the water has depth enough to float your boat with you in it. Some shallower shoreline sections grow quite thick with vegetation, but most are sandy and readily accessible to either paddler or swimmer.

Large stands of pitch pine and black oak surround the ponds, along with white pine, hemlock, and spruce, planted by the Civilian Conservation Corps in the 1930s. Nickerson State Park—created in 1934 when the commonwealth acquired the Roland Nickerson estate, the largest private holding of forestland on the Cape—also sports numerous hiking and biking trails that wind through the forest; the scenic Cape Cod Rail Trail passes through the park's north end. On this trail you can bike approximately 25 miles. Going southwest, the trail leads to Dennis; heading northeast, then north, you reach the Cape Cod National Seashore Marconi Area. Occupying the bed of an abandoned railway, this ideal bicycle trail covers generally flat terrain with minimal road crossings. You can obtain a trail map and rent bicycles at the park.

Nickerson State Park ponds, stocked with trout and bass, are popular for fishing. A world-record American eel, caught at Cliff Pond in 1992, weighed 8 pounds, 4 ounces, and measured 46 inches in length and 10.5 inches in girth. While not popular today, except in sushi bars, eel formed a large part of the nineteenth-century New England diet and came to be known as "Derryfield beef." The eel, a unique fish, breeds in the Sargasso Sea, then returns inland until reaching adulthood—a life cycle opposite that of most anadromous fish. Eel can live for thirty to fifty years, and those in Cliff Pond were probably cut off from the sea decades ago.

19

Nauset Marsh and Salt Pond Bay
Eastham, MA

MAPS: Massachusetts Atlas, Map 61
   USGS Quadrangle, Orleans

AREA: 1,300 acres

CAMPING: Nickerson State Park, 508-896-3491;
   reservations: 877-422-6762 or www.ReserveAmerica.com

INFORMATION: Cape Cod National Seashore, Salt Pond Visitor
   Center, 508-255-3421; tide charts, www.maineharbors.com

HABITAT TYPE: tidal estuary, salt marsh

EXPECT TO SEE: herons and egrets, shorebirds, black duck,
   fiddler crab, salt marsh plants

TAKE NOTE: little development; too shallow for motors in most
   places; check with rangers at Salt Pond Visitor Center about
   tide and wind conditions before venturing out; novice paddlers
   should avoid this area

GETTING THERE

Salt Pond. From Route 6 at the rotary where the limited-access highway ends, continue 2.8 miles, and turn right onto Salt Pond Landing.

   Salt Pond Visitor Center. From Salt Pond Landing, go north on Route 6 for 0.2 mile to Doane Road. The Salt Pond Visitor Center is 100 feet down Doane Road.

Salt Pond Bay in Nauset Marsh provides very enjoyable paddling in a fascinating salt marsh ecosystem, at least at high tide. Low tide exposes vast areas of mud flats that could leave you stranded. We paddled here twice on falling tides and both times had to drag our boats through rapidly retreating waters. Fortunately, the mud underfoot was quite solid. At high tide you can paddle around this area quite easily, but watch out for strong tidal currents in some channels. Also, wind can cause problems as it blows unimpeded over vast expanses of salt marsh and low-lying islands.

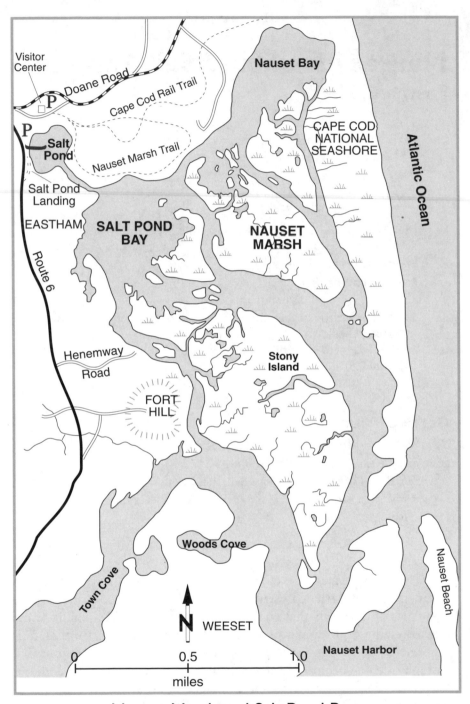

Nauset Marsh and Salt Pond Bay

Cape Cod National Seashore—a 40-mile-long preserve of dunes, beach, and estuary between Chatham and Provincetown—includes Nauset Marsh. Established in 1961, the national seashore provides superb hiking, bicycling, swimming, and fishing opportunities for tens of thousands of visitors each year, though few people think of paddling here. Salt Pond, where you launch, was once a freshwater kettle pond, but the ocean broke through, and tides now feed the pond twice daily through a narrow channel connecting it to Salt Pond Bay and the large Nauset Marsh estuary.

Nauset Marsh, a classic tidal estuary, is rich in birdlife, woodland mammals, marine animals (including quahogs, oysters, mussels, and various fish), and the unusual plants that comprise this ecosystem. As you get out into the bay, note the thick masses of peat that gulls and sandpipers scour for food on the many islands that dot this huge marsh. We spent many hours looking with binoculars at myriad birdlife, including skeins of cormorants, several gull species, black duck, kingfisher, great blue heron, snowy egret, semipalmated plover, black-bellied plover, lesser yellowlegs, and sanderling. On one trip, we watched fifty harbor seals near the break between Coast Guard and Nauset Beaches (harbor seals winter in this area, but most head to Maine to raise their young).

If you find yourself here at low tide, you can enjoy wonderful hiking near the Salt Pond Visitor Center or, farther north, within Cape Cod National Seashore. Nauset Marsh Trail leads from the Salt Pond Visitor Center along the east side of Salt Pond, and then along the edge of Salt Pond Bay. This mile-long trail provides a great way to learn to identify some of the more common flora here: black oak, pitch pine, black locust, eastern red cedar (juniper), beach plum, winterberry, saltmeadow grass, and salt marsh cordgrass. Pick up a trail map at the visitor center.

Also, you can bicycle the scenic, 25-mile-long Cape Cod Rail Trail that connects the visitor center with Nickerson State Park. Occupying the bed of an abandoned railway, this ideal bicycle trail covers generally flat terrain with minimal road crossings and interruptions. You can pick up a map of the trail, plus rent bicycles, at Nickerson State Park.

A lesser yellowlegs scurries along the shore of Nauset Marsh.

Martha's Vineyard

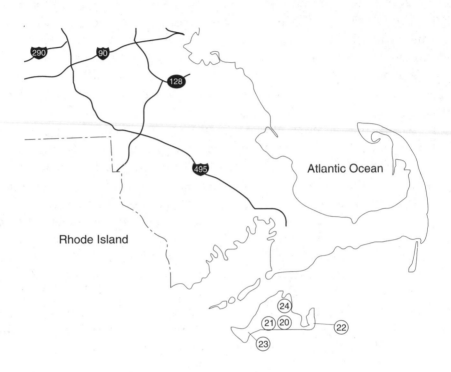

Atlantic Ocean

Rhode Island

Paddling the Vineyard's Ponds

Long known for sailing, beachcombing, bed-and-breakfast hopping, gift shopping, and general vacationing, Martha's Vineyard also offers truly spectacular paddling. We include descriptions of six bodies of water in this guide. Most people reach Martha's Vineyard via ferry out of Woods Hole. Rates in 2003: $110 round-trip for car and driver, plus $11 per passenger; reservations are highly recommended.

Anyone wishing to paddle on Martha's Vineyard must think about timing. The population increases from about 12,000 in winter to more than 60,000 during summer. Unless you reserve early, the ferry, inns, and campsites will be full. Many visitors scoot around on mopeds when not shopping, contributing to traffic problems. A possible solution: schedule your visit before mid-June or after Labor Day. You might not get warm sun during off-season visits, but you will have less competition for space.

In general, we do not recommend the Vineyard to novice paddlers. Sailboarders love the Vineyard for a reason—wind—and sudden weather changes crop up often. Ponds open to the sea can suffer from extremely strong tidal currents—in some places the tidal current moves faster than you can paddle. Combined with a strong breeze, this can engender very hazardous paddling conditions. Use caution and good sense when paddling here so that you can fully enjoy what the Vineyard offers. Wear PFDs, especially with children—simply having PFDs onboard is not sufficient.

20

Edgartown Great Pond
Edgartown, MA

MAPS: Massachusetts Atlas, Maps 68 and 69
USGS Quadrangles, Edgartown

AREA: 860 acres

CAMPING AND ACCOMMODATIONS: One private campground:
Martha's Vineyard Family Campground—in Vineyard Haven,
508-693-3772. Accommodations: American Youth Hostel,
508-693-2665; Martha's Vineyard Chamber of Commerce,
508-693-0085 or www.mvy.com.

INFORMATION: For ferry reservations, contact the Steamship
Authority at 508-477-8800, 508-693-9130, or
www.steamshipauthority.com. For tide charts, see
www.maineharbors.com.

HABITAT TYPE: saltwater pond, salinity depends on how long it
has been cut off from the ocean

EXPECT TO SEE: gulls, herons and egrets, sandpipers, osprey,
otter, blue crab, snapping turtles, salt marsh plants, black gum

TAKE NOTE: motors allowed on some ponds; minimal development; wind and tide can create hazardous conditions—novice
paddlers should avoid this area on windy days; wear PFD;
respect private property

GETTING THERE

From Main Street in Edgartown, go 1.8 miles (1.8 miles) west on Edgartown–West Tisbury Road, and turn left onto Meeting House Way. Go 1.4 miles
(3.2 miles) on a rough, sandy road, then take a sharp right onto a less traveled,
unmarked, sand road. Go 0.8 mile (4.0 miles) to the access. Be careful not to
block the access points used for loading by commercial shellfish harvesters.

One of our favorite paddling spots in all of Massachusetts, Edgartown
Great Pond has very little development, lots of wildlife, a 10-horsepower
limit, and more than 15 miles of shoreline to explore. The pond's south
edge backs up against a barrier beach that separates it from the Atlantic

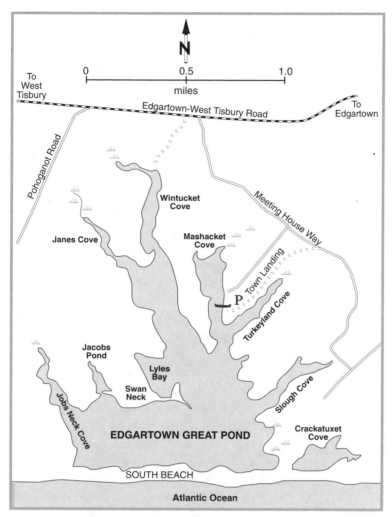

Edgartown Great Pond

Ocean, and you can hear waves crashing just across the low dunes. The beach isolates the pond from the ocean, freeing it from tidal currents.

Edgartown Great Pond and Tisbury Great Pond stand among the best remaining examples anywhere of great salt ponds, a geologic feature of coastal outwash plains. The rippling topography on Martha's Vineyard resulted from glacial streams depositing till as they flowed. As glaciers receded northward, meltwater flowed south off the glaciers, creating streams carrying silt and sand, which they deposited to form the outwash plains found here and on Nantucket, Cape Cod, and Long Island. Moving coastal sands then sealed off the south end of these ponds with barrier beaches.

The varying salinity in great salt ponds results in considerable plant and animal diversity. Periodically, storms wash open a channel between the pond and ocean or just wash over the dunes, allowing mixing of the water. Hurricane Bob in 1991, for example, swept ocean water over the barrier beach, thoroughly mixing Edgartown Great Pond's water with seawater in a few hours. More predictably, anglers open a channel several times a year because, without periodic saltwater mixing, the water would not remain saline enough for shellfish. At the tips of some Edgartown Great Pond coves, freshwater ecosystems harbor salt-intolerant plants, such as cranberry, woolgrass, and grass pink (a type of orchid). Salt-tolerant species, such as salt marsh grasses (*Spartina spp.*), glasswort, and marsh orach, grow along the main pond.

Piping plover and least tern, both threatened species, nest on the dunes here. Osprey nest on several platforms around the pond, and numerous warblers and other songbirds nest in the surrounding area. Paddling here in September, we saw many great blue heron, snowy and great egrets, black-crowned night-heron, black-backed and herring gulls, and various sandpipers and plovers. We also had the good fortune to see a family of five otters. Look for otters early in the morning or toward dusk.

Janes Cove seems the most remote of the Edgartown Great Pond coves. We saw the otters and a pair of large snapping turtles here. Note the thick moss hanging from some of the old red maples and bettle-bung trees (a local name for black gum). Jobs Neck Cove, with just one house on it, also looks great. As you paddle along the shore, watch for blue crabs scurrying away. Specimens up to 8 inches across occur here (note the bright blue claws of some individuals).

Settlers fished here as early as 1660, primarily for alewife. A school of alewives feeding at the surface of calm water looks like a mass of bubbles breaking the surface. They enter the pond through the South Beach opening in spring to spawn, leaving in fall when the barrier beach breaches. Anglers also catch yellow and white perch, eel, and occasional trapped oceanic fish such as striped bass, flounder, and blue-fish. Today the primary commercial fishery in Edgartown Great Pond is shellfish: oysters and steamer clams.

Paddling the full perimeter of Edgartown Great Pond could easily take a full day, especially if you spend time studying its varied plants and wildlife. Remember to respect private property. Except for the public landing on Mashacket Neck, the entire shoreline is privately owned: no camping and no strolling along South Beach allowed.

～21～

Tisbury Great Pond
Chilmark and West Tisbury, MA

MAPS: Massachusetts Atlas, Maps 68 and 69
USGS Quadrangles, Tisbury Great Pond and Vineyard
Haven

AREA: 790 acres

CAMPING AND ACCOMMODATIONS: One private campground:
Martha's Vineyard Family Campground—in Vineyard Haven,
508-693-3772. Accommodations: American Youth Hostel,
508-693-2665; Martha's Vineyard Chamber of Commerce,
508-693-0085 or www.mvy.com.

INFORMATION: For ferry reservations, contact the Steamship
Authority at 508-477-8800, 508-693-9130, or
www.steamshipauthority.com. For tide charts, see
www.maineharbors.com.

HABITAT TYPE: saltwater pond, brackish water

EXPECT TO SEE: gulls, herons and egrets, osprey, otter, sandpipers, blue crab, salt marsh grass, oaks, pitch pine

TAKE NOTE: motors allowed on some ponds; moderate development; wind and tide can create hazardous conditions—this
area is not recommended to novice paddlers; wear PFD;
respect private property

GETTING THERE

From Main Street in Edgartown, go west for 7.7 miles (7.7 miles) on Edgar-
town–West Tisbury Road, and turn left onto New Lane (coming from West
Tisbury, New Lane is 0.3 mile past the Old Country Road intersection).
New Lane, initially paved, quickly becomes Tiah Cove Road. Go 1.2 miles
(8.9 miles), and turn right onto Clam Point Road at the sign for Sepiessa
Point. Park on the left; carry your boat about 200 yards down to the water.
An access at the end of Clam Point Road has limited parking.

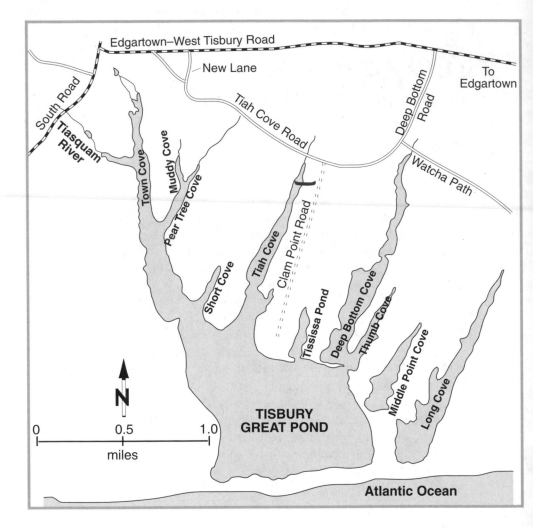

Tisbury Great Pond

With long fingerlike coves that head away from the barrier beach, Tisbury Great Pond closely resembles Edgartown Great Pond, with one important difference: Tisbury suffers from more development. To get a feel for what it would be like to paddle on Tisbury, see the Edgartown Great Pond entry. Martha's Vineyard Land Bank owns property along Tiah Cove, which contains the public access.

～22～

Pocha Pond
Edgartown, MA

MAPS: Massachusetts Atlas, Maps 68 and 69
   USGS Quadrangle, Edgartown

CAMPING AND ACCOMMODATIONS: One private campground:
   Martha's Vineyard Family Campground—in Vineyard Haven,
   508-693-3772. Accommodations: American Youth Hostel,
   508-693-2665; Martha's Vineyard Chamber of Commerce,
   508-693-0085 or www.mvy.com.

INFORMATION: For ferry reservations, contact the Steamship
   Authority at 508-477-8800, 508-693-9130, or
   www.steamshipauthority.com. For tide charts, see
   www.maineharbors.com. For information on Long Cove, Cape
   Poge Wildlife Refuge, Wasque Reservation, or Mytoi Japanese-
   style garden, contact The Trustees of Reservations at 508-693-
   7662 (for Cape Pogue—508-627-7689) or www.thetrustees.org.

HABITAT TYPE: saltwater pond and marsh

EXPECT TO SEE: gulls, herons and egrets, cormorants, sea ducks,
   osprey, mussels and seaweed along banks, salt marsh grass,
   glasswort, sea lavender, black gum, scrub oak, pitch pine

TAKE NOTE: motors allowed on some ponds; limited development; wind and tide can create hazardous conditions—this
   area is not recommended to novice paddlers; wear PFD;
   respect private property

GETTING THERE

From Edgartown, take the ferry to Chappaquiddick Island ($8 plus $2 per passenger in 2003). Go east on Chappaquiddick Road for 2.4 miles (2.4 miles),
and continue straight onto Dyke Road (dirt) when the paved road curves
sharply right and turns into School Road. Go 0.6 mile (3.0 miles) to the access
at Dyke Bridge.

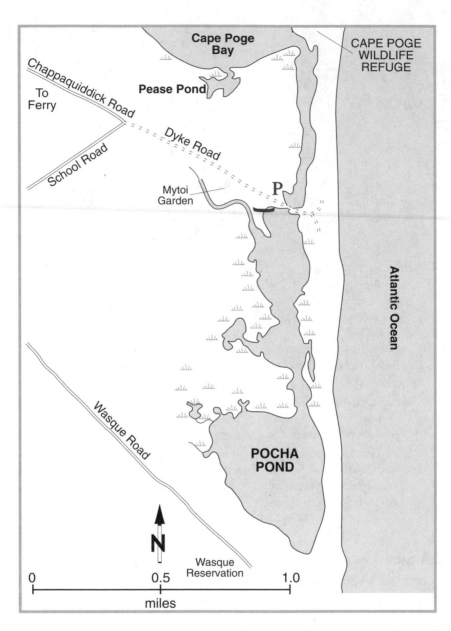

Cape Poge Bay

Pease Pond

CAPE POGE WILDLIFE REFUGE

Chappaquiddick Road

To Ferry

Dyke Road

School Road

Mytoi Garden

P

Atlantic Ocean

Wasque Road

POCHA POND

N

Wasque Reservation

0   0.5   1.0
miles

Pocha Pond

This pond and the connecting channel into Cape Poge Bay provide wonderful paddling and public access across the Cape Poge dunes to several miles of beautiful, remote ocean beach. From the access, you can paddle south into Pocha Pond. A couple of houses near the end of Dyke Road and a few at the south end represent the only development along here, amid acres of wonderful salt marsh.

Paddling here on a September morning, we saw dozens of great blue heron, great and snowy egrets, gulls, and cormorant, plus a few black scoter and kingfisher. Salt marsh plants found here include sea lavender (*Limonium carolinianum*), glasswort (*Salicornia virginica*), and salt marsh grass (*Spartina patens* and *S. alterniflora*). Pocha Pond links to the sea via the Cape Poge Gut, so only plants that withstand salt-water flooding survive here. On the exposed peat at low tide, beneath the salt marsh grass, grow various seaweeds and mussels and, in the water, sponge colonies, various crabs, and mollusks (we found some very large whelk shells). Past the open marsh, you will see pitch pine, scrub and swamp white oaks, and black gum.

Just southwest of Dyke Bridge, a narrow inlet creek invites exploration. Watch out for mollusk-encrusted rocks and shell conglomerates here, particularly near low tide. A *Phragmites* marsh inhabits the end of this little creek, along with a dense grove of sweet gum, whose leaves turn brilliant crimson in early fall.

North of Dyke Bridge, the channel narrows along Toms Neck (an area called the Lagoon) but opens up into Cape Poge Bay. In a strong breeze, the bay gets quite rough. With winds from the south, you can reach Pease Pond without too much difficulty (at low tide, exposed sand banks present obstacles). You can also land on the Atlantic side of the Lagoon or Cape Poge Bay and hike along the beach, though four-wheeler trails along here preclude having a wilderness experience. Also, note that poison ivy grows in profusion amid the dunes. Waves crash the sandy shores of this beautiful beach. Surf fishing here for stripers and blues is considered among the best on the Atlantic Coast—and you may find some interesting things washed up on the beach; on a 1992 visit, we came across the remains of a whale.

Menemsha Pond and Quitsa Pond
Chilmark and Gay Head, MA

MAPS: Massachusetts Atlas, Maps 68 and 69
  USGS Quadrangle, Squibnocket

AREA: Menemsha Pond, 660 acres

CAMPING AND ACCOMMODATIONS: One private campground:
  Martha's Vineyard Family Campground—in Vineyard Haven,
  508-693-3772. Accommodations: American Youth Hostel,
  508-693-2665; Martha's Vineyard Chamber of Commerce,
  508-693-0085 or www.mvy.com.

INFORMATION: For ferry reservations, contact the Steamship
  Authority at 508-477-8800, 508-693-9130, or
  www.steamshipauthority.com. For tide charts, see
  www.maineharbors.com.

HABITAT TYPE: saltwater pond, open to ocean

EXPECT TO SEE: gulls, herons and egrets, sea ducks, osprey, salt
  marsh grass, sea lavender

TAKE NOTE: motors allowed on some ponds; moderate development; wind and tide can create hazardous conditions (strong
  rip current at jetty, north end of Menemsha Pond)—this area
  is not recommended to novice paddlers; significant road
  noise; wear PFD; respect private property

GETTING THERE

Quitsa Pond. From the junction of Menemsha Cross Road and South Road in Chilmark, go southwest on South Road for 1.3 miles to the access at the bridge.

  Menemsha Pond. From the junction of Menemsha Cross Road and North Road northwest of Chilmark, go southwest on North Road for 0.5 mile (0.5 mile), and turn right onto Basin Road. Go 0.3 mile (0.8 mile) to the parking at Dutcher Dock. Hand launch just before the jetty.

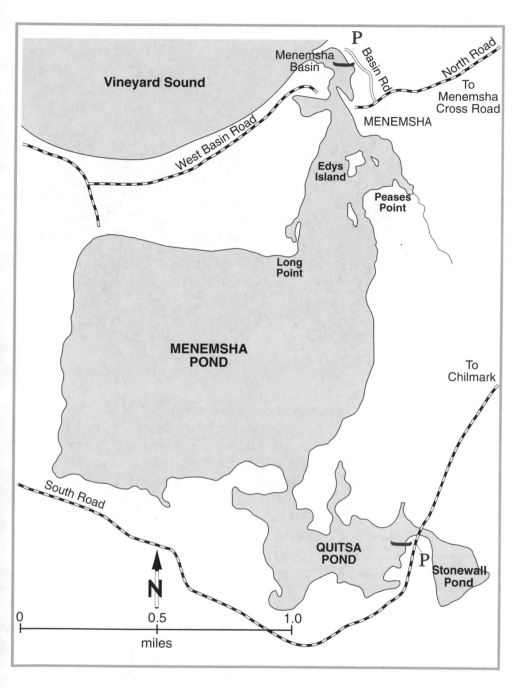

Menemsha Pond and Quitsa Pond

The sun sets over Quitsa Pond on a relatively calm midsummer evening.

From the water, you can view a classic New England fishing village at the north end of Menemsha Pond. Some fishing boats that dock there run very large. Smaller fishing and sailing boats moor along the perimeter of both Menemsha and Quitsa Ponds. Despite the development, we recommend paddling here for its scenic beauty. You could use the access at the end of Dutcher Dock near the large public beach area at the north end of Menemsha Pond, but because of strong tidal currents on Menemsha Creek leading into the pond, we recommend the access on Quitsa Pond. If you paddle up to Menemsha's north end, use caution there to avoid strong tides.

24

Sengekontacket Pond
Edgartown and Oak Bluffs, MA

MAPS: Massachusetts Atlas, Maps 68 and 69
   USGS Quadrangle, Edgartown

AREA: 1,040 acres

CAMPING AND ACCOMMODATIONS: One private campground:
   Martha's Vineyard Family Campground—in Vineyard Haven,
   508-693-3772. Accommodations: American Youth Hostel,
   508-693-2665; Martha's Vineyard Chamber of Commerce,
   508-693-0085 or www.mvy.com.

INFORMATION: Felix Neck Wildlife Sanctuary—Massachusetts
   Audubon Society, 508-627-4850 or www.massaudubon.org.
   For ferry reservations, contact the Steamship Authority at
   508-477-8800, 508-693-9130, or
   www.steamshipauthority.com. For tide charts, see
   www.maineharbors.com.

HABITAT TYPE: saltwater pond

EXPECT TO SEE: gulls, herons and egrets, osprey, hawks, blue
   crab, salt marsh plants

TAKE NOTE: motors allowed on some ponds; limited development; signficant road noise; much of shoreline is conserved;
   wind and tide can create hazardous conditions—novice paddlers should use great care; wear PFD; respect private property

GETTING THERE

From the junction of Edgartown and Vineyard Haven Roads in Edgartown,
go north for 2.0 miles on Edgartown–Oak Bluffs (Beach) Road to the access
on the left. You could also hand launch from several other locations along
the road.

Located between Oak Bluffs and Edgartown, this large pond suffers from
a fair amount of development and road noise but offers nice paddling
nonetheless. Numerous marshy coves and islands along the western

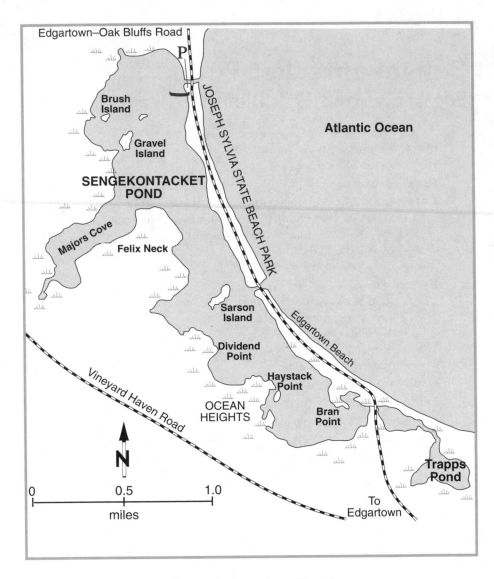

Sengekontacket Pond

shore beg to be explored. On Felix Neck near the pond's midpoint (reachable from Vineyard Haven Road), the Massachusetts Audubon Society maintains the Felix Neck Wildlife Sanctuary. Fortunately, you don't have to be able to pronounce the pond's Indian name to paddle on it.

Central
Massachusetts

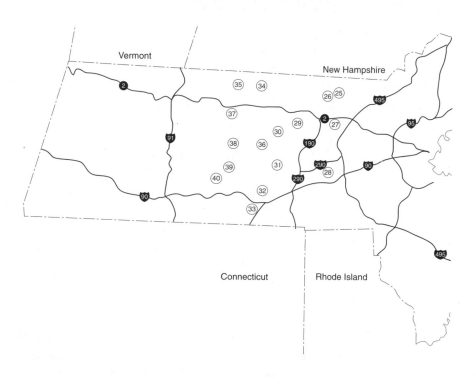

25

Nashua River
Groton and Pepperell, MA

MAPS: Massachusetts Atlas, Map 27
  USGS Quadrangle, Pepperell
LENGTH: 5 miles
CAMPING: Willard Brook State Forest and Pearl Hill State Park,
  978-597-8802; reservations: 877-422-6762 or
  www.ReserveAmerica.com
HABITAT TYPE: dammed-up meandering river, shrubby marsh-
  lands, many islands and protected bays
EXPECT TO SEE: muskrat, mink, waterfowl, marsh birds, aquatic
  vegetation, varied shrubs
TAKE NOTE: little development; motors allowed; take care to
  avoid getting lost

GETTING THERE

From Pepperell, go south on Route 111. When Route 111 joins Route 119, go east for 0.4 mile, turning left just after crossing the bridge over the Nashua River. Access is immediately on the left at the Groton Conservation Land.

An alternate hand-carry access, maintained by the Pepperell Conservation Commission, is on Canal Street, 0.1 mile south of Route 113 in Pepperell.

This dammed-up section of the Nashua River, lying halfway between Fitchburg and Lowell, would take an entire day to explore fully. Twists and turns among the many islands, coupled with adjacent oxbows and side channels, turn this inundated marshland into a giant 5-mile-long maze. If you have limited time and want to avoid getting lost, take along a compass and a photocopy of the map.

A shrubby, marshy shoreline provides cover for numerous ducks, geese, and other birds. We saw lots of beaver activity and several muskrat. As we paddled along, we thought we saw a beaver swimming, until it hustled out onto a 25-foot-long, horizontal dead tree and ran for shore. It turned out to be a gorgeous reddish gray mink that dove for

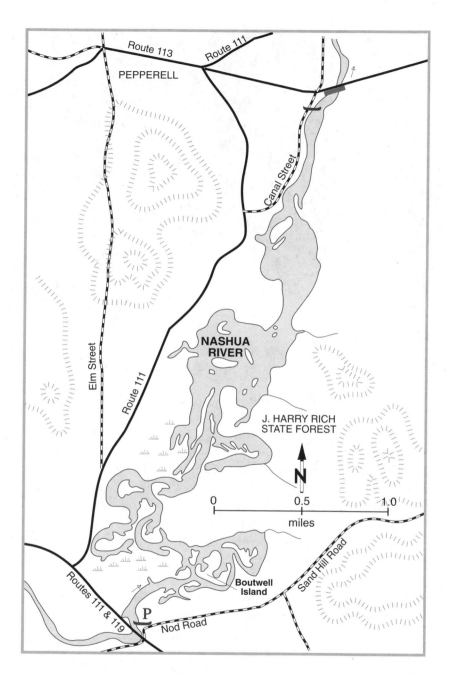

Nashua River

A mink eyes us warily from a shoreside stump.

cover into the dead tree's stump. If you sit patiently, chances are a mink will pop back into view after a few minutes to check you out, as this one did. Satisfied that we were interlopers, it dove back into the stump.

Though shrubs and cattails cover much of the marshy shoreline, a large number of majestic white pines tower overhead, especially along the eastern shore in the J. Harry Rich State Forest, giving the entire area a substantial wilderness feel. The state allows motors but limits their speed to 22 miles-per-hour—an odd number it seems.

We loved paddling here in spring, listening to the returning songbirds staking out their nesting territories and the choruses of spring peepers. Its gorgeous setting, large size, and plentiful wildlife make it one of the best places to paddle in eastern Massachusetts, though use care to avoid getting disoriented in the maze of channels.

Muskrat
Denizen of the Cattail Marsh

Toward dusk on marshy ponds and estuaries, as you paddle past tall stands of cattails and *Phragmites,* watch for a V rippling out across still water. You can distinguish a muskrat from its larger cousin, the beaver, by the way it swims. A beaver swims with only its large, broad head above water. A muskrat swims with its head above water and with its narrow tail snaking rapidly from side to side behind it. While generally wary, muskrats may seem oblivious to their surroundings. They have bumped into our boats, and they have sat unconcernedly as we photographed them from a short distance away.

The muskrat, *Ondatra zibethicus,* in the order Rodentia along with beaver, is more closely related to voles, rats, some mice, and lemmings in the family Cricetidae. Its common name derives from the strong musky scent emitted from glands in its groin during breeding season. They grow to a foot long, have an 8- to 10-inch scaly tail, and weigh 2 to 4 pounds. Males and females look identical, except under close examination.

Using both their hind feet and their vertically flattened tails for propulsion, muskrats swim adeptly. They can remain underwater for up to 15 minutes, covering distances up to 150 feet. Like beaver, their lips split behind the four incisors, allowing them to cut stems without swallowing water. Their diet consists of cattails and other common marsh plants, such as bulrush, waterlily, pickerelweed, arrowhead, and swamp loosestrife. They supplement this vegetarian diet with mussels, crayfish, snails, tadpoles, and other aquatic animals, particularly in winter when vegetation is scarce. Being ever wary of predators, muskrats usually cut their food and take it to a safer place to eat, such as a specially constructed feeding platform or, in winter, on top of ice. Though chiefly nocturnal, they can be seen during the daytime as well. Unlike beaver, they rarely venture more than 200 feet for food.

Muskrats build two types of houses: dens and lodges, depending on local conditions. They dig dens in the bank of a pond or river and always place the entrances below water level. On reservoirs and ponds with fluctuating water levels, these underwater entrances may be exposed at certain times of year. Muskrats use tunnels and dens for many generations and develop them into elaborate labyrinths. Tunnels up to 200 yards long have been found, and these can damage earthen dams, levees, and dikes. Individual nesting chambers typically measure 6 by 8 inches and contain shredded plant material.

They build lodges in shallow open water or marsh—places where bank dens cannot be built—of vegetation and mud collected from the immediate vicinity resemble small beaver lodges. An underwater entrance connects to the chamber, typically about a foot in diameter. Unlike beavers, muskrats build solid lodges and then tunnel them out later.

While muskrat lodges do not afford good protection from predators during warmer months, once the mud freezes in winter they become impenetrable fortresses. Muskrats use some lodges only in winter, when a large lodge may house as many as eight or nine muskrats, possibly congregating to keep warm. Most lodges last only a year, then collapse as the vegetation rots. In addition to lodges, muskrats build feeding platforms from the same materials; these smaller structures provide safe places to eat collected food.

Muskrats breed prolifically. Females typically have two or three litters in a single season and may have even more in the South, where they breed year-round. They can breed again just a few days after giving birth. After a gestation period of about thirty days, four to six nearly hairless, blind kits are born in the den or lodge. They open their eyes after two weeks, begin swimming in their third week, and become totally independent after four or five weeks. In fact, if the mother has another litter at that time, she will forcibly evict the youngsters, even injuring them in some cases to drive them away. Rapid population growth can lead to stress, competition for food, territory battles, and illnesses. Sometimes disease wipes out entire muskrat populations. Commonly, only a third of muskrat young survive into their first winter.

While muskrats may congregate in winter, they disperse in spring. During April and May, some individuals may travel as far as 20 miles overland looking for a new territory, leading to some muskrat roadkills.

Trappers have long sought muskrats for their soft fur, but their prolific reproduction and lower visibility protected them from population depletion, unlike beaver. Trappers nearly drove beaver to extinction in the late 1800s. Muskrats have proved hardy, able to survive, even prosper, in suburban and urban areas—wherever they find a bit of cattail marsh.

~ 26 ~

Squannacook River
Groton and Shirley, MA

MAPS: Massachusetts Atlas, Map 27
   USGS Quadrangles, Ayer and Townsend
LENGTH: 3 miles
CAMPING: Willard Brook State Forest and Pearl Hill State Park,
   978-597-8802; reservations: 877-422-6762 or
   www.ReserveAmerica.com
HABITAT TYPE: dammed-up meandering river, extensive
   marshlands
EXPECT TO SEE: muskrat, waterfowl, marsh birds, aquatic
   vegetation, varied shrubs, overhanging trees
TAKE NOTE: no development; too shallow for motors

GETTING THERE

From the junction of Routes 13 and 119 in Townsend, go east on Route 119 for 3.0 miles (3.0 miles), and turn right onto Townsend Road. Access is 2.5 miles (5.5 miles) from Route 119 at the West Groton Water Supply District plant on the right. Turn in by the yellow fire hydrant.

From Route 225 in West Groton, go north for 1.1 miles on Townsend Road to the access on the left.

Paddling through Squannacook River Wildlife Management Area, you may become entranced with the peacefulness, away from the bustle of everyday life. Marshlands head off like fingers in the lower reaches, providing ample opportunity for exploration. Birdlife fills the area, and—judging by the number of anglers—trout must fill the waters. The side channels abound with fragrant waterlily, along with lesser amounts of yellow pondlily, water shield, pondweed, and pickerelweed.

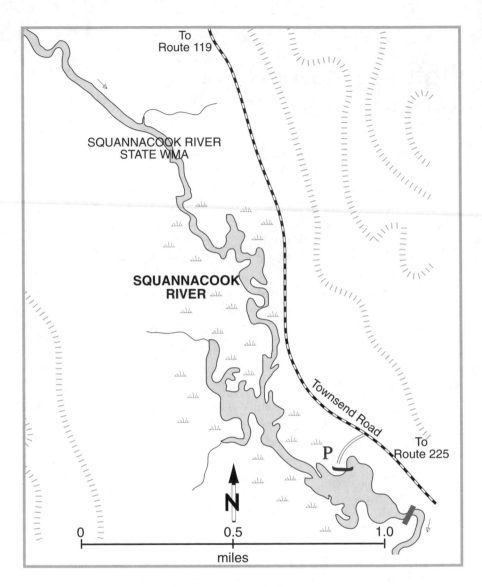

To
Route 119

SQUANNACOOK RIVER
STATE WMA

SQUANNACOOK
RIVER

Townsend Road

To
Route 225

P

N

0   0.5   1.0
miles

Squannacook River

We found an enormous beaver lodge with winter stores of freshly cut boughs jammed butt-first into the mud. Beaver swim out under the winter ice, retrieving branches to gnaw the bark that sustains them. We watched the occasional muskrat harvest streamside grasses for winter. Great blue herons patrolled the coves, and we scared up a few flocks of wood ducks as we intruded on their territories.

Unconcerned, a muskrat watches us paddle by.

Paddling upstream away from the dam, side channels disappear, and the canopy closes in over the narrow, twisting river. Besides the occasional white pine, deciduous trees hold sway. We paddled the Squannacook on a truly gorgeous, misty but balmy autumn day. Fall colors filled the air, and migrating sparrows filled the streamside vegetation. We navigated upstream through the slow current until a ledgy rapids blocked our way, then sat there soaking in the golden color of the streamside ferns and regretting our need to turn around.

~27~

Nashua River and the Oxbow National Wildlife Refuge

Bolton, Harvard, Lancaster, and Shirley, MA

Maps: Massachusetts Atlas, Maps 27 and 39
USGS Quadrangles, Ayer and Hudson

Length: 9.5 miles

Camping: Willard Brook State Forest and Pearl Hill State Park,
978-597-8802; reservations: 877-422-6762 or
www.ReserveAmerica.com

Habitat Type: meandering, slow-flowing river

Expect to See: muskrat, wood duck, painted turtle, whitetailed
deer, varied trees and shrubs

Take Note: a little development north of Route 2; too shallow
for motors

GETTING THERE

From Route 2, Exit 38A, go south on Routes 110/111 for 1.6 miles (1.6 miles),
and turn right onto Route 110 when they split. Go south on Route 110 for
2.0 miles (3.6 miles) to the sign for Oxbow National Wildlife Refuge, and turn
right onto Still River Depot Road. Access is just over the tracks in 0.5 mile
(4.1 miles); after crossing the tracks, jog right, then left.

This Nashua River section flows from Bolton Flats Wildlife Management
Area north through Oxbow National Wildlife Refuge and Fort Devens,
and passes under the Route 2 bridge. The two natural areas, along with
now closed Fort Devens, have protected the river from development. The
river has three distinct areas. Upstream from the access—up through
Bolton Flats WMA—the narrow, shallow, sandy-bottomed river has many
overhanging branches, lots of downed timber to negotiate, and moderate
current in a few places. During times of high water, you may have to paddle the upper section in one direction. We enjoyed paddling the upper
section in late summer because of reduced current and boat traffic.

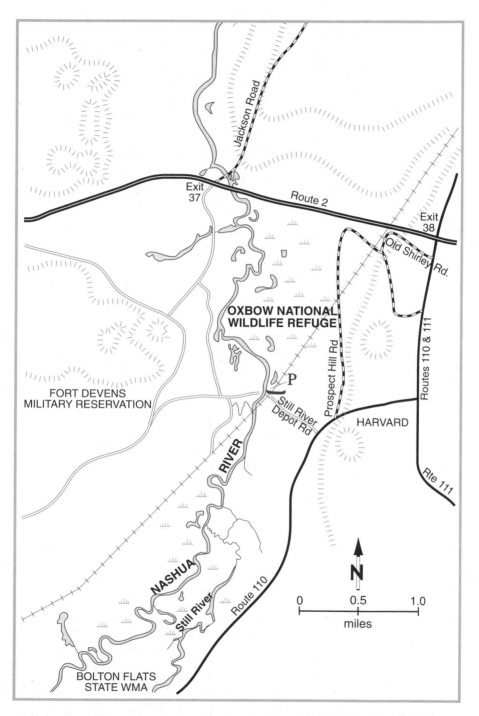

Nashua River and the Oxbow National Wildlife Refuge

The middle section between the Oxbow NWR access and Route 2 flows between Fort Devens on the west and Oxbow NWR on the east. A wooded shoreline encloses the narrow, winding river, with multiple-stemmed silver maple branches draped over the water, making it difficult to get by in a few spots. Though silver maple dominates the shore here, we also saw many sycamore and gray birch. A flock of a couple of dozen wood ducks took off from a tree as we paddled near, and we also came upon a large flock of mallards. Deer came down to the water to drink; several muskrats harvested pickerelweed and streamside grasses, seemingly oblivious to passing boats. We watched a large snapping turtle feed on underwater vegetation, while dozens of painted turtles basked on branches and logs.

The section farthest downstream—north of Route 2— runs much wider and deeper than the previous sections. The banks boast greater tree-species diversity. With the sky unfettered by overhanging branches, we watched a beautiful red-tailed hawk circle overhead. A Cooper's hawk chased songbirds off through the woods, and we looked in vain for cuckoos that might be feeding on the abundant tent caterpillar nests on gray birches. On the way back to the access, we checked out a beaver dam on a bay off to the Fort Devens side that harbored huge patches of pickerelweed.

28

Assabet Reservoir
Westborough, MA

MAPS: Massachusetts Atlas, Map 39
   USGS Quadrangle, Marlborough
AREA: 333 acres
HABITAT TYPE: wooded, marshy reservoir
EXPECT TO SEE: great blue heron rookery, osprey nest, mute swan
TAKE NOTE: many submerged and partially submerged stumps
   keep motors away; limited development; stay well back from
   the rookery to avoid disturbing nesting birds

GETTING THERE

From I-495, Exit 23, go west on Route 9 for 3.3 miles (3.3 miles), and exit onto Route 135. Turn right at the stop sign (south) toward Westborough. Go 0.7 mile (4.0 miles) on Route 135, and turn right onto Maynard Street. Continue on Maynard Street, go under the railroad tracks, bear right onto Fisher Street after 0.6 mile (4.6 miles), and then take an almost immediate left onto Mill Street. Parking is on the right after 0.4 mile (5.0 miles).

Assabet Reservoir, just a few miles from busy Route 9 in Westborough, provides a wonderful place to paddle. Thousands of closely spaced dead trees and stumps, left over from the creation of this flood-control reservoir in 1969, keep out motorboats. Though stumps make paddling here a challenge, the few remaining standing dead trees provide great nesting habitat for birds.

Great blue heron, osprey, and tree swallow nest here. Unfortunately, in the last ten years many dead trees have fallen, reducing the size of the great blue heron rookery. When we paddled here in 1992, nearly two dozen heron nests perched precariously among the spindly tops; in 2002 only nine nests remained, along with a wonderful addition, an osprey nest. Stay well back from the rookery to avoid disturbing nesting birds.

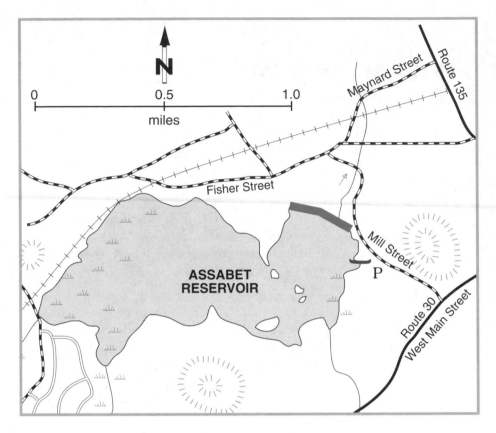

Assabet Reservoir

The reservoir's fairly open eastern end gives way to a forest of protruding and submerged stumps once you round the point of land extending down from the north. In places you will literally have to weave your boat around these trees to get through. Some of the once abundant tree swallows still nest in the remaining dead trees, keeping the mosquito population somewhat in check.

The shallow, stump-filled waters of Assabet Reservoir—15 feet at the deepest—provide plenty of cover for fish. Someone caught a 6-pound largemouth bass during our first trip here. Cattails and bulrush

Great blue heron nests perch precariously atop standing dead trees on the west end of Assabet Reservoir.

line most of the marshy perimeter, with water shield floating on open water. Looking at the reservoir, you might guess that thick muck covers the bottom; somewhat surprisingly, sand coats much of the bottom instead. Piles of freshwater mussels provide evidence of many raccoon meals. Willow, alder, red maple, red oak, and aspen surround the reservoir. A number of scattered islands add scenic beauty but offer little in the way of access for rest or a picnic. Along with swallows, great blue heron, and osprey, keep an eye out for green heron, cedar waxwing, wood duck, and lots of painted turtles.

29

Paradise Pond
Princeton, MA

MAPS: Massachusetts Atlas, Map 26
USGS Quadrangles, Fitchburg and Sterling
AREA: 61 acres
CAMPING: Willard Brook State Forest and Pearl Hill State Park,
978-597-8802; Lake Denison State Recreation Area and
Otter River State Forest, 978-939-8962; reservations:
877-422-6762 or www.ReserveAmerica.com
HABITAT TYPE: wooded pond
EXPECT TO SEE: mountain laurel in bloom in June; pitch pine
TAKE NOTE: no development; no motors

GETTING THERE

From the West. From Route 2, Exit 25, go south on Route 140 for 4.1 miles (4.1 miles), and turn sharply back left onto Fitchburg Road (Route 31 north). In 0.2 mile (4.3 miles) and for the next 0.5 mile (4.8 miles) after that, there are several access points on the right.

From the East. From Route 2, Exit 28, go south on Route 31 for 3.1 miles to the first of several access points on the left.

Bordering Leominster State Forest, undeveloped and free of motors, Paradise Pond provides an idyllic place to paddle. With an undulating shoreline and several islands and coves to explore, you could spend a few hours on this small pond, especially in mid-June when the abundant mountain laurel puts on a spectacular display. Route 31, though not heavily traveled, occasionally intrudes on the peace and quiet.

Vegetation includes a number of species that you rarely see this far north: swamp honeysuckle, a fairly late-blooming azalea with tubular sticky white flowers; sweet pepperbush, a late-blooming shrub with clusters of small, fragrant white flowers that you can still find in bloom at the end of August; and sassafras.

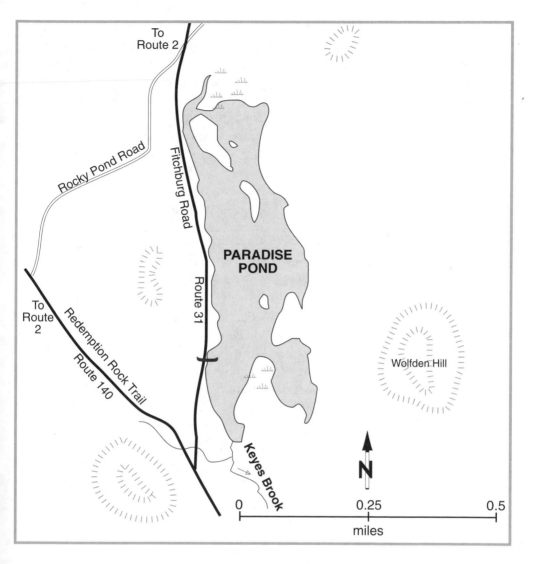

To
Route 2

Rocky Pond Road

Fitchburg Road

Route 31

PARADISE
POND

To
Route
2

Redemption Rock Trail

Route 140

Keyes Brook

Wolfden Hill

N

0   0.25   0.5
miles

Paradise Pond

The islands on Paradise Pond are quite interesting and very much worth visiting. Instead of white pine and the various deciduous trees that comprise most of the woods around the pond, pitch pine—a three-needled pine with large plates of bark on older trees—dominates the islands. A thick bed of needles in the open understory provides ideal locations for a picnic lunch.

In some sections, water shield covers the surface; you can easily distinguish this from other waterlilies because the stem extends down from the center of the oval leaves. Feel the slippery stems and the undersides of the leaves. Carnivorous plants occur here, as well. In the water you will see lots of bladderwort, and if you look carefully you will find sundews on floating logs and sphagnum hummocks. We also saw a water snake here, entwined on a branch over the water.

The ruins of an old mill building stand at the southern tip of the pond; an 1870 map shows this as the E. B. Walker Saw Mill. Earlier maps show other sawmills to the northwest on the Keyes Brook branch of the Stillwater. An old country road ran closer to this river route than the present Route 140, also known as Redemption Rock Trail. Early colonial negotiators chose Princeton as the site for a prisoner redemption at "Redemption Rock," off Route 140, less than a mile north of the junction with Route 31, deep in the woods. It was here in 1675 that Mary Rowlandson, who had been captured during the midwinter massacre at Lancaster and held in Quebec for eight weeks, was freed for twenty pounds sterling and some whiskey.

On the east side of Paradise Pond, Leominster State Forest provides some great hiking on old logging roads and trails that wind through needle-carpeted open woodland. You'll see lots of wildflowers here in spring.

～ 30 ～

Moosehorn Pond
Hubbardston, MA

MAPS: Massachusetts Atlas, Map 37
  USGS Quadrangle, Sterling
AREA: 67 acres
CAMPING: Lake Dennison State Recreation Area and Otter River
  State Forest, 978-939-8962; Willard Brook State Forest and
  Pearl Hill State Park, 978-597-8802; reservations:
  877-422-6762 or www.ReserveAmerica.com; Tully Lake: The
  Trustees of Reservations, 978-249-4957 or www.thetrustees.org
HABITAT TYPE: northern fen
EXPECT TO SEE: wood duck, great blue heron, northern fen plants
TAKE NOTE: little development; hand launch limits motors;
  paddle quietly amid marshy islands to minimize disturbance
  of nesting wood ducks

GETTING THERE

From Route 2, Exit 22, go south on Route 68 for 7.5 miles (7.5 miles), and turn left onto Old Princeton Road (this left is 0.6 mile south of the flashing yellow light on Route 68 in Hubbardston). Go east on Old Princeton Road for 1.6 miles (9.1 miles) to the access on the left (less than 100 yards beyond the junction of Old Princeton Road with Simonds Hill and Healdville Roads).

Moosehorn Pond, though small, is interesting and definitely worth a visit. Only one house, set well back from the water, interrupts the pond's otherwise pristine shoreline. Spongy mats of sphagnum and dense stands of leatherleaf, punctuated by occasional tall tamarack spires, lend a very "northern" feel to this marshy pond. Sundews, marsh ferns, and occasional pitcher plants hide amid the sphagnum.

Along with tamarack, look for red maple, white and gray birches, white pine, red oak, American chestnut, sassafras, witch hazel, blueberry, winterberry (a member of the holly genus), and sweet pepperbush. Fragrant waterlily, yellow pondlily, water shield, and pondweed leaves

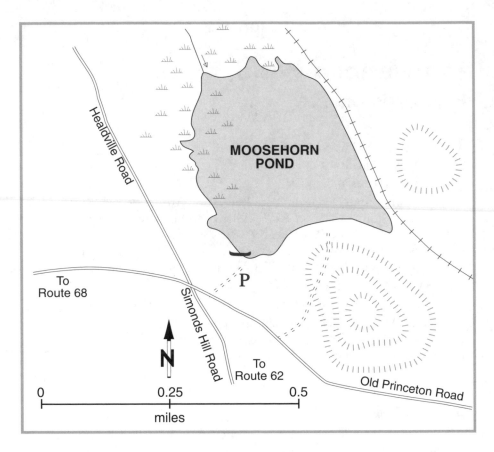

Moosehorn Pond

float on the water's surface. Paddle quietly through the marshy islands to minimize disturbance of nesting wood ducks; look for great blue heron stalking frogs, bass, pickerel, and yellow perch.

During most seasons you can paddle considerably farther north than the border of the pond shown on the map—though floating sphagnum mats, half-submerged logs, and grassy hillocks impede your progress. Indeed, on the pond's northern section, poling would prove far more effective than paddling. Old but still-used railroad tracks run along the pond's eastern side.

31

Eames Pond
Paxton, MA

MAPS: Massachusetts Atlas, Map 37
  USGS Quadrangle, Worcester North
AREA: 74 acres
CAMPING: Wells State Park, 508-347-9257; reservations:
  877-422-6762 or www.ReserveAmerica.com
HABITAT TYPE: shallow, marshy pond
EXPECT TO SEE: beaver, muskrat, great blue heron, waterfowl,
  other marsh birds, rafts of aquatic plants
TAKE NOTE: limited development; hand launch, shallowness, and
  vegetation keep motors out

GETTING THERE

From the junction of Routes 31, 56, and 122 at the stoplight in Paxton, go north
on Route 122 for 1.4 miles to the access on the left, just before the culvert.

With much of the shoreline protected by Moore State Park, Eames
Pond offers a wonderful paddling opportunity, especially if you don't
mind making your way through endless seas of lily pads. Beaver maintain something of a channel—guarded by pickerelweed and arrowhead—that wends its way through what is truly a carpet of fragrant
waterlily. As we paddled down the pond, we noticed what looked like a
small island near the eastern shore; upon closer inspection, it turned
out to be a massive beaver lodge at least 25 feet long, with abundant
branches stored underwater as a winter larder.

In contrast to most of the fragrant waterlily seen on ponds in
Massachusetts, the *tuberosa* subspecies grows here. Note the huge green
leaves, some spanning a foot. Fragrant waterlily occurs as two subspecies: *Nymphaea odorata odorata* and *N.o. tuberosa*. Most guidebooks
list these as separate species, but taxonomists have recently lumped
them into one. The more common subspecies, *odorata*, bears much

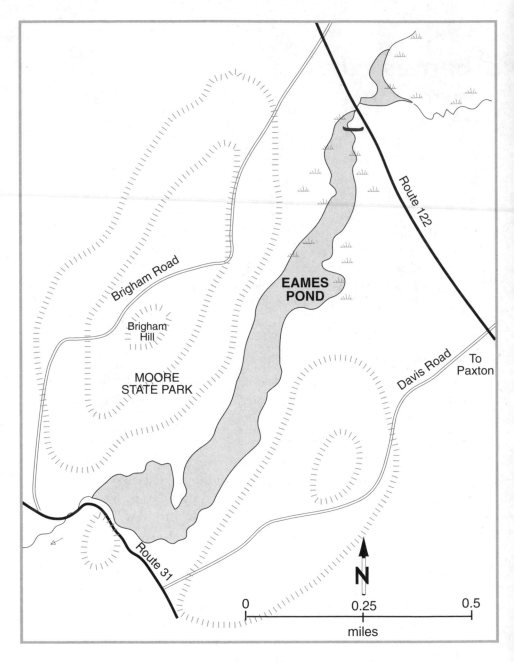

Eames Pond

When we paddled Eames Pond in mid-August, we were surrounded by purple-flowered bladderwort.

smaller leaves, with both the leaves and the flower sepals tinged with purple. *Tuberosa* produces large green leaves and green sepals.

As you paddle into the pond's southern reaches, fragrant waterlily gives way to water shield and pondweed. Most striking by far, though, when we paddled here in mid-August, was a truly stupendous amount of purple-flowered bladderwort (*Utricularia purpurea*) in bloom, more than we had seen on all other ponds combined. The entire south end radiated a purple glow that could be seen for hundreds of yards. Paddling closer, as an incredibly sweet odor wafted toward us on a gentle breeze, floating yellow-brown pondweed leaves provided a wonderful contrast to the sea of tiny purple flowers, borne on slender 4-inch stalks. We reveled in this gorgeous setting, not wanting to paddle back to the access. We also wondered if the *tuberosa* would eventually take over the southern end, as well, crowding out the huge mats of purple-flowered bladderwort.

Though few people paddle this wonderful pond, many people hike the several trails that course through Moore State Park. We prefer the paddling, especially when we see goldfinch and great blue heron among the bur-reed, joe-pye weed, sweetgale, buttonbush, wild rice, and dwarf red maples in this broad marsh. But we will never get over the sight of those purple-flowered bladderwort.

32

Quaboag Pond, Quaboag River, and East Brookfield River

Brookfield, East Brookfield, Warren, and West Brookfield, MA

MAPS: Massachusetts Atlas, Maps 48 and 49
  USGS Quadrangle, Warren

AREA/LENGTH: Quaboag Pond, 541 acres;
  Quaboag River, 9 miles;
  East Brookfield River, 2 miles

CAMPING: Wells State Park, 508-347-9257;
  reservations: 877-422-6762 or www.ReserveAmerica.com

HABITAT TYPE: marshy rivers

EXPECT TO SEE: beaver, muskrat, turtles, osprey, waterfowl,
  marsh birds, aquatic vegetation, varied shrubs

TAKE NOTE: development and motors on pond; little development on rivers

---

GETTING THERE

Access points are given in order, starting upstream.

Quaboag Pond, North End. From the junction of Routes 9 and 148 in Brookfield, go east on Route 9 for 1.1 miles (1.1 miles), and turn right onto Quaboag Street. Access is on the right in 1.4 miles (2.5 miles).

Route 148. From the junction of Routes 9 and 148 in Brookfield, go south on Route 148 for 0.6 mile to the access on the left, just before the bridge.

Route 67. From I-90, Exit 8, head south on Route 32, and turn left onto Route 20 east in Palmer; turn left onto Route 67 north. From Warren, take Route 67 north for 2.4 miles to the access and picnic area on the left, just before the junction with Route 9.

Warren. Just after crossing the bridge in Warren, turn left onto Old West Brookfield Road (River Street), and go 0.3 mile to Lucy Stone Park on the left. This is a take-out point only (for when you have two vehicles); going downstream from here will take you into dangerous whitewater.

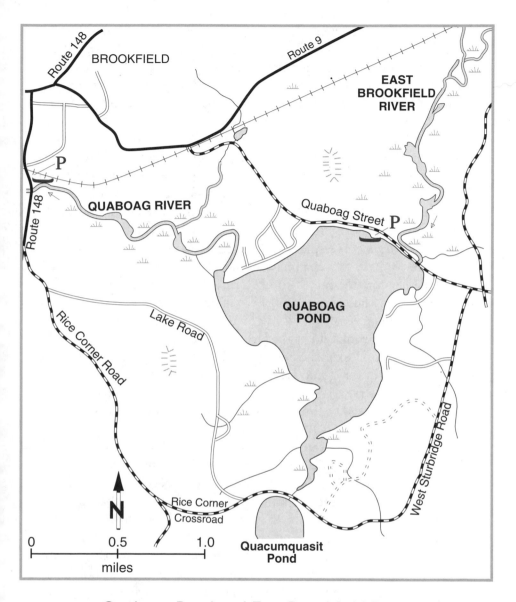

Route 148
BROOKFIELD
Route 9

EAST
BROOKFIELD
RIVER

P

Route 148

QUABOAG RIVER

Quaboag Street P

Lake Road

**QUABOAG
POND**

Rice Corner Road

West Sturbridge Road

N

Rice Corner
Crossroad

0   0.5   1.0
miles

**Quacumquasit
Pond**

Quaboag Pond and East Brookfield River

East Brookfield River. Because of development and water-skiers, we would avoid Quaboag Pond, except as access to the East Brookfield River (or Sevenmile River). We love paddling the inlet and outlet rivers, both of which provide an extraordinary undeveloped, wildlife-rich paddling resource. East Brookfield River flows into Quaboag Pond at the northeastern tip. Traveling upstream from the Quaboag Street bridge, the slow-flowing East Brookfield hugs the road for a few hundred yards, then turns north and east. Initially, the wide channel winds through Allen Marsh, the sides thick with pickerelweed, grasses, sedges, and buttonbush. Fragrant waterlily, yellow pondlily, and pondweed leaves float on the water's surface. Bladderwort and Eurasian water-milfoil flow in the current beneath. Though rarely visible, freshwater mussels thrive in the sandy bottom. Look for painted turtles and the less common stinkpot turtle along here—we saw a stinkpot perched on a protruding branch well above the water's surface. Wood ducks raise their broods here, and great blue herons patrol the shorelines. You may see muskrats harvesting streamside grasses as you paddle along.

Farther north, the channel narrows and becomes more defined, with fewer backwater ponds to explore. About 2 miles upriver, after reaching a fork, fallen trees and beaver dams impede your progress, though with perseverance you might make it to Lake Lashaway (left fork) or to East Brookfield (right fork); still, portaging over the numerous deadfalls would likely be quite an ordeal. In the upper stretches, we saw a beaver swimming midday and an osprey with fish.

Quaboag River. At Quaboag Pond's northwestern tip, the Quaboag River rises, beginning its westward journey to its confluence with the Ware and Swift Rivers, where they form the Chicopee River. Quiet meandering flat water, through wide marshlands teeming with wildlife, marks this 9-mile section of river. Paddling down and back takes at least a full day, especially if you stop to revel in the gorgeous scenery and to watch the ubiquitous wildlife. For more than the first half of the journey, the Quaboag River winds its way through marshy Quaboag Wildlife Management Area. Thick shrub vegetation lines the banks, and underwater vegetation forms thick mats. Clumps of swamp loosestrife, some extending for hundreds of yards along the shore, arch gracefully out over the water. Along this stretch of river, trees line the higher ground, a few hundred yards across the marsh.

Paddling farther downstream one evening, where trees and taller shrubs encroach on the shores, we saw seven beaver beginning their nightly branch-gathering forays. We listened to hermit thrush, catbird, towhee, song sparrow, and cardinal call from the dense undergrowth, and to veery singing off in the woods. We watched muskrat swim about and a deer come down for a drink. Swamp rose grows in

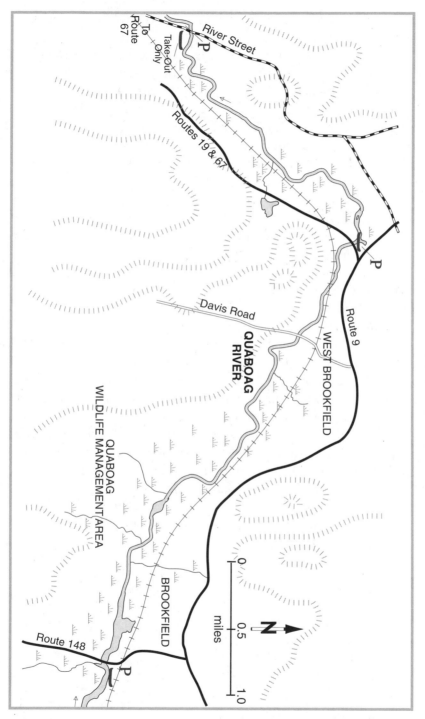

Quaboag River

River Street

To
Route
67

Take-Out
Only

P

Routes 19 & 67

P

Route 9

Davis Road

WEST BROOKFIELD

QUABOAG
RIVER

QUABOAG
WILDLIFE MANAGEMENT AREA

BROOKFIELD

Route 148

P

0   0.5   1.0
miles

N

profusion, and some huge swamp white oaks occur along the banks in the downstream sections.

After paddling through expansive marshes, the river narrows, and trees line the banks. When you reach the section with several large rocks in succession jutting above the surface, the current picks up. Turn around here, especially during times of high water. If you have two cars, you can paddle down to the take-out at Lucy Stone Park in Warren.

In years long past, the Quaboag River served as a major thoroughfare for the region's Native Americans. A short portage connected Quaboag Pond to the nearby Quinebaug River, which runs south through Nipmuk and eastern Niantic country to meet other tributaries of the Pawcatuck River system, which in turn meanders from southern Rhode Island through Narragansett country. In this way, Native American nations of this south coastal region could communicate, trade, and journey north to Quaboag Pond, then turn west and down the Chicopee River to Connecticut country.

In the uprising known as King Philip's War, Native American nations along this route ravaged the more isolated English settlements. Old Brookfield, a frontier village about 8 miles to the northwest on Foster Hill, became an easy target. On August 2, 1675, Quaboag warriors ambushed an armed team of English negotiators from Boston, there to extract a pledge of neutrality amid growing warfare in southeastern New England. The retreating English took hasty refuge with Brookfield's families in their largest structure, Ayres' Tavern. Ephraim Curtis, a scout of that party, finally crept through a determined siege in which all other structures were burned, to bring about eventual rescue from Marlborough. Fifty women and children and thirty-two men held the tavern, while two sets of twin babies were born within. The settlers soon abandoned the town for safer and more central Hadley, in today's "Pioneer Valley" near Amherst.

～33～

East Brimfield Lake, Quinebaug River, Holland Pond, and Long Pond

Brimfield, Holland, and Sturbridge, MA

MAPS: Massachusetts Atlas, Maps 48 and 49
  USGS Quadrangles, Brimfield, Holland, and Sturbridge
AREA/LENGTH: Holland Pond, 85 acres;
  East Brimfield Lake and Long Pond, 420 acres;
  Quinebaug River, 3 miles
CAMPING: Wells State Park, 508-347-9257;
  reservations: 877-422-6762 or www.ReserveAmerica.com
HABITAT TYPE: slow, marshy, peaceful river
EXPECT TO SEE: muskrat, waterfowl, marsh birds, aquatic
  vegetation, lots of swamp rose on river, tree-lined lakeshore
TAKE NOTE: no motors on river; lakes congested with
  motorboats

GETTING THERE

Holland Pond. From the junction of Routes 20 and 148 in Fiskdale, go west for 1.7 miles (1.7 miles) and turn left onto Holland–East Brimfield Road. Turn right onto Morse Road in 2.0 miles (3.7 miles) at the Canoe Trail sign. In 0.2 mile (3.9 miles), turn sharply back left onto the access road; the Canoe Trail access is 0.3 mile (4.2 miles) around to the right, skirting the north shore of Holland Pond.

Long Pond Access; Route 20, North Side. From the junction of Routes 20 and 148, go west on Route 20 for 0.7 mile to the access on the right, just across from the entrance to Streeter Road Beach.

Brimfield Lake Access; Route 20, South Side. Continue on beyond the Long Pond access for 0.4 mile to the access on the left.

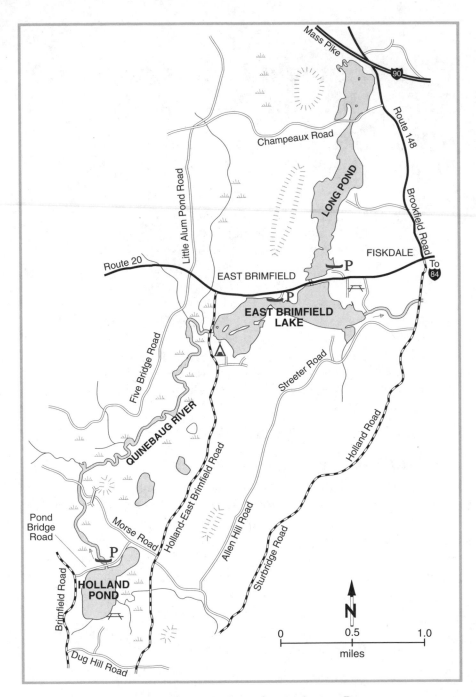

East Brimfield Lake, Quinebaug River, Holland Pond, and Long Pond

Near historic Old Sturbridge Village you can enjoy a full day of paddling on the various bodies of water that collectively comprise East Brimfield Lake. The slow-flowing Quinebaug River connects Holland Pond to the south with Long Pond to the north. With limited time, we would paddle the quieter and less congested Quinebaug River, putting in at the Holland Pond access. With more time, we would paddle the 12-mile round trip up to the north end of Long Pond and back to Holland Pond.

Small but very attractive Holland Pond has just a few houses on the west side, well away from and above the water. Two sandy beaches—a small one near the outlet and another larger one across the pond at the Holland Pond Recreation Area—offer a respite from the summer heat.

From Holland Pond, depending on water level, you may have to carry over the road into the Quinebaug River. The river passes some farmland near the north end but mostly winds through thick marshes filled with birdlife. Ferns grow thickly along sections of the bank, and in the few places where wooded slopes rise steeply from the water, you will see mountain laurel beneath the red oak and white oak canopy. Underwater vegetation fills the shallows. When we paddled here in July, swamp rose bloomed in profusion along the banks, while pickerel-weed and waterlilies bloomed on the water. You will scarcely notice the current, because the water level drops only about 3 feet in 3 miles.

We would not spend much time on East Brimfield Lake south of Route 20 given the looming dam at the east end, a public beach and picnic area, a large and well-used boat ramp, a popular private campground, and the highway running along much of it. We would stick to the river or head immediately up to Long Pond, north of Route 20.

Long Pond extends about 1.5 miles north from the Route 20 access, almost to I-90. White pine, red and white oaks, sugar and red maples dominate the heavily wooded shoreline. Unfortunately, Eurasian water-milfoil has crowded out some of the native vegetation; some development has also sprouted along the east shore. Two-thirds of the way up, you have to paddle under very low Champeaux Road bridge; marshy coves, floating pond vegetation, ferns along the banks, and lots of birds abound along the more interesting northern shoreline. A red oak and white pine grove juts out into the water, making a great picnic area on the northwestern side of Long Pond. Though shielded pretty well by trees, I-90 vehicle noise intrudes on the northern end of the pond.

While in the area, you can visit historic Old Sturbridge Village, a living museum portraying New England life in the 1830s.

34

Millers River, Otter River, and Lake Denison
Templeton and Winchendon, MA

MAPS: Massachusetts Atlas, Map 25
   USGS Quadrangles, Athol, Royalston, and Winchendon
AREA/LENGTH: Lake Denison, 82 acres;
   Millers River, 7.5 miles;
   Otter River, 3 miles
CAMPING: Lake Denison State Recreation Area and Otter River
   State Forest, 978-939-8962; reservations: 877-422-6762 or
   www.ReserveAmerica.com; Tully Lake: The Trustees of
   Reservations, 978-249-4957 or www.thetrustees.org
HABITAT TYPE: meandering unspoiled rivers, shrubby marshlands
EXPECT TO SEE: waterfowl, marsh birds, snapping turtle,
   muskrat, beaver, aquatic vegetation, varied shrubs
TAKE NOTE: no motors; no development

GETTING THERE

Lake Denison. From the junction of Routes 12 and 202 in Winchendon, go south on Route 202 for 1.8 miles (1.8 miles), and turn diagonally right onto Main Street as Route 202 curves left. Go south on Main Street for 1.7 miles (3.5 miles) to the Lake Denison access on the left.

   Millers and Otter Rivers. Continue south on Main Street from the Lake Denison access for 0.1 mile (3.6 miles), and turn right onto New Boston Road. The access is in 0.3 mile (3.9 miles) on the left, just over the bridge.

Bounded by the Birch Hill Wildlife Management Area and the Otter River State Forest, these two rivers offer an unspoiled paddle through red maple, alder, red-willow dogwood, and buttonbush swamps. Because we loved the seclusion, we paddled here three times in 2001 and once in 2002. In spring the current flowed swiftly enough to make paddling upstream difficult in some places. We paddled nearly 3 miles

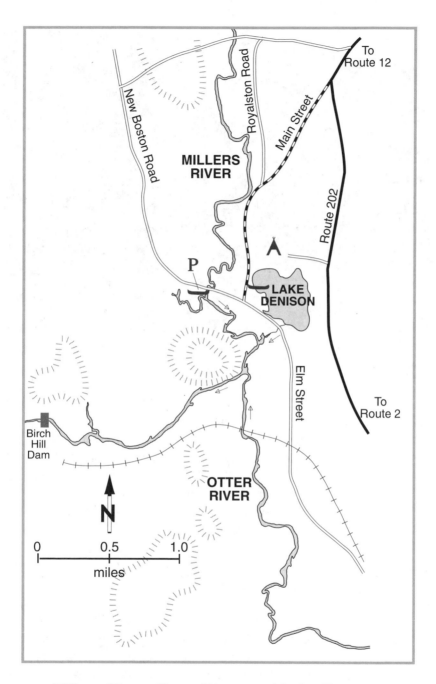

Millers River, Otter River, and Lake Denison

Except during times of high water, this section of Millers River can be paddled in both directions.

up the Millers River until a massive logjam blocked our way. On return trips in summer and fall, several beaver dams filled the channels. Spring floods wash out the dams, followed by rebuilding in summer.

Beaver have also impounded the north-flowing Otter River, necessitating portages to reach broad upstream meadows. Many species of ferns grow along the bank, including cinnamon, interrupted, royal, and marsh ferns. Marsh birds occur here in profusion. In mid-June, wood ducks, Canada geese, and mallards herded broods of young away from approaching boats. Great blue herons fed in the shallows, and killdeer nested on mudflats on the river's upper reaches. Crows mobbed a great horned owl, several snapping turtles fed just below the clear water's surface, and muskrats harvested streamside vegetation as we paddled by.

These rivers go up with rains and back down relatively quickly. Stay out of the river if you cannot paddle upstream easily. At times of high water, steer clear of trees in the water—they could cause you to capsize. Better yet, paddle Lake Denison instead. Receding glaciers formed this kettle-hole lake; a large chunk of glacier submerged in glacial till gradually melted, leaving a shallow lake with sandy shores and bottom, ideal for swimming.

35

Tully Lake and East Branch Tully River
Athol and Royalston, MA

MAPS: Massachusetts Atlas, Map 24
  USGS Quadrangle, Royalston
AREA/LENGTH: Tully Lake, 243 acres;
  East Branch Tully River, 3 miles
CAMPING: Tully Lake: The Trustees of Reservations, 978-840-
  4446 or www.thetrustees.org; Lake Denison State Recreation
  Area and Otter River State Forest, 978-939-8962; reserva-
  tions: 877-422-6762 or www.ReserveAmerica.com
HABITAT TYPE: Tully Lake, dammed-up river, shrubby marsh-
  lands, many islands, protected bays; Tully River, marshlands
  and beaver swamps
EXPECT TO SEE: muskrat, beaver, aquatic vegetation, varied
  shrubs, ferns
TAKE NOTE: no development; motors allowed (with 10 HP limit)
  on Tully Lake; no motors on Tully River

GETTING THERE
Tully Lake. From Route 2, Exit 17, go north on Route 32, through Athol, for 5.9 miles to the Tully Lake access on the right.
  Tully River. From the Tully Lake access, go north on Route 32 for 0.5 mile (0.5 mile) and turn right onto Doane Hill Road. Go 0.9 mile (1.4 miles) to the access on the left, just over the bridge.

Tully Lake. Located in north-central Massachusetts, not far from the New Hampshire border, Tully Lake is known to few people outside the immediate area. A highly varied shoreline, with dozens of islands and deep winding coves to explore, provides a wonderful paddling experience. A primitive, walk-in camping area at the north end provides an added bonus.

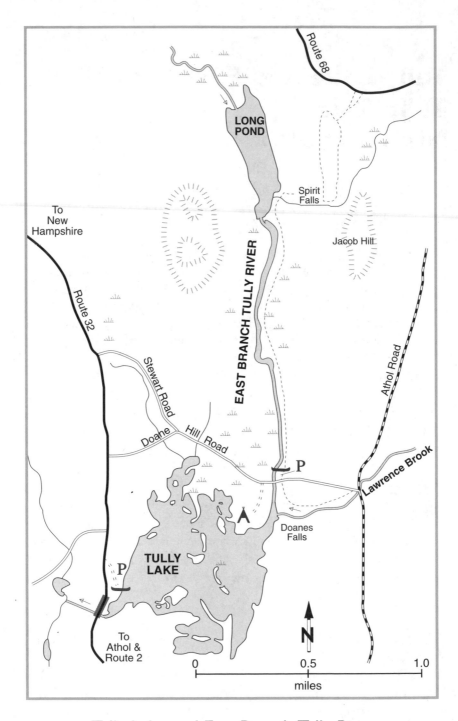

Tully Lake and East Branch Tully River

Along the shore, white pine predominates, mixed with red maple, hemlock, red and white oaks, some quaking aspen, and white birch, along with a fairly dense border of shrubs, including buttonbush, various heaths, alder, blueberry, and—in places—cranberry, with tiny oval leaves, dwarfed by large cranberries in late summer and fall. Farther from shore the woods open up, providing great picnicking and hiking opportunities on 18 miles of trails. On the large island near the lake's south end, we found a few highbush blueberries absolutely covered with berries during a visit in early August. Along with the more common white pine, scrub oak—a species more common on dry, sandy hills—grows near the south end of the lake.

East Branch Tully River. Underwater vegetation sways in the current, but otherwise you would hardly know which way the East Branch of the Tully River flows. Sweetgale, grasses, royal fern, buttonbush, and other shrubs grow thickly along the banks of this wide, gorgeous marsh. Look for fragrant waterlily, yellow pondlily, pondweed, and water shield along the edges and for pitcher plant on the sphagnum hummocks.

On our paddle up and back in early June, muskrats had uprooted many of the tender shoots of pickerelweed. As hermit thrushes called from the woodlands, we saw several beaver; they had also girdled many of the streamside hemlocks, killing them, which eventually will make way for more palatable species. Beaver are especially visible here in the evening.

Rounding the last bend paddling north, the river opens up into serene Long Pond, surrounded by thick woodland. The pond marks the end of open water. You can continue on beyond the power line at the pond's north end, portaging over repeated beaver dams.

Near the south end of Long Pond on the east side, you can pull your boat up and hike to Spirit Falls along Spirit Brook Trail. Though most spectacular in early spring and after rains, Spirit Falls is worth the short hike anytime. You can also hike from the Tully River access both to Doanes Falls on Lawrence Brook and to Spirit Falls.

36

Ware River and East Branch Ware River
Barre and Rutland, MA

Maps: Massachusetts Atlas, Map 37
  USGS Quadrangles, Barre and Sterling
Length: East Branch, North Rutland, 2.0 miles;
  East Branch, upstream from Barre Falls Dam, 2.3 miles;
  Ware River, downstream from Barre Falls Dam, 3.0 miles
Camping: Lake Denison State Recreation Area and Otter River
  State Forest, 978-939-8962; Willard Brook State Forest and
  Pearl Hill State Park, 978-597-8802; reservations:
  877-422-6762 or www.ReserveAmerica.com; Tully Lake: The
  Trustees of Reservations, 978-249-4957 or www.thetrustees.org
Habitat Type: marshy, slow-flowing rivers
Expect to See: beaver, muskrat, great blue heron,
  Canada goose, mallard, other marsh birds, raptors
Take Note: minor development on East Branch, North
  Rutland; no development on other sections; no motors

The Ware River presents several opportunities for quietwater paddling in areas where current allows travel in both directions. We include three nearby sections here, including one downstream of Barre Falls Dam on the Ware River and two upstream of the dam on the East Branch. We found these sections to be thick with wildlife, with very few other boaters in evidence. We cover them in order from upstream to downstream.

EAST BRANCH, NORTH RUTLAND
GETTING THERE
From Route 2, Exit 22, go south on Route 68, and turn left onto River Road, 1.4 miles (1.4 miles) after the junction of Routes 62 and 68. The unmarked access is on the right in 0.6 mile (2.0 miles), just before the Pout & Trout Campground.

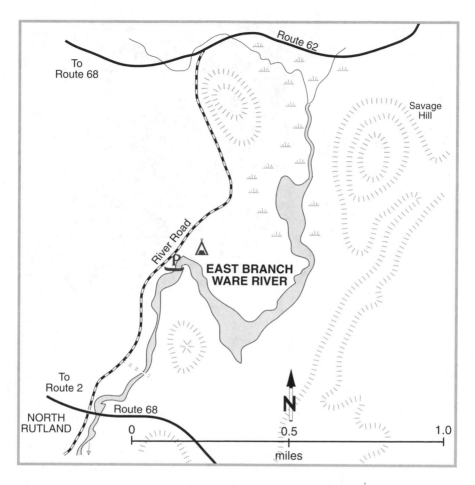

East Branch, North Rutland

From the boat access, you can paddle a short way downstream, through a few backyards, until you come to a small falls and a covered bridge. We enjoyed watching the phoebes and other birds that congregate just above the bridge, but the far more interesting section lies upstream from the access. You will encounter negligible current here as you work your away through extensive marshes, banks thick with grasses and shrubs. Red maple, white pine, and other trees line the faraway shoreline, which leads to scenic hillsides in the background.

Paddling here in the morning, you will see muskrat rooting up the ubiquitous pickerelweed; in the evening you should see beaver dragging branches for dam repair, to increase the size of their already huge

A great horned owl watches us closely as we paddle by.

lodges, or to store them, butt end stuck into the mud outside their lodges. You can paddle up beyond a series of beaver dams, but only the adventuresome will want to go very far—the streambed narrows and logjams occur with frequency.

We watched a large snapping turtle hanging lazily, fishing in the open channel, as dozens of yellow warblers sang from the streamside shrubbery. Painted turtles scrambled out onto logs to sun, as red-winged blackbirds squabbled over breeding territories. We found nesting Canada geese and mallards and watched a red-tailed hawk circle overhead. Amazingly, we saw three bitterns, which usually stay well hidden.

EAST BRANCH, UPSTREAM FROM BARRE FALLS DAM
GETTING THERE

From the junction of Routes 62 and 68, go west on Route 62 for 2.2 miles (2.2 miles) to the Barre Falls Dam access road on the left. The access is from the picnic area parking lot in 1.1 miles (3.3 miles), just after crossing the dam.

From the downstream access described below, turn left (east) onto Route 122, go 0.3 mile (0.3 mile), and turn left onto Coldbrook Road. Go north for 3.0 miles (3.3 miles) to the picnic area parking lot.

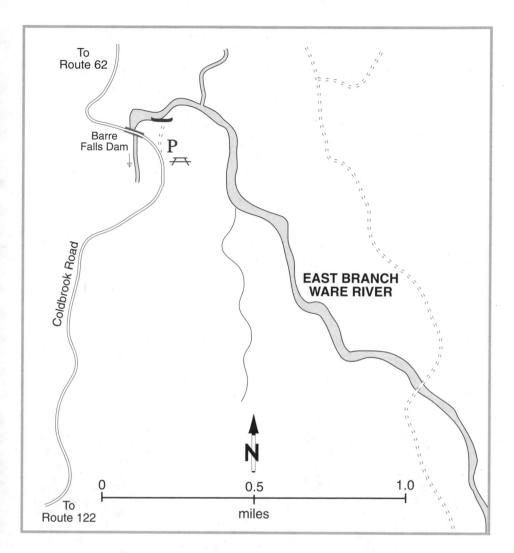

East Branch, Upstream from Barre Falls Dam

Do not attempt to paddle upstream from the dam unless you crave adventure. A 100-plus-yard carry down to the water from the picnic area awaits you; moreover, you have to carry back up when you may be sore from paddling. The river above the dam also can have a fair amount of current. Though we could paddle against it fairly easily, some tight, narrow turns presented a real challenge when the current pushed the bow away from our intended direction. After paddling slightly less than a mile upstream, we had to carry over a beaver dam, which gave us access to about another mile of river. By the time we finished paddling here, we knew that we had done some work.

You undoubtedly will not have much company if you choose to paddle this wide, shrubby, treeless marsh. Expect to see the same marsh birds as on other sections. You will also see red and white pine plantations, sometimes red on one side and white on the other side of the river.

WARE RIVER, DOWNSTREAM FROM BARRE FALLS DAM
GETTING THERE

From the junction of Routes 62, 32, and 122 in Barre, go south on Routes 32 and 122 for 1.2 miles (1.2 miles) to the Y, and go left onto Route 122. The access is on the left in 3.2 miles (4.4 miles), just before the bridge.

As we paddled through this wildlife paradise, a sphinx-type moth hover-fed on arrowwood flowers, and we studied iridescent green damselflies, tiger swallowtails, and several species of dragonflies. A great horned owl watched us warily from a streamside perch as we paddled

A tiger swallowtail sips nectar from a streamside flower.

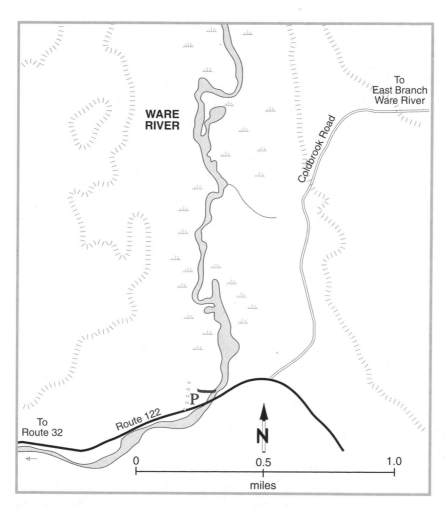

WARE
RIVER

Coldbrook Road

To
East Branch
Ware River

To
Route 32

Route 122

P

N

0   0.5   1.0

miles

Ware River, Downstream from Barre Falls Dam

by, and we watched a coyote burst forth from cover to chase a duck that had hidden in the pickerelweed along the shore. The Ware River also boasts the largest fish-species diversity in central Massachusetts.

The pondweed and pickerelweed, with yellow pondlily in protected coves, seem to withstand spring runoff, and we could paddle against the current, but we visited when the river was low enough that we often scraped our paddle blades on the bottom in the shallow areas. At times of high water, the current would make paddling here too much of a chore. The beaver that prune back the streamside alders burrow into the banks, rather than build the typical lodge that would wash away in a flood.

37

Lake Rohunta
Athol, New Salem, and Orange, MA

MAPS: Massachusetts Atlas, Map 24
  USGS Quadrangle, Orange
AREA: 383 acres
HABITAT TYPE: shallow pond, wooded shores
EXPECT TO SEE: osprey, wood duck, Canada goose,
  aquatic vegetation
TAKE NOTE: shallow water and abundant aquatic vegetation
  limit motors; limited development

GETTING THERE
Access to Lake Rohunta is on the northeast side of Route 2, less than a mile
east of Exit 16 (Route 202 south).

Anyone who drives across central Massachusetts on Route 2 has probably wondered about Lake Rohunta. We had driven by it many times before taking the time to check it out thoroughly. From the highway, the main lake appears to extend north from Route 2, but far more water actually lies to the south. While some houses occur along the lake at its widest sections, few motorboats ply these shallow, weedy waters. The surrounding woods may entice you to spread out a picnic lunch—particularly on the east side of the lake north of Route 2. The quite open pine and hemlock woods harbor dense carpets of needles and acid-loving laurels and blueberry bushes along the shore.

Our first time here, we spent a wonderful half day paddling the north end of the lake and the southern section down as far as Branch Bridge Road (where a small culvert blocks passage to the lake's southernmost section), exploring the diverse aquatic vegetation, watching painted turtles bask in the sun, and gorging ourselves on plentiful blueberries in July's waning days. We paddled through acres of fragrant waterlily, yellow pondlily, water shield, pickerelweed, pondweed, and two types of

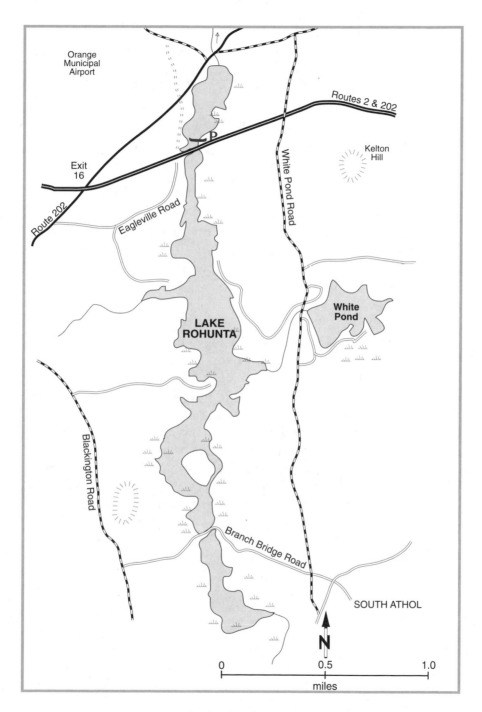

Lake Rohunta

bladderworts, with buttonbush along the shores. In the most protected coves, the remains of trees killed during the lake's creation jutted above the water's surface. On the mossy tussocks around these stumps, we found two species of sundews, round-leaved and spatulate-leaved. On the upper side of their leaves, these tiny carnivorous plants sport sticky hairs that catch small insects. Enzymes in the leaves digest the insects to help nourish the plant.

The farther south you paddle, the shallower and weedier it gets. When we visited here in late April, an osprey fished the clear water as aquatic vegetation just began to emerge, and we paddled unfettered. But by midsummer, floating vegetation, which covers more than 90 percent of the water's surface, impedes the paddling. Near the south end, we worked our way around a large, heavily wooded island. Though staying right presents an easier path, we found thicker stands of blueberry on the left.

While plowing through the pickerelweed and yellow pondlilies requires some work, you may see some exciting wildlife. We saw black ducks, Canada geese, a pair of broad-winged hawks (which may nest on the island), and a few wood ducks flying to safety as we paddled near. Early in the morning, look for mink or even a river otter here.

Local historians believe that the name *Rohunta* comes from one Rodney Hunt, who operated a hydropower facility at the waterway's south end in the late 1800s. The area also has a bit of postcolonial history: in 1787 Daniel Shays led a straggling band of rebellious farmers along this way in retreat from Springfield. It marked the last desperate hurrah of "Shay's Rebellion," when farmers in western Massachusetts, suffering under post-Revolution economic depression, protested the imprisoning of debtors by occupying the Springfield courthouse—an action that alarmed even President Washington. The uprising was quickly quelled, and Shays, a reluctant leader, escaped to Vermont, where he was eventually pardoned.

Osprey
Fish Hawk Back from the Brink

Osprey, or fish hawk, live near dozens of the lakes, ponds, and estuaries covered in this guide. Though we often see them on inland waterways perching or diving for fish, we see them in much larger numbers along the coast, where you may also observe them nesting.

The osprey, *Pandion haliaetus*, the sole species in the family Pandionidae, occurs on all continents except Antarctica. The bird, dark brown to almost black above and white below, soars with a characteristic M-like shape on a nearly 6-foot wingspread.

Osprey feed exclusively on fish. They soar or hover at a height of about 150 feet, using their keen eyesight to locate fish near the water's surface, then dive, crashing into the water feet first. There, they catch and grasp fish with their specially adapted feet, which have sharp, spiny projections.

They generally mate for life and return to the same nesting site each year. Males arrive first from the Gulf states or Latin American wintering grounds, followed a week later by the females. Returning males sometimes engage in a sky dance, repeatedly flying steeply up, hovering with tail fanned and talons extended, then diving down. This may be courtship behavior, a territorial display, or both.

Traditionally, osprey have nested in tall, dead trees, but more recently they have taken to hundreds of artificial nesting platforms that have been erected since the early 1970s in southern New England. The stick nest typically measures about 5 feet in diameter and 2 to 7 feet thick, depending on age. To collect sticks, the male uses an interesting technique: he alights near the end of a dead branch and breaks it off. The female collects most of the nest lining material (moss, bark, twigs, grass, seaweed).

The female lays two or three eggs—whitish with reddish brown blotches—over a period of several days. The chicks hatch after a thirty-four- to forty-day incubation period, during which the female does most of the sitting. Because the young hatch over several days, they vary in size. Though osprey often fledge two or three young, in a year of food shortages the larger chick will outcompete its smaller siblings and may be the sole survivor. The male osprey does virtually all the fishing during the incubation and nestling stage. Young osprey take to flight after seven or eight weeks, but they do not become fully independent for another month or two. After migrating south, the young spend two winters and the summer between in the wintering ground. Returning to the vicinity of their natal haunts the following year, they may pair up and begin nest building, but they do not breed until their third year.

The bald eagle, far less adept at fishing, often tries to steal the osprey's fish. We often spot gulls in hot pursuit, as well. A far more significant enemy, however, has been humankind and its chemical warfare against insect pests.

We introduced the "miracle" insecticide DDT in 1947 and used it widely on coastal salt marshes to control mosquitoes. Over the years, DDT, an extremely long-lived chlorinated hydrocarbon, accumulated in fatty tissue of animals. Small fish ate sprayed insects, larger fish ate smaller fish, and so on, gradually moving up the food chain to osprey. At each step, ingested DDT was stored in fatty tissue rather than excreted. At the top of the food chain, osprey ate many DDT-laced fish over a long lifespan and suffered from very high DDT concentrations. Those levels resulted in eggshell thinning and consequent extremely high rates of nesting failure. Osprey populations plummeted. Along the Connecticut River delta, for example, the osprey population dropped from 200 nesting pairs in 1938 to 12 by 1965. By the end of the 1960s, the bird had nearly disappeared from the eastern United States. The realization that DDT caused this decline led to its ban in the early 1970s. Since that time, osprey populations have gradually recovered.

Though osprey seem to be thriving, they still face threats from dwindling habitat, high-speed boating, and water pollution. Some evidence exists of increased competition from gulls since area landfills have closed. Osprey still ingest pesticides on their wintering quarters where we still apply environmentally dangerous chemicals such as DDT. With international efforts to eliminate use of such chemicals worldwide and with better controls on water pollution here, we will be able to enjoy watching the osprey hover over our waterways for many years to come.

～ 38 ～

Pottapoag Pond and Quabbin Reservoir, North End
Hardwick, New Salem, and Petersham, MA

MAPS: Massachusetts Atlas, Maps 24 and 36
   USGS Quadrangles, Barre and Orange
AREA: Pottapoag Pond, 568 acres
CAMPING: Erving State Forest, 978-544-3939; reservations:
   877-422-6762 or www.ReserveAmerica.com; Tully Lake: The
   Trustees of Reservations, 978-249-4957 or www.thetrustees.org
HABITAT TYPE: part of Quabbin Reservoir; wooded shoreline,
   some islands and protected bays
EXPECT TO SEE: bald eagle, towering pines, gorgeous scenery
TAKE NOTE: no development; motors up to 20 HP allowed on
   Pottapoag but not North End; launch fee charged (in 2002,
   $4 per vehicle, $2 per boat); fishing license required (one-day
   license available for $5 on-site); boats must be at least 12 feet
   long; Pottapoag Pond may be unsuited to novices due to wind
   and waves

POTTAPOAG POND
GETTING THERE

From the junction of Routes 32 and 32A in Petersham, go south on Route 32A
for 9.8 miles, and turn right onto Session Road. After 0.4 mile (10.2 miles),
turn right onto Greenwich Road (do not go straight onto Muddy Brook Road).
Mellon Road comes in from the right after 1.4 miles (11.6 miles); after another
0.5 mile (12.1 miles), turn right onto the access road (Gate 43). Access is in
another 1.8 miles (13.9 miles).

Nestled among the hillsides of central Massachusetts, Pottapoag Pond
presents a rare opportunity to paddle in stunning, pristine surroundings. Here and on the North End, hand-paddled craft have their only
access to the wild hinterlands of the Quabbin Reservoir complex, the

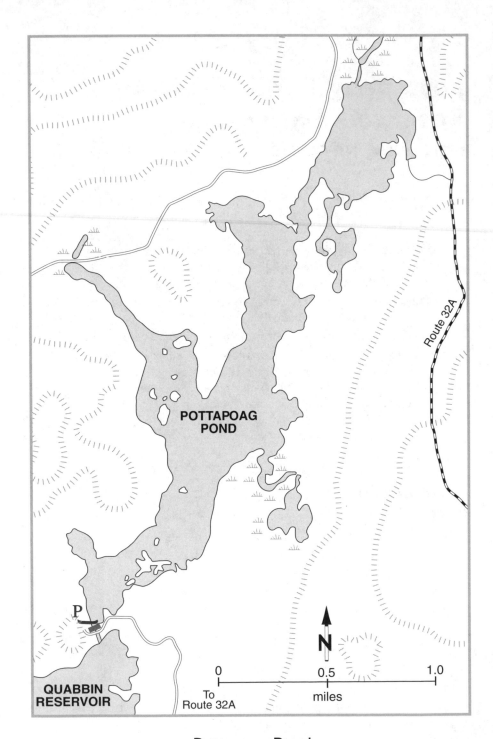

Pottapoag Pond

water supply for 40 percent of Massachusetts. Shallow protected coves provide hours of paddling among carpets of ferns under towering, lichen-covered pines. Beaver have removed almost all deciduous trees along the shoreline, and we could see their new work farther up the hillsides. We prefer to paddle here midweek when fishing activity is low. Expect to spend an entire day if you intend to explore the entire shoreline and all of the coves.

We reveled in the huge amounts of floating heart found here— perhaps the largest amount we have seen in New England. *Nymphoides cordata* has small heart-shaped leaves, up to 2 inches across, borne singly on long tendrils. Most aquatic plants occur in water shallower than about 4 feet; floating heart can inhabit much deeper water. Each stem can bear a few small white flowers in midsummer.

The shallow, protected coves, some filled with stumps, harbor rafts of water shield, fragrant waterlily, yellow pondlily, pondweed, and yellow iris. When we paddled here in spring, veery, common yellowthroat, eastern towhee, yellow warbler, red-winged blackbird, grackle, song sparrow, white-breasted nuthatch, eastern kingbird, Baltimore oriole, eastern wood-pewee, and cedar waxwing all sang from the hillsides and undergrowth as they established breeding territories. We also saw Canada geese with young, mallards, wild turkey, and a pileated woodpecker. The highlight, though—with apologies to Sandburg—was a majestic bald eagle clasping a craggy perch with crooked hands on a pine-covered island.

A note of caution: the main lake, elongated north to south, has 2 miles over which wind-driven waves can build, making paddling unpleasant and possibly dangerous in windy conditions. Novice paddlers beware.

QUABBIN RESERVOIR, NORTH END
GETTING THERE
From Route 2, Exit 16, go south on Route 202 for 1.9 miles (1.9 miles), and turn left onto Route 122. Access at Gate 31 is on the right in 1.4 miles (3.3 miles).

The sole parts of vast Quabbin Reservoir open to paddlers include Pottapoag Pond and the much smaller, unnamed, north-end reservoir described here. Unlike Pottapoag Pond, the north end excludes

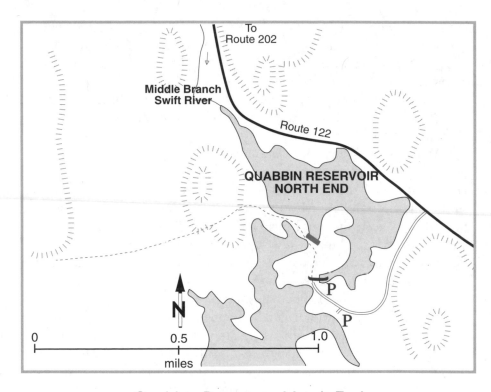

Quabbin Reservoir, North End

motors. You might want to paddle here on the same day that you paddle Pottapoag to avoid paying fees to gain access to a small body of water. You could also paddle here when stiff winds preclude paddling on Pottapoag Pond. A sizable peninsula juts out from the southern shore, providing wind protection and interesting coves to explore.

When we paddled here, tree swallows cruised the water's surface, picking off insects, and early warblers—palm and yellow-rumped—cruised the waterside foliage for early-emerging insects. Birds seemed to congregate along the inlet stream's shore for the 100 paddleable yards above the first beaver dam.

In places, dense pockets of small pines fought for light in the understory, and leatherleaf bloomed along the shore in late April. A small amount of road noise from Route 122 occasionally broke the stillness along the scenic hillsides, but tall hemlocks and pines shield the pond pretty well in most places. Occasional patches of mountain laurel cropped up here and there, and wood ducks jumped to the air as we approached.

39

Muddy Brook and Hardwick Pond
Hardwick, MA

MAPS: Massachusetts Atlas, Map 36
   USGS Quadrangle, North Brookfield
AREA/LENGTH: Hardwick Pond, 66 acres;
   Muddy Brook, 1.6 miles
HABITAT TYPE: reservoir and slow-flowing, marshy river
   through beaver swamp
EXPECT TO SEE: many birds, broods of Canada goose and wood
   duck, red-tailed hawk, muskrat, beaver
TAKE NOTE: limited development and motors on Hardwick
   Pond only

GETTING THERE

From the North. From the junction of Routes 32 and 32A in Petersham, take Route 32A south for about 10.0 miles to Hardwick. In Hardwick, turn right onto Greenwich Road. After 0.3 mile (0.3 mile), turn left onto Patrill Hollow Road, and continue for 3.2 miles (3.5 miles) to the junction with Thayer and Greenwich Roads. Turn left onto Greenwich Road, go south for 1.2 miles (4.7 miles), and turn sharply back to the left onto Hardwick Pond Road. Access is at road's end in 0.3 mile (5.0 miles).

From the South. From Route 9 in downtown Ware, turn north onto North Street (traffic light), and go 1.3 miles (1.3 miles) to the stop sign and T at Greenwich Road. Turn right onto Greenwich Road, and go north for 2.4 miles (3.7 miles) to the second Hardwick Pond Road on the right, just after the Hardwick–Ware town line. Hardwick Pond Road ends at the access in 0.3 mile (4.0 miles).

Going north out of Hardwick Pond, paddle up slow-flowing, picturesque Muddy Brook through a broad beaver marsh, a valley filled with shrubs and songbirds. Cardinals, catbirds, yellowthroats, and yellow

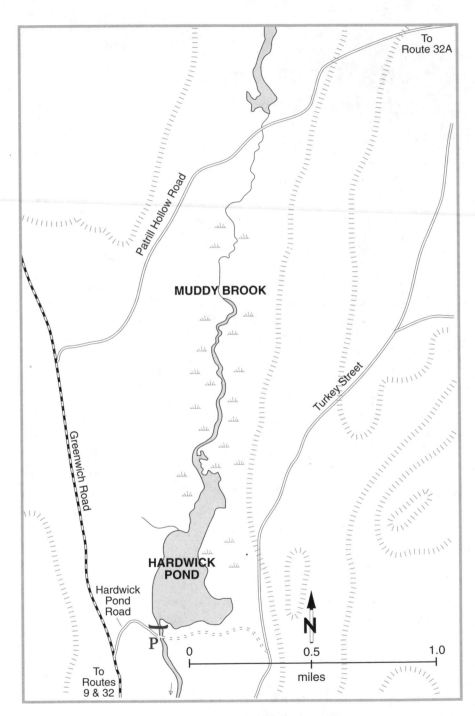

To
Route 32A

Patrill Hollow Road

MUDDY BROOK

Turkey Street

Greenwich Road

HARDWICK POND

Hardwick
Pond
Road

P

To
Routes
9 & 32

N

0   0.5   1.0
miles

Muddy Brook and Hardwick Pond

warblers call from dense undergrowth, and scores of red-winged black-birds sing from the marshes in early June. Shrubs line the banks and cover the islands and hummocks along the side channels of the marsh, with an occasional red maple sprouting up here and there.

At high water you can paddle over drowned-out beaver dams, but you should be prepared to portage over some dams. One dam had a thick growth of swamp rose on and around it. Another had a beaver working on the dam at 4:15 in the afternoon; the beaver climbed off the dam, swam over to us, gave us the hairy eyeball, slapped its tail on the water, and dove for cover—strong evidence that the brook's upper reaches receive few visitors.

After we had paddled a mile or more up the brook, we came to a 5-foot-high beaver dam. Portage through open woods around the right side of the dam onto a shrub-filled lagoon with standing dead trees, nesting wood ducks, great blue heron, snapping turtle, red-tailed hawk, and cedar waxwings. We also saw a relatively rare yellow-billed cuckoo here. We found the main channel above the lagoon with some difficulty and had to bushwhack through shrubs as we paddled and pulled ourselves along, noting the beauty of fern-clad banks. We spotted patches of royal, interrupted, cinnamon, and hay-scented fern. Though you can paddle up to Patrill Hollow Road, most of us will get tired of portaging over logjams and beaver dams and pulling our way through shrubs long before reaching the road.

The lake itself pales in comparison with the pristine brook, but you can also paddle down the outlet a way. You will undoubtedly have to lie down in your boat to make it under the bridge; try not to disturb the phoebe nesting under there.

40

Swift River
Belchertown and Ware, MA

Maps: Massachusetts Atlas, Maps 36 and 48
USGS Quadrangles, Palmer and Winsor Dam
Length: 4.5 miles
Camping: Swift River lean-tos: Department of Fisheries and
Wildlife, 413-323-7632; Wells State Park, 508-347-9257;
reservations: 877-422-6762 or www.ReserveAmerica.com;
Tully Lake: The Trustees of Reservations, 978-249-4957 or
www.thetrustees.org
Habitat Type: slow-flowing wooded river
Expect to See: many birds, broods of Canada goose and
mallard, muskrat
Take Note: some development; shallow water and hand launch
limit motors

Getting There

From the junction of Routes 9 and 202 in Belchertown, go east on Route 9
for 3.8 miles (3.8 miles), and turn right onto East Street. Go south for 2.2 miles
(6.0 miles), and turn left onto Cold Spring Road. The boat access is to the
right of the footbridge in 0.1 mile (6.1 miles).

Though clusters of houses impinge somewhat on the Swift River, most
of the section included here has a very wild feel to it. Swift River's clear
water, outlet for the mighty Quabbin Reservoir, meanders along slowly
with a very modest low-flow volume mandated by law. Shallow water,
masses of aquatic vegetation, and occasional downed trees and logjams
limit motors. We watched muskrats harvest grasses and pickerelweed
and saw evidence of beaver in the pruned-back streamside alders.

What we reveled in most, though, was the huge number of birds
of many species. We saw wild turkey, broods of mallard and Canada
goose, treetop Baltimore orioles singing their melodious songs, tufted

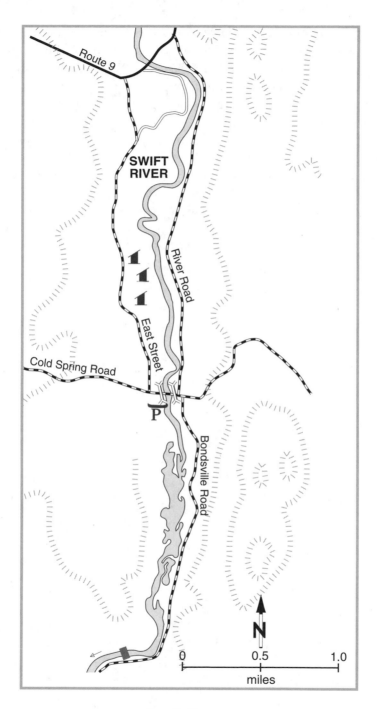

Route 9

SWIFT
RIVER

River Road

East Street

Cold Spring Road

P

Bondsville Road

N

0   0.5   1.0
miles

Swift River

titmouse, grackle, blue jay, flicker, kingfisher, veery, eastern kingbird, eastern wood-pewee, red-winged blackbird, robin, catbird, cardinal, song sparrow, yellow-rumped warbler, yellowthroat, northern waterthrush, goldfinch, crow, mourning dove, and great blue heron.

The river contains lots of aquatic vegetation, especially in late summer, which shows that high water rarely scours the channel. Pickerelweed, pondweed, and fragrant waterlily grow in profusion against the wooded shoreline. Downstream from the access in the section backed up by a dam, lots of inlets, islands, and coves beg to be explored. Upstream from the access, the Department of Fisheries and Wildlife maintains four lean-tos along the river within the Herman Covey WMA that you can use for free but must reserve in advance.

Western Massachusetts

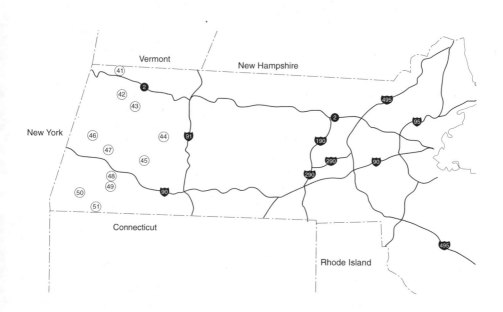

Vermont

New Hampshire

New York

Connecticut

Rhode Island

41

Mauserts Pond
Clarksburg, MA

MAPS: Massachusetts Atlas, Map 21
   USGS Quadrangle, North Adams
AREA: 44 acres
CAMPING: Clarksburg State Park, 413-664-8345; Savoy Mountain
   State Forest, 413-664-9567; Mount Greylock State Reservation,
   413-499-4262; Mohawk Trail State Forest, 413-339-5504;
   reservations: 877-422-6762 or www.ReserveAmerica.com
HABITAT TYPE: wooded reservoir in a state park;
   swimming beach
EXPECT TO SEE: yew, bladderwort, beaver activity, deep woodlands
TAKE NOTE: no motors

GETTING THERE

From Route 2, take Route 8 north from North Adams for 3.0 miles (3.0 miles), and turn left onto Middle Road, following signs to Clarksburg State Park. The park entrance is on the right after another 0.2 mile (3.2 miles). The access is to the right, past the contact station, by the beach.

This small pond in Clarksburg State Park, just south of the Vermont border in northwestern Massachusetts, provides a wonderful opportunity for family camping, hiking, and paddling. Exploring the entire shoreline by boat won't take long, which will leave plenty of time to explore this heavily wooded 3,400-acre park by foot. Clarksburg State Forest, a few miles to the west, has more trails and access to a gorgeous section of the Appalachian Trail.

Red maple dominates the pond's shoreline, though you will also see black cherry, white and gray birches, white pine, and hemlock. Shrubs include highbush blueberry, winterberry—with bright red berries in autumn—sheep laurel, and American yew (*Taxus canadensis*), an unusual creeping shrub that seldom gets taller than about 3 feet and

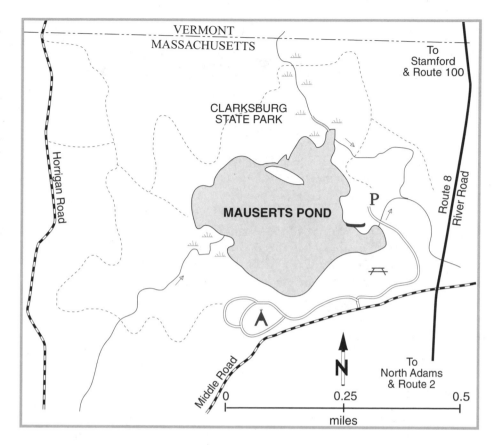

Mauserts Pond

bears red berries in late summer. Cattail, bur-reed, grasses, and active beaver lodges sprout up in the marshy areas along the northern shore. You can squeeze your way a short distance up several of the inlet creeks and along a narrow channel that snakes behind the spit of land extending into the pond from the northern shore (a good spot to see the yew).

As you paddle along the sandy shoreline, keep an eye out for fresh-water mussels, some with thin-walled shells more than 5 inches long. In the shallow water look for carnivorous bladderworts (*Utricularia spp.*), which send yellow or purple flowers above the water's surface on slender stalks. See the section on Carnivorous Plants (page 236) for information on the inner workings of these fascinating plants.

42

Bog Pond and Burnett Pond
Savoy, MA

MAPS: Massachusetts Atlas, Map 21
USGS Quadrangles, Cheshire (Burnett Pond) and North
Adams (Bog Pond)
AREA: Bog Pond, 40 acres
CAMPING: Savoy Mountain State Forest, 413-664-9567; Clarksburg
State Park, 413-664-8345; Mount Greylock State Reservation,
413-499-4262; Mohawk Trail State Forest, 413-339-5504;
reservations: 877-422-6762 or www.ReserveAmerica.com
HABITAT TYPE: swampy fen in state forest
EXPECT TO SEE: pitcher plant, terrestrial bladderwort, sundew,
deep woodlands, Canada goose; moose are a possibility
TAKE NOTE: no motors; no development

GETTING THERE

Bog Pond. From the junction of Routes 2 and 8 in North Adams, go east on Route 2 for 4.4 miles (4.4 miles), and turn right onto Central Shaft Road, at the sign for Savoy State Forest. Go south on Central Shaft Road (it changes to Florida Road, then Burnett Street, both unmarked), and jog right after 2.0 miles (6.4 miles), following state forest signs. In 3.9 miles (10.3 miles), as Burnett Street ends, go straight (north) onto unmarked New State Road for 1.2 miles (11.5 miles) to the access on the left.

From the east, go west on Route 2, turn left onto Central Shaft Road 2.0 miles after The Summit (tower, restaurant, views), and follow directions as above.

Burnett Pond. From the junction of Burnett Street and New State Road, go south on New State Road for 0.8 mile to the unmarked access on the right at a gate. Hike 100 yards down to the pond.

Savoy Mountain State Forest, one of the best places to see moose in Massachusetts, certainly warrants a visit, particularly during the heat of summer. Bog Pond, at an elevation of 1,858 feet, and nearby Burnett Pond are both nearly 1,300 feet higher than nearby valleys. Consequently,

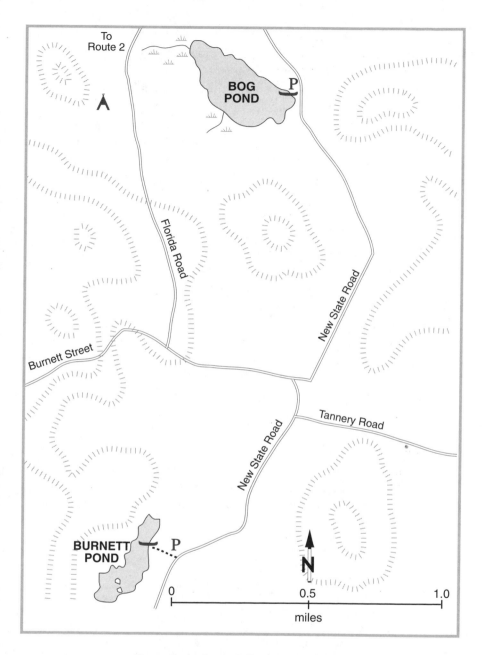

To
Route 2

BOG
POND

P

Florida Road

New State Road

Burnett Street

Tannery Road

New State Road

BURNETT
POND

P

N

0   0.5   1.0

miles

Bog Pond and Burnett Pond

they can be several degrees cooler because of the so-called adiabatic lapse rate. The sun's heating of valley floors sends warm air masses skyward, expanding as they rise. Because the rising mass's heat content remains constant, as it does work expanding against adjacent air masses, it cools. Dry air masses cool at the rate of 5.4 degrees F per 1,000 feet, while more humid air masses cool at 3.6 degrees. So, depending on humidity, on sunny days the shores of Bog Pond should be between about 5 and 7 degrees cooler than the surrounding lowlands. In addition, cooling breezes often flow strongly across Bog Pond because no mountains lie to the west.

Bog Pond lies in a gorgeous setting, with lots of boggy islands to explore at your leisure. Fragrant waterlily, water shield, and water celery cover the water's surface, while hemlock, balsam fir, and red maple cover the shoreline. A large beaver lodge perches on a sphagnum-covered island, along with three carnivorous plants: purple pitcher plant, round-leaved sundew, and large patches of a beautiful terrestrial yellow-flowered bladderwort (Utricularia cornuta) that blooms in mid-July. The pond's shores—covered with ostrich fern, leatherleaf, sweetgale, sheep laurel, and several other shrubs—also provide habitat for a host of marsh birds, including yellowthroat, yellow warbler, cedar waxwing, song sparrow, black-capped chickadee, Canada goose, and great blue heron.

When we paddled here, beaver had dammed the spillway, raising the water level by more than a foot. Even with the added depth, this small, shallow pond demands that you paddle it slowly, savoring the marsh's plants and animals. We also give directions above to nearby Burnett Pond, which, with its higher proportion of conifers, has a more northern boreal feel to it, perhaps explaining the frequent moose sightings there.

～ 43 ～

Plainfield Pond
Plainfield, MA

MAPS: Massachusetts Atlas, Map 21
   USGS Quadrangle, Ashfield
AREA: 65 acres
CAMPING: Clarksburg State Park, 413-664-8345; Savoy Mountain State Forest, 413-664-9567; Mount Greylock State Reservation, 413-499-4262; Mohawk Trail State Forest, 413-339-5504; reservations: 877-422-6762 or www.ReserveAmerica.com
HABITAT TYPE: shrubby wooded pond
EXPECT TO SEE: mallard, floating heart, mountain laurel, deep woodlands
TAKE NOTE: no motors; limited development

GETTING THERE

From the junction of Routes 2 and 8A in Charlemont, go south on Route 8A for 9.5 miles (9.5 miles), and turn right onto Routes 8A/116. Go 0.9 mile (10.4 miles) to the access on the right, just past the town beach.

From Adams, go east on Route 116 to the junction with Route 8A south. Stay straight on Routes 8A/116, and go 4.9 miles to the access on the left.

From Pittsfield, go east—and from Northampton, go west—on Route 9 to the junction with Route 8A. Turn north onto Route 8A, and go 9.3 miles to the access on the left.

At the access, very tame mallards with broods greeted us, a sure sign that residents using the town beach feed these birds. Massive quantities of floating heart *(Nymphoides cordata)*, with tiny white flowers and heart-shaped leaves less than 2 inches across, also greeted us as we paddled out from the access. Rarely do we see these delicate aquatic plants growing in such profusion. Thick stands of shrubs layer the shoreline, with a profusion of highbush blueberry and mountain laurel, as well as lesser quantities of swamp azalea and arrowwood. When

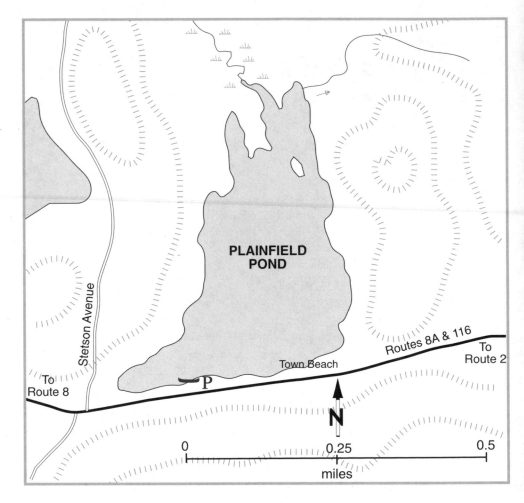

Plainfield Pond

we paddled here in mid-July, arrowwood's umbel-like purple berries and blueberry's urnlike white flowers lent color to the shore, but we wished that we had visited earlier when the mountain laurel and swamp azalea bloomed.

Plainfield Pond perches high on the Berkshire plateau, surrounded by forests of spruce, paper birch, white pine, red maple, and hemlock. These trees populate some large, gorgeous, fractured granite slabs, some posing as islands, on the pond's north end. The pond's very clear water, harboring lots of freshwater mussels, gives way to yellow-brown water as you enter the marshes on the north end. Sweetgale, with lesser

Young mallards congregate near the access, a sure sign that people feed them.

amounts of leatherleaf and swamp rose, lines the low banks, and beaver keep a channel open through the pickerelweed, water shield, yellow-flowered bladderwort, and yellow pondlily.

Beaver had gnawed away the bark of some hemlocks, killing them, a phenomenon that we have seen in several other locations. Apparently, if you run out of the good stuff, you kill off the bad stuff in the hope that more palatable species will replace them. Next time you see a dense stand of hemlock, take a good look at the understory. Few hardwoods—preferred beaver food—take root under hemlocks.

Upper Highland Lake
Goshen, MA

MAPS: Massachusetts Atlas, Map 34
USGS Quadrangle, Goshen
AREA: 56 acres
CAMPING: DAR State Forest, 413-268-7098;
reservations: 877-422-6762 or www.ReserveAmerica.com
HABITAT TYPE: wooded pond
EXPECT TO SEE: hemlock groves, beaver, woodland songbirds
TAKE NOTE: no motors; limited development

GETTING THERE

From the South. From Northampton, take Route 9 west; in Goshen, turn right onto Route 112, and go north for 0.7 mile (0.7 mile) to the DAR State Forest entrance (Moore Hill Road) on the right. Access is on the left in 0.4 mile (1.1 miles).

From the North. From Greenfield, take Route 2 west—and from North Adams, take Route 2 east—to Shelburne Falls, and go south on Route 112 for 13.7 miles to the entrance on the left.

Nestled within the Daughters of the American Revolution (DAR) State Forest in the Berkshires, Upper Highland Lake offers a great getaway spot for a relaxed weekend of camping, paddling, and hiking. Groves of gorgeous hemlocks, with streams of light filtering through the canopy, await hikers on the many trails that traverse the 1,020-acre DAR State Forest. The fifty-two campsites, including some that are wheelchair-accessible, fill up well before the weekend, so we recommend reservations. This small lake, with no development on it other than recreational facilities and a private camp near the northwest corner—a fresh-air camp for urban children—offers quiet paddling in scenic surroundings.

The shoreline vegetation consists primarily of deciduous trees—birch, maple, beech, and some oak—with many white pine and hemlock

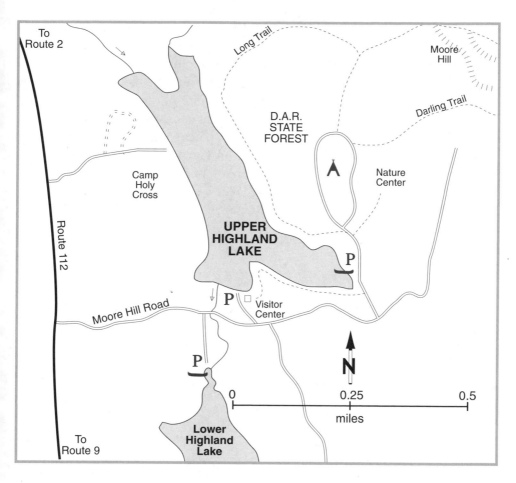

To
Route 2

Long Trail

Moore
Hill

Darling Trail

D.A.R.
STATE
FOREST

Nature
Center

Route 112

Camp
Holy
Cross

**UPPER
HIGHLAND
LAKE**

P

Moore Hill Road

P

Visitor
Center

P

N

To
Route 9

P

**Lower
Highland
Lake**

0   0.25   0.5
miles

Upper Highland Lake

mixed in. The woolly adelgid, which has gradually marched northward, threatens the eastern hemlocks here and in the rest of New England. Highbush blueberry, mountain laurel, and other shrubs grow along the shore. An inlet and a cove extending to the northwest await exploration. A beaver lodge perches between the cove and inlet, which you might want to visit around dusk or dawn to look for beaver.

Just to the south and also largely within DAR State Forest lies the somewhat larger Lower Highland Lake. The state prohibits gasoline-powered motorboats here as well, but considerable development crowds the southern shores.

A ranger recalled finding a World War II photograph showing the boot-shaped Upper Highland Lake from the fire tower atop Moore Hill (on the east side of the lake and accessible by road or trails). Spotters used the tower, like others throughout southern New England in this uneasy time, to watch for warplanes. The photo shows a nearly bare summit with young growth of hemlock and pine, reminders that much of this area had once been cleared for sheep raising. Enlargement of the dams by the Civilian Conservation Corps increased the size of both lakes, turning these small reservoirs—used for powering silk mills at Goshen—into the lovely paddling lakes we find today.

～ 45 ～

Littleville Lake
Chester and Huntington, MA

MAPS: Massachusetts Atlas, Map 34
  USGS Quadrangle, Chester
AREA: 275 acres
CAMPING: Chester-Blandford State Forest, 413-354-6347; DAR
  State Forest, 413-268-7098; reservations: 877-422-6762 or
  www.ReserveAmerica.com
HABITAT TYPE: long, narrow, wooded reservoir
EXPECT TO SEE: scenic, undulating hillsides; woodland songbirds
TAKE NOTE: no development; boats must be at least 12 feet
  long; motors allowed, 10 HP limit

GETTING THERE

From Northampton. Go west on Route 66 (initially West Street) for about 13.6 miles (13.6 miles), and turn left onto Route 112. Go south for 2.2 miles (15.8 miles); just after crossing the Westfield River, take an immediate right onto Goss Hill Road at the sign for Littleville Lake. In 0.7 mile (16.5 miles), continue right on Goss Hill Road. The access is on the left in another 0.7 mile (17.2 miles).

From the South. Take Route 20 to Route 112 in Huntington. Go north on Route 112 for 1.4 miles, and turn left just before it crosses the Westfield River, at the sign for Littleville Lake. Follow directions as above.

Northern Access. From the junction of Routes 20 and 112, go north on Route 112 for 0.1 mile (0.1 mile), and turn sharply left onto Basket Street/Fisk Avenue, just after crossing the bridge. Follow the river for 1.5 miles (1.6 miles), and turn right onto Skyline Trail. Go 2.5 miles (4.1 miles), and turn right onto East River Road. Go 2.0 miles (6.1 miles), and turn right onto Kinne Brook Road to the Dayville access in 0.8 mile (6.9 miles).

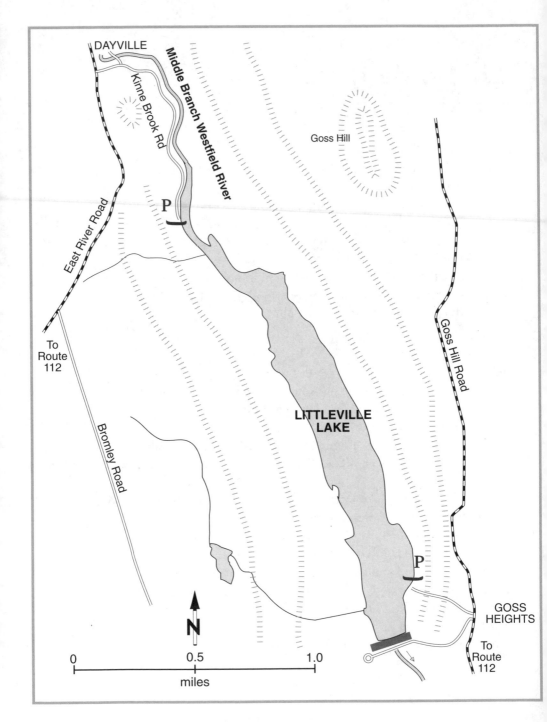

DAYVILLE

Middle Branch Westfield River

Kinne Brook Rd

Goss Hill

East River Road

P

To
Route
112

Goss Hill Road

Bromley Road

LITTLEVILLE
LAKE

P

GOSS
HEIGHTS

To
Route
112

N

| 0 | 0.5 | 1.0 |

miles

Littleville Lake

Created in 1965 when the U.S. Army Corps of Engineers built a flood-control dam on the Middle Branch of the Westfield River—to stem serious flooding that had occurred since the 1600s—Littleville Lake offers superb paddling, fishing, and picnicking in a scenic valley. To build the dam, a local fairground had to be relocated; today's Dayville Fair continues to be a local high point in mid-September. The lake doubles as a backup water supply for Springfield, about 30 miles downstream, but has yet to be drawn upon since its completion.

The wooded hills of the 1,567-acre area contain typical woodland tree species, including sugar and red maples, white ash, red oak, black and gray birches, quaking aspen, white pine, ironwood, and sycamore. The rocky shoreline leads to fairly steep wooded banks. A few marshy areas occur at the north end, along with the inlet. Signs of an abandoned farm appear about two-thirds of the way up the lake: old apple trees, stone walls, and pastures growing up into woodland. We found beaver and other wildlife to be more plentiful near the north end. You can paddle up the crystal-clear inlet river a short distance, but it becomes shallow fairly quickly with a lot of exposed rocks.

Anglers ply these waters for largemouth bass, yellow perch, and rainbow trout. Paddling around early one evening with the light just right, we saw about a dozen foot-long bass lurking beneath the surface along the west shore.

Despite the general lack of inlets and coves to explore, Littleville Lake offers a pleasant morning or afternoon of paddling, with plenty of places to stop for a picnic. The Corps prohibits swimming, wading, and camping.

46

Housatonic River and East Branch Housatonic River
Hinsdale, Lee, Lenox, Pittsfield, and Washington, MA

MAPS: Massachusetts Atlas, Maps 32 and 33
  USGS Quadrangles, East Lee and Pittsfield East

LENGTH: Housatonic River, 10 miles;
  East Branch Housatonic River, 5 miles

CAMPING: October Mountain State Forest, 413-243-1778;
  Beartown State Forest, 413-528-0904; Tolland State Forest,
  413-269-6002; Pittsfield State Forest, 413-442-8992;
  reservations: 877-422-6762 or www.ReserveAmerica.com

HABITAT TYPE: dammed-up meandering river, shrubby
  marshlands; forested hillsides; some farmland

EXPECT TO SEE: beaver, muskrat, mallard, Canada goose, wood
  duck, marsh birds, aquatic vegetation, varied shrubs, box
  elder, silver maple

TAKE NOTE: little development; electric motors allowed

HOUSATONIC RIVER
GETTING THERE

New Lenox Road. From Pittsfield, go south on Route 7, and turn left onto New Lenox Road. The John F. Decker canoe access is on the right in 1.4 miles (0.6 mile after the East Street/New Lenox Road junction).

Lenox Station. From the junction of East Street and New Lenox Road, take East Street south for 2.9 miles (2.9 miles), and turn left onto Housatonic Street. Take Housatonic Street 0.9 mile (3.8 miles) to the access, which is at a footbridge at the junction of Housatonic Street, Willow Creek Road, and Crystal Street. To get here directly from Pittsfield or from the south, from Routes 7 and 20, at the stoplight take Housatonic Street east for 1.3 miles to the access.

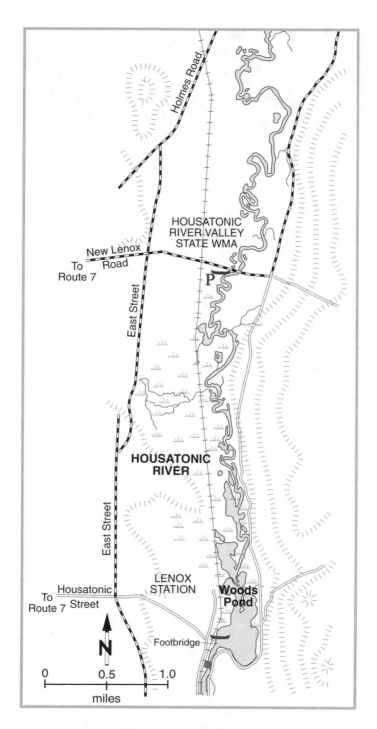

Holmes Road

HOUSATONIC
RIVER VALLEY
STATE WMA

New Lenox
Road

To
Route 7

P

East Street

HOUSATONIC
RIVER

East Street

LENOX
STATION

Woods
Pond

Housatonic
Street

To
Route 7

N

Footbridge

0   0.5   1.0

miles

Housatonic River

We saw many pairs of Canada geese raising their broods along the banks of the Housatonic River.

This very popular canoeing and kayaking stream teems with paddlers on busy summer weekends, making wildlife viewing more difficult. We recommend paddling here in spring or fall or during the week in summer months. You can escape the crowds somewhat by paddling off into the numerous, very large oxbows, leaving behind the troops of paddlers intent on just making it down the river. Though the current barely flows by midsummer, paddling here during spring high water may necessitate a one-way trip. At times of high water, you can also paddle upstream from Lenox Station/Woods Pond; myriad bays and side channels sheltered by scenic hillsides beg to be explored. If we had limited time, we would paddle upstream from Lenox Station.

The relatively tame mallard brood that greeted us at the access did not seem to mind the paddlers, and we did manage to see abundant birdlife—the usual marshland species, including several broods of wood duck. Though we did not paddle here in the evening, judging from the size and number of lodges, beaver must be a routine evening sight. While the Housatonic Valley Wildlife Management Area protects the river valley marshlands, the October Mountain State Forest protects the gorgeous forested hillsides to the east.

Except for farmland near New Lenox Road, trees cover the shoreline, arching out over the water—and over the abundant, diverse shrubs and vines lining the shore. Silver maple dominates in some areas, its branches serving as launchpads for deerflies (a sight predator). We also saw willow, basswood, box elder, and many others. Thick patches of ostrich fern waved in the slight breeze, and wildflowers bloomed in profusion. As we listened to song sparrows calling from the underbrush and watched a phoebe bob its tail from a streamside perch, we understood why this is such a popular area. We had a hard time understanding, however, how so much trash could accumulate behind the numerous deadfalls; perhaps it had washed downstream from Pittsfield after heavy rains.

Paddling upstream from New Lenox Road, after about a mile you will reach several power lines and a complex of buildings on the right, a research station of the Electrical Power Research Institute. Several years ago we visited this facility to talk with researchers about their work with electromagnetic fields (EMF) for an article that Alex was writing for his publication *Environmental Building News* on the effects of EMF on human health. EPRI had an entire house set up using different code-compliant wiring configurations to see how much EMF each produced.

EAST BRANCH HOUSATONIC RIVER
GETTING THERE

From Pittsfield, go east on Route 9. Route 8 joins for a few miles; when the roads split, take Route 8 south. From the junction with Route 143, continue south on Route 8 for 1.1 miles to the access on the right, just before the bridge.

In contrast with the Housatonic River, few venture onto the East Branch, which intrepid explorers who don't mind getting in and out of their boats will love. When we paddled upstream (south) from the access in early June, we had to portage over thirteen beaver dams to get to the upper meadow just south of Ballard Crossing Road. We recommend that you paddle here in shorter boats and only when high water has drowned out at least some of the beaver dams.

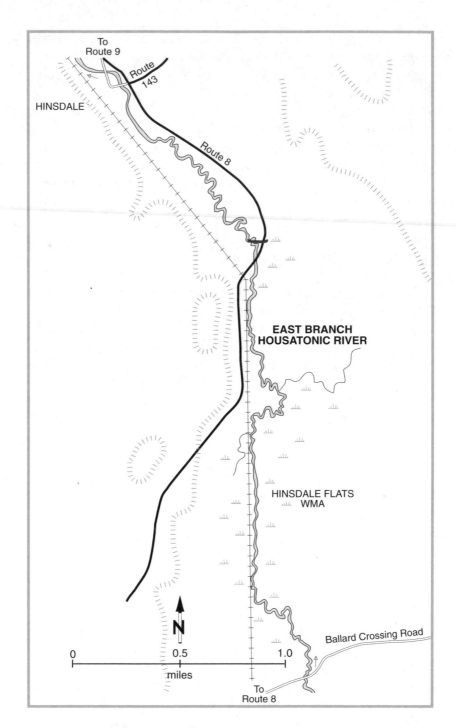

To
Route 9

Route
143

HINSDALE

Route 8

EAST BRANCH
HOUSATONIC RIVER

HINSDALE FLATS
WMA

N

Ballard Crossing Road

0   0.5   1.0

miles

To
Route 8

East Branch Housatonic River

A railroad embankment parallels the East Branch for more than a third of the distance covered here, reducing its scenic value to paddlers, though the entire area falls within the confines of the Hinsdale Flats Wildlife Management Area. We found the area alive with wildlife, particularly in the evening when beaver become active. We saw lots of waterfowl and all the usual marsh birds, including kingbirds on the nest; beaver, muskrat, painted and snapping turtles, mussels, and crayfish; and many species of shrubs and aquatic plants. We particularly enjoyed the broad expanse of meadow with meandering stream just north of Ballard Crossing Road.

The stretch between the access and Hinsdale offers no respite from beaver dams. We have to admit that we tired of beaver-dam portages—we had just done thirteen up and thirteen back!—and did not have the patience to paddle and portage all the way to Hinsdale.

47

Buckley Dunton Lake
Becket, MA

MAPS: Massachusetts Atlas, Map 33
USGS Quadrangle, East Lee
AREA: 195 acres
CAMPING: October Mountain State Forest, 413-243-1778;
Beartown State Forest, 413-528-0904; Tolland State Forest,
413-269-6002; Pittsfield State Forest, 413-442-8992;
reservations: 877-422-6762 or www.ReserveAmerica.com
HABITAT TYPE: wooded reservoir
EXPECT TO SEE: mountain laurel, blueberries, beaver, woodland
songbirds
TAKE NOTE: barely submerged stumps, rocks, and poor access
limit motors; limited development

GETTING THERE

From I-90, Exit 2, go east on Route 20 for 4.0 miles (4.0 miles), and turn left onto Becket Road, which becomes Tyne Road as you climb up over Becket Mountain and cross the Appalachian Trail. Go downhill, veering left onto Yokum Road as Tyne Road goes right after 1.9 miles (5.9 miles). After another 0.6 mile (6.5 miles), turn left onto the access road just before a multi-vehicle garage. The sign, Buckley Dunton Reservoir—Day Use Only, is sometimes blocked by vegetation. The turn is right across from Leonhardt Road. The put-in is in 0.5 mile (7.0 miles).

Buckley Dunton Lake nestles amid the Berkshires in the southeast corner of October Mountain State Forest, Massachusetts' largest tract of publicly owned land, which includes a 9-mile Appalachian Trail segment that passes over nearby scenic peaks. The damming of Yokum Brook in the 1800s to provide power for downstream mills created the lake.

Trees and shrubs typical of the moderately high Berkshire mountains dot the lake's heavily wooded shoreline, including hemlock, white

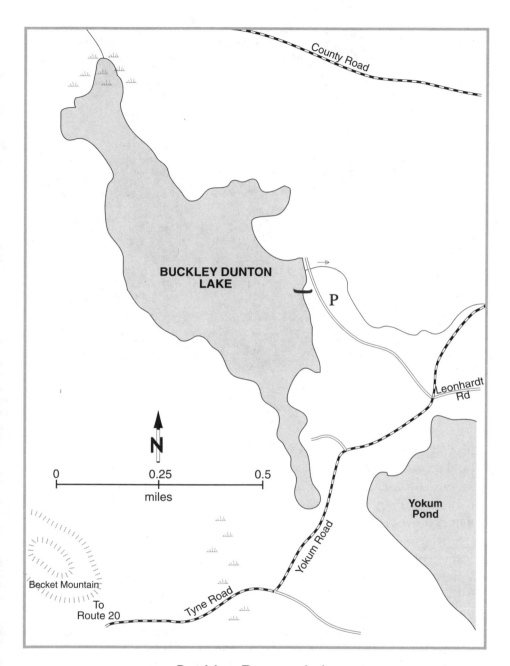

County Road

BUCKLEY DUNTON LAKE

P

Leonhardt Rd

N

0   0.25   0.5

miles

Becket Mountain

To
Route 20

Tyne Road

Yokum Road

Yokum
Pond

Buckley Dunton Lake

The heavily wooded hillsides of October Mountain State Forest surround Buckley Dunton Lake.

pine, spruce, red and sugar maples, black cherry, ash, gray and yellow birches, and alder. Look for large patches of mountain laurel in bloom in late June and blueberries in fruit in late July or August. Large boulders that jut out into the water invite picnic stops, but thick vegetation makes most of the shoreline quite impenetrable.

Rotting logs and tree stumps in the shallow, marshy north end force you to meander along carefully. Yellow pondlily, fragrant waterlily, pondweed, blue flag, and cattail grow here. Also, look carefully for diminutive carnivorous sundews on mossy hillocks. Listen for bullfrogs in spring, and in the evening or early morning you may see the lake's resident beaver. We also saw ruffed grouse here. On nice weekends you may see and hear heavy use of trails by off-road vehicles and see a fair number of people out fishing on the lake.

48

West Branch Farmington River
Otis, MA

MAPS: Massachusetts Atlas, Map 45
    USGS Quadrangle, Otis

LENGTH: 1.3 miles

CAMPING: Tolland State Forest, 413-269-6002; Beartown State
    Forest, 413-528-0904; Granville State Forest, 413-357-6611;
    October Mountain State Forest, 413-243-1778; Chester-
    Blanford State Forest, 413-354-6347;
    reservations: 877-422-6762 or www.ReserveAmerica.com

HABITAT TYPE: meandering, slow-flowing stream through broad
    beaver marsh

EXPECT TO SEE: beaver and many marsh birds, especially
    red-winged blackbird, yellow warbler, common yellowthroat

TAKE NOTE: no motors; no development

GETTING THERE

From I-90, Exit 2, go east on Route 20, and turn right onto Route 8. Go south
for 2.8 miles (2.8 miles), and turn right onto Ed Jones Road, just after the chicken
farm. Go 0.1 mile (2.9 miles) to the access on the left, just before the bridge.

This stretch of the West Branch of the Farmington River downstream
from Ed Jones Road represents what most small streams must have
looked like before our ancestors wiped out the beaver in the Northeast in the 1800s. From releases of a few animals in the early 1900s,
beaver have reclaimed much of their original habitat. We love paddling through this broad beaver marsh, but paddle here only if you
don't mind portaging over beaver dams. When we visited in early
June, high water allowed us to paddle over several drowned-out dams,
but we still had portages, one over a dam at least 3 feet high. We paddled by a huge beaver lodge with many succulent branches stored
underwater for winter food; on the backside, a large northern water
snake sunned itself.

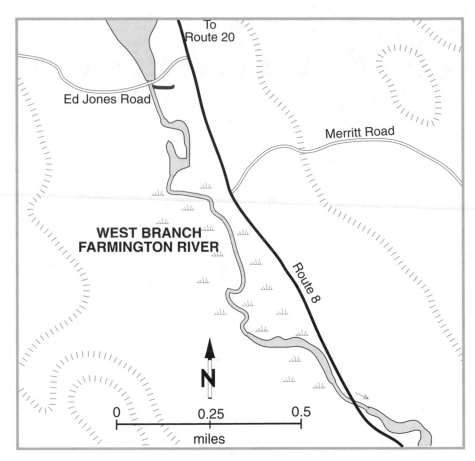

West Branch Farmington River

Few trees, other than a few red maples, grow in this marsh because of raised water levels behind the beaver dams. Shrubs and ferns grow in profusion, with high species diversity, including royal and marsh ferns, sweetgale, alders, and swamp azalea in bloom in early June. In the water, look for yellow pondlily and pickerelweed throughout and clumps of arrowhead and streaming leaves of water celery in the lower reaches.

We startled a great blue heron, which took flight.

Birds brought the marsh alive, as tree and barn swallows skimmed the water's surface, while multitudes of red-winged blackbirds, yellow warblers, and common yellowthroats called from streamside perches. We also saw eastern kingbird, chimney swift, cedar waxwing, great blue heron, wood duck, goldfinch, and several other species.

Beaver
Resident Wetlands Engineer

The beaver, *Castor canadensis*, is one of the most remarkable animals found in New England's waters. Unlike many other animals, beavers actively modify their environment. The sole representative of the family Castoridae, this 30- to 100-pound rodent—the largest rodent in North America—descends directly from a bear-sized ancestor that lived a million years ago.

Quietwater paddlers frequently see beaver dams and lodges, especially on more remote lakes and ponds. This industrious mammal uses branches pruned from streamside trees or downed timber to construct dams and lodges. Beaver work mostly under cover of darkness, especially in areas heavily frequented by humans. In the wilds, however, beaver work away in broad daylight. We mention in our lake, pond, and stream descriptions where we have seen beaver abroad during the day.

Beaver build dams to raise a stream's or pond's water level, providing the resident colony with access to trees growing farther away. The deeper water also allows beaver to cache branches underwater for winter retrieval, even when thick layers of ice cover their winter stores. They also dig small canals through marsh and meadow to transport branches from distant trees. Just as we find paddling easier than carrying a boat, beaver prefer swimming with a branch—taking advantage of water's buoyancy—to carrying it overland. They usually prune off leafy twigs to reduce drag.

Studies show that the sound of flowing water guides beaver in their dam building. In one experiment, researchers played a tape of gurgling water; beaver responded by jamming sticks into locations from which the sound emanated, even though no water actually flowed there. Beaver dams can be very large, more than 10 feet high and hundreds of feet long. The largest dam ever recorded, near the present town of Berlin, New Hampshire, spanned 4,000 feet and created a lake with forty lodges!

Beaver dams benefit many other species, providing important habitat for waterfowl, fish, moose, muskrat, and other animals. Plus, the dams provide flood control, minimize erosion along streambanks, increase aquifer recharge, and improve water quality by allowing silt to settle out and by providing biological filtration through aquatic plants. We credit beaver with creating much of America's best farmland by damming watercourses, thus allowing nutrient-rich silt to accumulate over many years. As the ponds fill in, meadows form.

The beaver lodge includes an underwater entrance and usually two platforms: a main floor about 4 inches above the water level, and a sleeping shelf another 2 inches higher. Beaver may construct the lodge in a pond's center, totally surrounded by water, but more commonly site it on the edge. Before the onset of winter, beaver cover much of the lodge with mud—which they carry on their broad tails while swimming—freezes to provide an almost impenetrable fortress. The river otter—the only predator that can get in—can swim through the underwater entrance. Beaver leave the peak more permeable for ventilation.

Near the lodge, in deep water, beaver store up a winter's worth of branches in an underwater food cache. They jam branches butt-first into the mud to keep them under the ice and then swim out of their lodges to bring back the stored branches to eat. While they prefer alder and willow, they also love the cambium layer—just beneath the bark—of such hardwoods as yellow birch, white ash, and black cherry. During spring and summer months, beaver eat primarily pond vegetation, shrubs, herbaceous plants along the shore, and even algae. We have watched them munching voraciously on yellow pondlily stems.

Beaver have adapted remarkably well to their aquatic lifestyle. They have two layers of fur: long silky guard hairs and a dense woolly underfur. Because they regularly groom this fur with a special comblike split toenail and keep it oiled, water seldom totally wets beaver's skin. Their noses and ears have special valves that keep them shut when underwater, and special folds of skin in the mouth enable beaver to gnaw underwater and carry branches in their teeth without getting water down their throats. Their back feet have fully webbed toes to provide propulsion underwater, and their tails provide rudder control, helping them swim in a straight line when dragging a large branch. Their respiratory and circulatory systems have adapted to underwater swimming, enabling a beaver to stay underwater for up to 15 minutes and swim 0.5 mile. Similar adaptations evolved independently in whales, seals, loons, and other air-breathing divers—though painted turtles rely on a very different mechanism for staying underwater (see the section on painted turtles on page 259). Finally, as with other rodents, their teeth grow constantly and remain sharp through use.

Castor oil, that medicinal cure-all of yesteryear, comes from special perineal scent glands. Beaver use the oily yellow liquid to waterproof their fur and to communicate. Along the banks of ponds and lakes, you may see mud mounds scented with this castoreum; it has a strong but not unpleasant smell and, in fact, forms a base ingredient in some expensive perfumes.

Beaver generally mate for life and maintain an extended family structure. Young stay with their parents for two years, so both yearlings and the current year's kits live with the parents in the lodge. Females usually bear two—sometimes three—kits between April and June. Born fully furred with eyes open, they can walk and swim almost right away, though they rarely leave the lodge until at least a month of age. The yearlings and both parents assist in bringing food to the kits as well as with dam and lodge construction.

The demand for beaver pelts, more than any other factor, was responsible for the early European exploration of North America. Trappers nearly exterminated them by the late 1800s, but last-minute legislative protection in the 1890s saved them from extinction. Trappers extirpated them in Connecticut in the mid-1800s, and the state began reintroducing them in 1914 as part of a restocking program. Then began what certainly might be history's most successful endangered species reintroduction program. Within a few decades, beaver had repopulated the entire state.

Although we have removed most of their natural predators—wolves, cougars, and bobcats—beaver populations have not rebounded to historic highs, mainly because of habitat loss and because their engineering activities often conflict with humans.

As you paddle along the shoreline of lakes or quiet rivers, keep an eye out for telltale signs of beaver, including gnaw marks on trees, distinctive conical stumps of cut trees, canals leading off into the marsh, alder branches trimmed back along narrow passages, and well-worn paths leading away from the water's edge where the hardworking mammals have dragged more distant branches to the water. Exploring a quiet beaver pond by canoe or kayak—carrying over the dam if necessary—often provides a substantial reward because it allows access to pristine ponds and marshes.

We see beaver most often in the late evening or early morning. Paddle quietly toward a beaver lodge around dusk. Wait patiently, and you are likely to see the animals emerge for evening feeding and perhaps construction work on a dam or lodge. When a beaver senses danger it slaps the water with its tail and dives with a loud *ker-chunk!* We hope that you will find it as exhilarating as we do to emerge from a tight bend in a marshy stream and come across a beaver pruning back the alders, or to drift silently toward a beaver at dusk, watching it go about its various activities.

49

Upper Spectacle Pond
Otis and Sandisfield, MA

MAPS: Massachusetts Atlas, Map 45
   USGS Quadrangle, Otis
AREA: 72 acres
CAMPING: Tolland State Forest, 413-269-6002; Beartown State
   Forest, 413-528-0904; Granville State Forest, 413-357-6611;
   Chester-Blanford State Forest, 413-354-6347; reservations:
   877-422-6762 or www.ReserveAmerica.com
HABITAT TYPE: wooded, mountain pond
EXPECT TO SEE: woodland birds, forested hillsides, water
   smartweed, pondweed
TAKE NOTE: hand-carry access limits motors; no development

GETTING THERE

From I-90, Exit 2, go east on Route 20, and turn right onto Route 8. Go
south for 5.5 miles (5.5 miles), and turn right onto Route 23 in Otis. Go west
for 3.4 miles (8.9 miles), and turn left onto Cold Springs Road. Go south for
0.8 mile (9.7 miles), and veer left onto unmarked dirt Webb Road. Access is
on the right fork in 1.0 mile (10.7 miles).

From Great Barrington, go east on Route 23. From the church, general
store, and post office in Monterey, it is another 3.7 miles to Cold Springs
Road on the right, just after Town Hill Road. Follow as above.

Passing through a deep hemlock woods, you end up at the access amid
a noble stand of large hemlock and white pine. Though white pine
occurs along the pond's shore, deciduous trees predominate here and
on scenic hillsides, with mountain laurel the dominant shrub. The
pond and its coves—including a beautiful island wooded with oaks—
require only an hour or two to explore fully. If geese haven't covered
the granite slabs on the northeast with excrement, these slabs make an
excellent picnic stop.

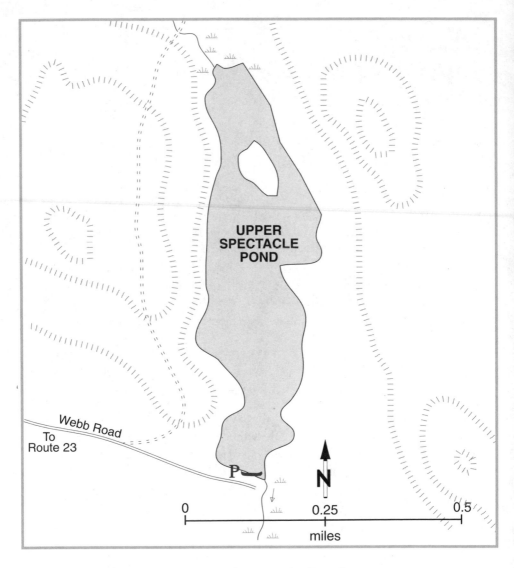

UPPER
SPECTACLE
POND

Webb Road
To
Route 23

P

N

0   0.25   0.5

miles

Upper Spectacle Pond

Water smartweed *(Polyganum amphibium)* and pondweed *(Pota-mogeton spp.)*—both featuring elongated, floating leaves and small, vertical puffs of flowers—grow in profusion side by side. They bear a superficial resemblance, but looking closely, you can note the leaf veination. Smartweed veins radiate out at roughly right angles to the midvein, whereas pondweed side veins start with the midvein at the stem and remain roughly parallel all the way to the tip.

Aquatic smartweed in bloom on Upper Spectacle Pond.

Lots of yellow-flowered and purple-flowered bladderwort occur here, notable because Eurasian water-milfoil has not inundated this pond and crowded out native species yet. Gelatinous bryozoa colonies, also susceptible to crowding, occur on many submerged logs and branches along the shore. As we paddled along, an immature bald eagle soared overhead, possibly from the nest at nearby Colebrook Lake to the south.

50

Threemile Pond
Sheffield, MA

MAPS: Massachusetts Atlas, Map 44
  USGS Quadrangle, Sheffield
AREA: 81 acres
CAMPING: Beartown State Forest, 413-528-0904; Tolland State
  Forest, 413-269-6002; Granville State Forest, 413-357-6611;
  October Mountain State Forest, 413-243-1778; reservations:
  877-422-6762 or www.ReserveAmerica.com
HABITAT TYPE: wooded pond; forested hillsides
EXPECT TO SEE: muskrat, Canada goose, wood duck, tree
  swallow, osprey, tamarack
TAKE NOTE: too weedy and shallow for motors; limited
  development; most lies within Threemile Pond Wildlife
  Management Area

GETTING THERE

From Great Barrington. From the junction of Routes 7, 23, and 41, go south on Route 7 for 0.9 mile (0.9 mile), turn left onto Brookside Road (which becomes Brush Hill Road, then Home Road), go 4.0 miles (4.9 miles), and turn left onto a different Brush Hill Road. Go 1.2 miles (6.1 miles) to the access on the right; watch for ruts and mud.

From Sheffield. From Route 7, go east on Maple Avenue (which becomes County Road) for 1.6 miles (1.6 miles), and turn left onto Home Road. Go 1.7 miles (3.3 miles), turn right onto Brush Hill Road, and go 1.2 miles (4.5 miles) to the access on the right.

A broad-winged hawk soared overhead and dozens of tree swallows darted from their nest boxes as we worked our way carefully down the rutted road to the access in early May. Spring peepers beckoned to us while an osprey dove for fish. When we ventured onto the northern section of this shallow, weedy pond, wood ducks flew off into the marsh, and Canada geese paddled out of sight.

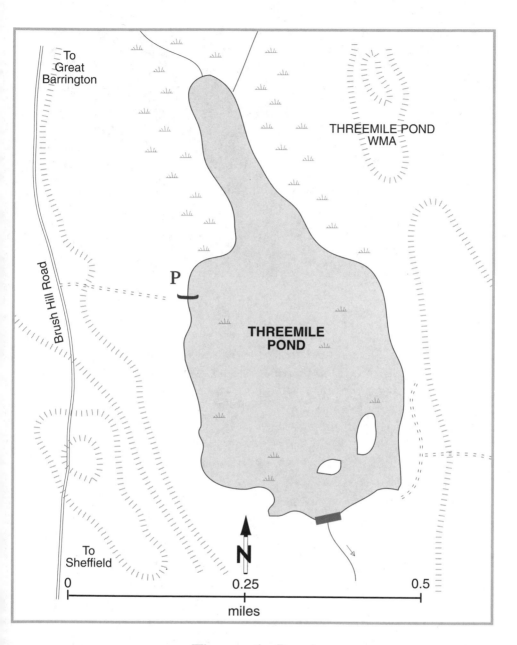

To
Great
Barrington

Brush Hill Road

P

THREEMILE POND
WMA

THREEMILE
POND

To
Sheffield

N

0   0.25   0.5
miles

Threemile Pond

A white-tailed skimmer, Plathemis lydia, *soaks up the sun on a dead tree on Three-mile Pond.*

On a late-June return trip, the osprey had vanished, no doubt because dense rafts of invasive Eurasian water-milfoil clogged the waterway, leaving precious little open water. Though we had to slog through this sea of vegetation, we still enjoyed forging our way down to the large island off the southeast shore. Densely foliated, the island harbors quite a few tall, thin tamaracks, a tree that withstands saturated soil, along with sphagnum mats, pitcher plants, cranberries, and large beaver lodge.

As we gazed back up the pond, with clumps of blooming mountain laurel here and there, we drank in the scenic beauty of unspoiled, undulating, deciduous-tree-covered hillsides that harbor a section of the Appalachian Trail. A couple of cabins on the southeast shore and a low earthen dam on the south end provide the only evidence of civilization (except for the invasive water-milfoil).

Returning to the boat access, we studied the several species of dragonflies that patrol the shallows and searched for frogs among the cattails. While you could paddle the entire perimeter of this pond in an hour, you could also linger, studying the myriad plants and wildlife in this picturesque spot.

～ 51 ～

Thousand Acre Swamp and East Indies Pond
New Marlborough, MA

MAPS: Massachusetts Atlas, Map 44
   USGS Quadrangle, South Sandisfield
AREA: Thousand Acre Swamp, 155 acres;
   East Indies Pond, 69 acres
CAMPING: Beartown State Forest, 413-528-0904; Tolland State
   Forest, 413-269-6002; Granville State Forest, 413-357-6611;
   reservations: 877-422-6762 or www.ReserveAmerica.com
HABITAT TYPE: shallow, marshy, tree-lined ponds
EXPECT TO SEE: beaver, waterfowl, aquatic vegetation, mountain
   laurel, scenic woods
TAKE NOTE: few motors; no development

THOUSAND ACRE SWAMP
GETTING THERE

From Great Barrington, take Routes 23/183 east; when they divide, take Routes 57/183 southeast for 5.8 miles (5.8 miles) to New Marlborough, and turn right onto New Marlborough–Southfield Road. Go 1.3 miles (7.1 miles), and turn left over the bridge onto Southfield-Norfolk Road (Route 272). Go 0.3 mile (7.4 miles), and turn left onto East Hill Road. In 1.8 miles (9.2 miles), turn right onto Hotchkiss Road, and go 1.4 miles (10.6 miles) to the access on the left. While it is also possible to reach Hotchkiss Road from Norfolk Road, reaching the access from this direction may not be feasible due to bridge closure.

This out-of-the-way, scenic pond offers wonderful paddling within the borders of Campbell Falls State Park. Interestingly, Campbell Falls itself lies well outside the park, which has no development or conveniences. Though we enjoyed paddling through the abundant vegetation of this stump-filled pond, we noted luxuriant growths of invasive Eurasian water-milfoil starting to crowd out the native water shield,

Thousand Acre Swamp

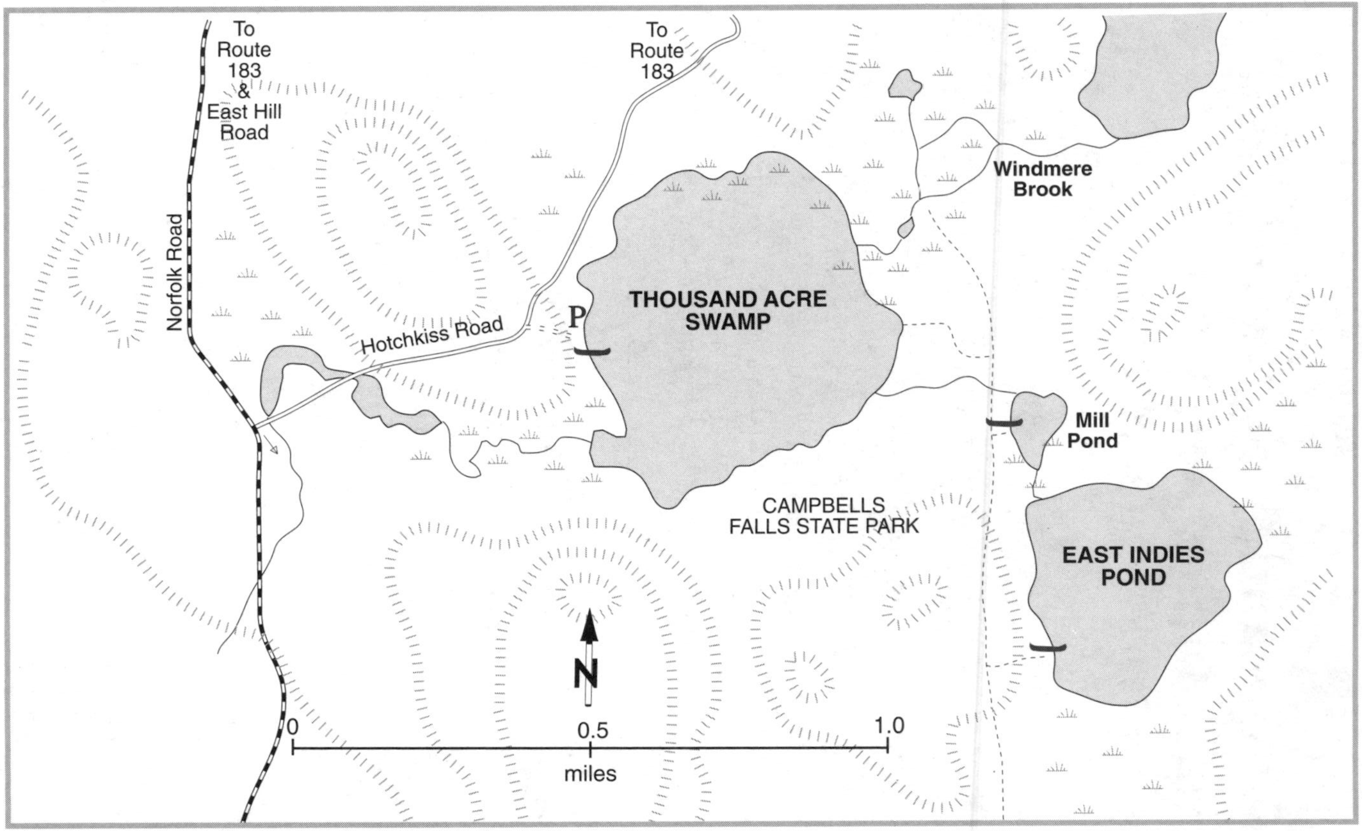

WINDMERE BROOK

EAST INDIES POND

Mill Pond

To Route 183

THOUSAND ACRE SWAMP

P

Hotchkiss Road

CAMPBELLS FALLS STATE PARK

To Route 183 & East Hill Road

Norfolk Road

N

0   0.5   1.0
miles

The marshy northwest entrance to secluded East Indies Pond.

fragrant waterlily, yellow pondlily, and pondweed. While some mountain laurel bloomed along the southern shore, it paled in comparison to the growth at East Indies Pond.

Mallards and Canada geese nest here, and if you visit in the evening you may see some of the resident beaver as they work over the wooded shores. In the woodland during a mid-June visit, we watched a wild turkey hen herding her brood of six young. Though we did not paddle it, the outlet stream where it crosses Hotchkiss Road south of the pond looks like a wonderful area to explore. We found loads of mussels on the sandy bottom, and we watched a great blue heron—up to its nithers in yellow pondlily—hunting fish and frogs. In early summer you may notice shallow depressions in the pond's sandy bottom, where black crappie keep their eggs aerated and protected from predators. You can paddle back into Windmere Brook about 150 feet, past a large beaver lodge to a beaver dam 3 feet high.

EAST INDIES POND
GETTING THERE

The 0.5-mile trail starts directly across the pond from the Thousand Acre Swamp access. Look for a grove of tall white pines that has been used as a campsite. From there, follow an ATV trail for about 600 paces to a T. Turn right, go about 60 paces, and cross the outflow stream. Continue uphill for another 100 paces to an obvious trail off to the water on the left (look for a big rock on the left). It's another 100 paces to Mill Pond. Alternatively, from the stream crossing, you can follow the ATV trail 1,000 paces to a fork; the left fork heads downhill for 400 paces to a fire grate and East Indies Pond.

Only attempt launching your boat on East Indies Pond if you crave adventure. Branches hang low over the ATV trails, making overhead portaging a challenge; a wheeled portaging cart would help. After you reach the access on Mill Pond, you have to portage over a couple of swampy beaver dams to get to East Indies Pond.

We were not prepared for what greeted us upon reaching the pond in late June—probably the most spectacular mountain laurel bloom we have ever seen. Mountain laurel, with stems reaching 15 and 20 feet tall, all in electric bloom, formed dense stands along much of the shoreline. Cruising the shoreline in this gorgeous setting, we hardly noticed the floating heart, water celery, pondweed, waterlilies, or the complete lack of Eurasian water-milfoil. We expect that you would see beaver here in the evening, judging by the size of the lodges on the two ponds. A few clearings along the west shore looked pretty enticing, as did some large granite boulders—perfect for an afternoon rest or picnic.

Rhode Island

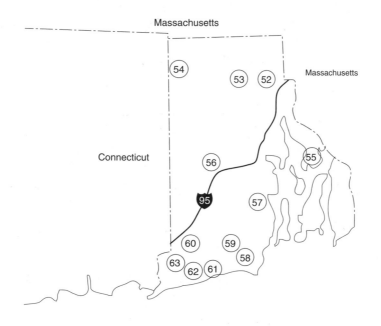

Olney Pond
Lincoln, RI

MAPS: Connecticut and Rhode Island Atlas, Map 65
   USGS Quadrangle, Pawtucket
AREA: 120 acres
CAMPING: George Washington Camping Area, 401-568-2013
HABITAT TYPE: wooded pond
EXPECT TO SEE: ducks, mute swan; shrubby, wooded shoreline;
   picnickers and strollers
TAKE NOTE: no motors weekends and holidays, otherwise 10 HP
   limit; recreational development only

GETTING THERE

From Route 146, about 4.0 miles north of I-95, take the Twin River Road exit for Lincoln Woods. Turn left at the end of the exit ramp, go 0.5 mile (0.5 mile), and turn right at the stop sign, entering the one-way, 2.6-mile loop road around the pond. The access is on the left in 1.4 miles (1.9 miles).

Just minutes from downtown Providence, Olney Pond offers surprisingly pleasant paddling. Gorgeous granite boulders—some striated with bands of quartz or blazoned with clusters of polypody fern—dot the heavily wooded shoreline. Only Lincoln Woods State Park recreational facilities occur along the pond—and herein lies the problem: Olney Pond abounds with recreational users on weekends and particularly nice days. Hikers, joggers, and bicyclists, many of whom come from nearby offices for a break during the day, fill the pond's perimeter road, removing any semblance of solitude.

Many sheltered coves beg to be explored, especially a particularly beautiful one at the pond's northern tip, where you must wend your way around huge boulders extending from the water. Red oak dominates the surrounding woods; other species include white oak, dogwood, white ash, hickory and, close to shore, red maple.

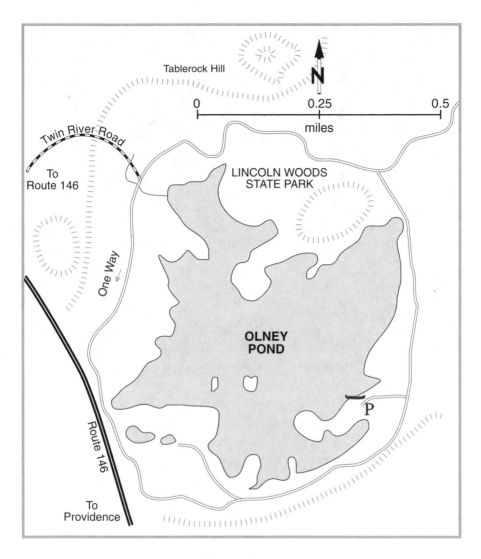

Olney Pond

At a trail junction near the pond's northernmost cove, a marker describes the Zachariah Allen Woodlot, planted in 1820. About 0.3 mile from here, to the northwest on Quinsnicket Hill, Allen took ownership of a 40-acre worn-out pasture and planted acorns and chestnuts in an early silviculture experiment. Today, more than 170 years later, a marker by an old spring describes this unusual businessman-botanist and his investment through planting acorns and chestnuts in plowed

Huge granite boulders lend scenic character to Olney Pond's shores.

soil. Even before the area became a state park, city folks from nearby Providence visited the woodlot via steam cars to Lonsdale or "electrics" from Pawtucket. Wildflowers and ferns, including such uncommon species as maidenhair spleenwort and smooth yellow violet, fill the Quinsnicket Hill woods.

～ 53 ～

Stillwater Reservoir
Smithfield, RI

MAPS: Connecticut and Rhode Island Atlas, Map 65
USGS Quadrangle, Georgiaville
AREA: 304 acres
CAMPING: George Washington Camping Area, 401-568-2013
HABITAT TYPE: shallow reservoir
EXPECT TO SEE: waterfowl; turtles; shrubby, wooded shoreline
TAKE NOTE: motors allowed, 10 HP limit; development in areas

GETTING THERE

Western Access. From I-295, Exit 7, go west on Route 44 for 0.6 mile (0.6 mile), and turn right onto Route 5. Go north (Route 116 joins from the left after 1.0 mile) for 2.2 miles (2.8 miles), and turn left onto Log Road. Go 0.4 mile (3.2 miles) to the access on the right.

Eastern Access. From above, instead of turning onto Log Road, continue north on Routes 5/116 for 0.5 mile (3.3 miles). At the T, turn left onto Routes 5/104. The access is on the left in 0.5 mile (3.8 miles), just after the bridge.

Alternately, from I-295, Exit 8, go north on Route 7, and turn left onto Route 116. At the T in 1.2 miles (1.2 miles), turn right onto Routes 5/104. Access is on the left in 0.3 mile (1.5 miles).

Mowry Conservation Area. From the Routes 5/104 access, continue north for 0.9 mile, and turn left onto Old Forge Road. The conservation area is on the right, with parking on the left.

Do not expect a wilderness experience on Stillwater Reservoir (also known as Wounasquatuck Reservoir and Stump Pond), but paddling here in the early morning or at midweek can be quite pleasant. Once heavily polluted and prone to severe summer draw-downs, Stillwater Reservoir has dramatically improved in recent years, following shutdown of several of the region's most polluting industrial facilities. Certain areas suffer from heavy development, but portions of the

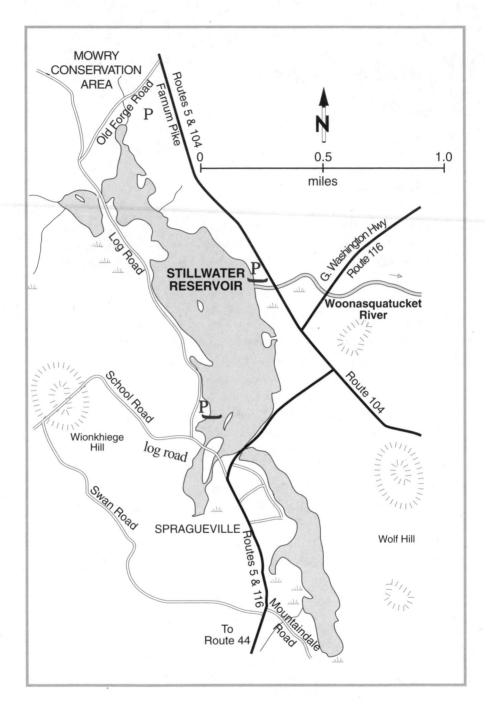

Stillwater Reservoir

reservoir feel relatively remote and wild. A little-used road extends along much of the western shore, and traffic from Routes 5/104 can be heard to the east.

During a morning paddle in mid-April, we saw as many as fifty painted turtles, a snapping turtle, mallards, a few Canada geese, and a pair of gorgeous wood ducks. Blueberries burst forth along the mossy banks in midsummer. For some reason, many red oaks have died along the west shore—perhaps pollution. While it's a bit disconcerting to see so many dead treetops, they provide a veritable paradise for woodpeckers and various cavity-nesting birds that rely on woodpecker holes, such as bluebird, tree swallow, great crested flycatcher, house wren, kestrel, chickadee, and wood duck. Anglers ply these waters for warmwater species.

If you feel adventurous, you might want to explore a small, isolated extension of the reservoir near the northwestern end. You can usually slip a boat through the culvert that runs under Log Road to reach this area, but the culvert may be too narrow for large canoes; even in a small boat, you have to pretty much lie down and pull yourself through. You will see a narrow island in this part of the reservoir with an out-of-place stone wall running down its center. At the reservoir's northern tip, you can reach a tiny segment of water by paddling under a wooden bridge. Though very shallow and weedy in summer, this area is thick with painted turtles.

We do not recommend paddling into the reservoir's southern extension, south of Routes 5/116, because of heavy development. Along with paddling opportunities, the nearby Mowry Conservation Area offers very nice hiking and picnicking off Old Forge Road, along the north end of the reservoir. A fast-flowing brook flows around huge boulders, one of which overhangs the brook.

54

Bowdish Reservoir

Glocester, RI

> **MAPS:** Connecticut and Rhode Island Atlas, Map 64
>   USGS Quadrangle, Thompson
> **AREA:** 226 acres
> **CAMPING:** George Washington Camping Area, 401-568-2013;
>   in CT: West Thompson Lake, 860-923-2982
> **HABITAT TYPE:** shallow reservoir
> **EXPECT TO SEE:** waterfowl; shrubby, wooded shoreline
> **TAKE NOTE:** motors limited to 10 HP; limited development; use
>   caution in wind

GETTING THERE

From the stoplight at the junction of Routes 44 and 102 in Chepachet, go west on Route 44 for 4.5 miles (4.5 miles) to the turn-off for the George Washington Camping Area. Turn right, and the access is the third left in 0.3 mile (4.8 miles).

A large bog stood at this site before Bowdish Reservoir flooded it out. Today a few floating sphagnum islands, the only remnants of the bog, appear near the center of the reservoir. When the water level rose, these mats broke loose and floated to the surface; tree roots anchor them in the reservoir's shallow waters. On these islands, look for rare bog plants usually seen much farther north, including black spruce (an extremely short-needled conifer), Atlantic white cedar, leatherleaf, bog laurel, bog rosemary, sundew, pitcher plant, and—rarest of all—a dwarf mistletoe that lacks roots and always grows in association with black spruce. These islands appear larger on older maps and may be disappearing.

Bowdish Reservoir does not exude wilderness. The southwestern edge, bounded by heavily traveled Route 44, supports some development. Even at the far-eastern end, by the George Washington Camping

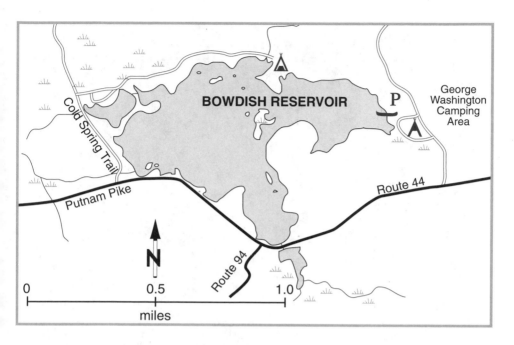

Bowdish Reservoir

Area, you can still hear cars and trucks. A mammoth private campground that caters to RVs extends along most of the northern shore, although quite a bit of space extends between heavily wooded sites.

Huge slabs of granite extend down into the water in places, and the small, private island in the reservoir's southern extension appears to be mostly solid rock. The forested land of the George Washington Management Area along the reservoir's eastern end remains readily accessible to hikers and picnickers. Several very nice trails, accessible from the boat launch area, course through the surrounding oak-hemlock forests for several miles. Dominant species include hemlock, white, red, and scarlet oaks, black birch, white pine, and mountain laurel. At the water's edge you will also find lots of highbush blueberry and sweet pepperbush, which has very fragrant late-blooming white flower spikes.

Carnivorous pitcher plants, Sarracenia purpurea, *grow on sphagnum hummocks on Bowdish Reservoir.*

The reservoir itself supports quite a bit of vegetation. Underwater plants include water-milfoil, fanwort, and bladderwort. Floating plants include water shield and yellow pondlily. Though the abundant aquatic vegetation damps waves somewhat, in a strong wind large waves build up across the open water, so use caution paddling here.

55

Brickyard Pond
Barrington, RI

MAPS: Connecticut and Rhode Island Atlas, Map 68
USGS Quadrangle, Bristol
AREA: 102 acres
HABITAT TYPE: wooded pond
EXPECT TO SEE: ducks, mute swan, osprey; shrubby, wooded shoreline; strollers
TAKE NOTE: motors allowed; limited development

GETTING THERE

From I-195, Exit 7, in East Providence, go south on Route 114 to the first stoplight, where Massasoit Avenue traverses the Barrington River (left or east) and Federal Road/Recycling Center goes west. Turn right onto Federal Road/Recycling Center, go 0.6 mile (0.6 mile) to Middle Highway, and turn left (south). Go 1.0 mile (1.6 miles) to the access road (American Legion Way) on the left. Turn left into the access in 0.2 mile (1.8 miles), behind the American Legion.

Brickyard Pond, in an urban area that abounds with housing developments and a golf course, offers a surprisingly wild place to paddle. An abandoned railroad bed converted into a beautiful hiking and biking trail borders the northern shore, and a few houses dot the southern shore. But a wooded shoreline and many shallow coves draped with grape arbors beg to be explored. Several islands provide more shoreline to investigate, making the pond seem much larger than its 102 acres.

Dozens of catbirds skulked among the dense grapevines and Virginia creeper in the fingerlike western coves, while goldfinches and gnatcatchers gleaned seeds and insects from shoreside vegetation. A downy woodpecker pulled apart heads of narrow-leaved cattail, probing

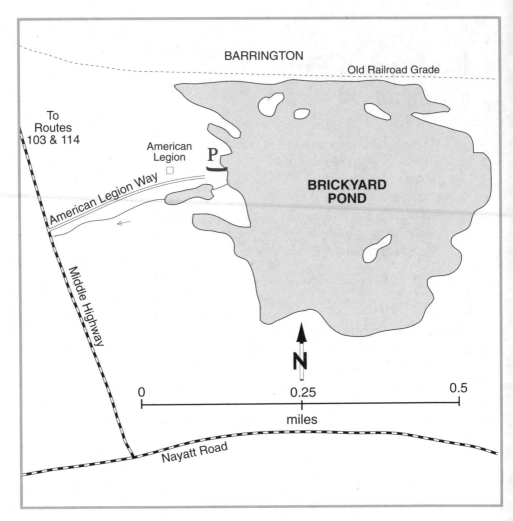

Brickyard Pond

for insects, while a diving osprey came up with a fish. Families of Canada geese fed in the shallows, two brightly colored male wood ducks took off in front of us, and we counted twenty-three mute swans. While beautiful, mute swans, introduced from Europe, aggressively compete with native species.

A downy woodpecker pecks apart a cattail, looking for insects.

Four oak species—red, pin, white, and swamp white—grace the shoreline, along with willow, sassafras, cottonwood, red and Norway maples, gray birch, and alder. We saw many other bird and plant species here and could have spent several hours exploring. As a spotted sandpiper fled before us, we reveled in the rich number of species harbored by this urban wildlife paradise.

56

Big River
Coventry and West Greenwich, RI

MAPS: Connecticut and Rhode Island Atlas, Map 67
USGS Quadrangles, Coventry Center and Crompton
LENGTH: 2.3 miles
CAMPING: Arcadia Management Area, 401-222-6800;
George Washington Camping Area, 401-568-2013
HABITAT TYPE: slow-flowing river through broad marsh
EXPECT TO SEE: waterfowl; dense aquatic vegetation;
wooded shoreline
TAKE NOTE: most motors stay north of Harkney Hill Road;
limited development

GETTING THERE

Northern Access. From I-95, Exit 6, go north on Route 3, and take the first left onto Harkney Hill Road. Go west on Harkney Hill Road for 1.1 miles to the Zeke's Bridge Fishing Access on the right, just before the bridge.

Southern Access. From I-95, Exit 6, go south on Route 3 for 1.3 miles (1.3 miles), and turn right onto Weaver Hill Road. Go north for 0.3 mile (1.6 miles), and turn right onto the unmarked dirt access road, which ends at the access site (stay right at the fork) in 0.7 mile (2.3 miles).

Most boaters here venture out from the northern access into Flat River Reservoir; a low bridge and abundant aquatic vegetation keep most motors out of the southern section of Big River. The river courses through a broad marsh, filled with aquatic vegetation and birdlife. Tons of fanwort and purple- and yellow-flowered bladderwort fill the water column, while pickerelweed, arrowhead, water celery, fragrant waterlily, yellow pondlily, pondweed, floating heart, and water shield crowd the water's surface, borne on an imperceptible current.

Along the shore, stands of Atlantic white cedar and white pine intermingle with the predominant deciduous trees. Stunted red maples, *Phragmites*, cattail, buttonbush, royal fern, sweetgale, alders, and other shrubs

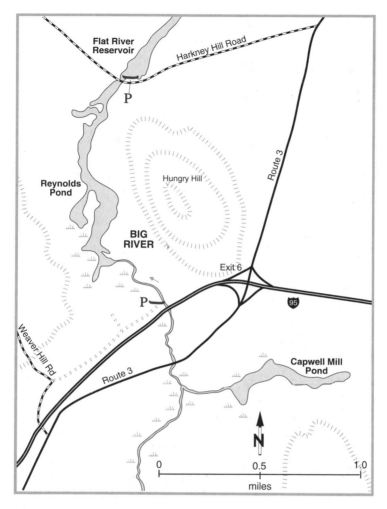

Big River

hang out over the water. Paddling south, you can explore a couple of large coves before the river channel narrows just before the culverts that slice through the I-95 embankment. Noise from the roadway far overhead does not intrude too much on the solitude. After passing under the Route 3 bridge, the riverbed narrows further through tight twisting turns. About 0.25 mile south of Route 3, narrow passageways block further progress.

We saw a couple of anglers in motorboats in the northern reaches, but as you progress upstream to the south, you should pretty much have the place to yourself. We spent most of our time identifying and photographing the various bladderwort species, but we also enjoyed seeing many of the marsh birds that congregate here.

57

Belleville Pond
North Kingstown, RI

> **MAPS:** Connecticut and Rhode Island Atlas, Map 71
>   USGS Quadrangle, Wickford
> **AREA:** 159 acres
> **CAMPING:** Arcadia Management Area, 401-222-6800;
>   Burlingame State Park, 401-322-8910
> **HABITAT TYPE:** shallow, marshy pond
> **EXPECT TO SEE:** waterfowl; dense aquatic vegetation,
>   wooded shoreline
> **TAKE NOTE:** motors limited by vegetation; no development

---

GETTING THERE

From Route 4, Exit 5A, go 2.6 miles (2.6 miles) east on Route 102, and turn right (south) onto Route 1. Go 0.8 mile (3.4 miles), and turn right onto Oak Hill Road. The access is through Ryan Park in 0.6 mile (4.0 miles) on the right. Stay left on the loop road to the marked access.

Belleville Pond boasts some of the best inland marsh habitat that we have seen. Waterfowl abound, and its shoreline provides hours of quiet exploration. The shallow water, highly productive biologically, supports the waterfowl populations, which draw in hunters in fall.

During an October visit—with both summer residents and migrants present—we saw pied-billed grebe, mallard, black duck, bufflehead, wood duck, American coot, green-winged teal, Canada goose, mute swan, cormorant, great blue heron, and marsh wren. During the warmer months, many painted turtles sun on logs. Marsh plants include cattail, *Phragmites*, swamp loosestrife, bulrush, pickerelweed, yellow pondlily, fragrant waterlily, water shield, duckweed, fanwort, and bladderwort. The underwater vegetation (fanwort and bladderwort primarily) grows densely in places, providing good habitat for such fish species as chain pickerel, largemouth bass, and yellow perch. A fish

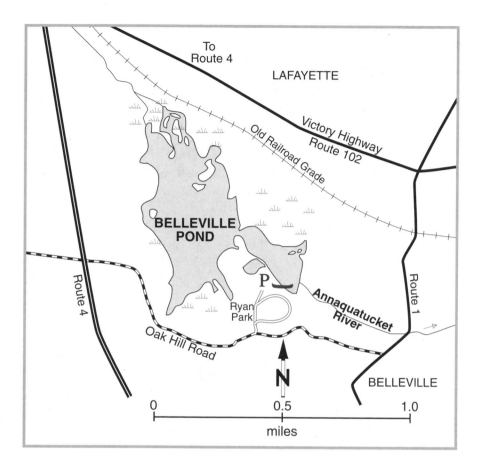

Belleville Pond

ladder at the outlet (Annaquatucket River, which flows 3 miles into Narragansett Bay) enables alewife to swim upstream into Belleville Pond to spawn.

At the pond's poorly defined north end, marshy islands abound. Quietly exploring around these islands and the increasingly narrow channels of open water between them, you should see lots of birds.

Around the less marshy sections of the pond, deciduous trees dominate: red, white, and scarlet oaks, red maple, aspen, gray birch, and black gum. On the more solid sections of shoreline, highbush blueberry, sweet pepperbush, and alder provide shelter and food for a wide variety of songbirds. You can hear Route 4 through the trees, but it doesn't detract too much from the solitude.

58

Tucker Pond
South Kingston, RI

MAPS: Connecticut and Rhode Island Atlas, Map 75
  USGS Quadrangle, Kingston
AREA: 101 acres
CAMPING: Burlingame State Park, 401-322-8910;
  Arcadia Management Area, 401-222-6800
HABITAT TYPE: wooded, natural kettle pond
EXPECT TO SEE: rosebay rhododendron, wooded shoreline
TAKE NOTE: motors limited to 10 HP; limited development

GETTING THERE

From the junction of Routes 110 and 138 in West Kingston, go south on Route 110 for 3.8 miles (3.8 miles), and turn left at the four-way stop sign onto Tuckertown Road. Go 0.5 mile (4.3 miles) to the access on the right.

From the junction of Routes 1 and 110, go north on Route 110, and turn right onto Tuckertown Road. Go 0.5 mile to the access on the right.

Tucker Pond, just to the southeast of Worden Pond in southern Rhode Island, has perhaps the most dramatic stand of rosebay rhododendron (*Rhododendron maximum*) that we have seen north of the southern Appalachians. This largest member of the heath family—which includes mountain laurel, azalea, blueberry, cranberry, and leatherleaf—covers most of the shoreline. Though we haven't been here when these 15- to 20-foot high rhododendrons bloom (typically late June or early July), they ought to be spectacular. On the pond's steeper south and east sides, they extend up quite high on the banks, with taller white oak, black gum, and pitch pine extending above—as if emerging from a sea of green.

About a dozen houses appear around the pond but do not seem terribly imposing, and the 10-horsepower limit keeps boating activity to quiet fishing. Because this natural kettle pond has no major inlet, the water level fluctuates with rainfall. In a dry year, the level can drop

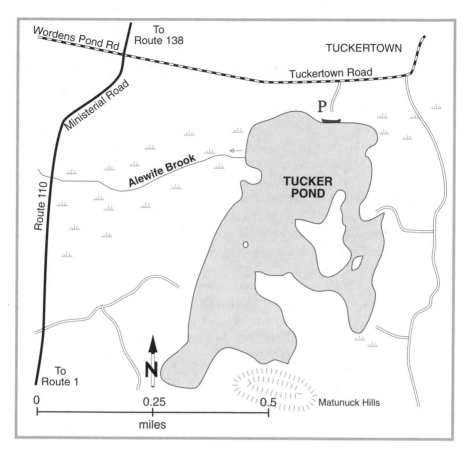

Tucker Pond

considerably. The last glacier, which receded 10,000 to 12,000 years ago, created the hilly area that extends south from Tucker Pond for a few miles, known as the Charlestown recessional moraine or the Matunuck Hills. Tucker Pond and the collection of smaller kettle ponds to the south, formed from chunks of glacial ice, have shoreline ecosystems (some protected by The Nature Conservancy) that support a number of plant species quite rare in Rhode Island. Enjoy these plants from your boat.

A band of floating plants surrounds much of the perimeter, but most of the pond consists of open water. Where rhododendrons don't dominate the shoreline, highbush blueberry, sweetgale, sweet pepperbush, and red maple occur. Swamp loosestrife, pickerelweed, and bulrush populate the few marshy coves. Several islands rise from the pond, including a large one (with a house fairly well hidden near the peak).

59

Worden Pond and Great Swamp
South Kingston, RI

> **MAPS:** Connecticut and Rhode Island Atlas, Maps 71 and 75
> USGS Quadrangle, Kingston
> **AREA/LENGTH:** Worden Pond, 1,075 acres;
> Chipuxet and Charles Rivers, 9 miles
> **CAMPING:** Arcadia Management Area, 401-222-6800;
> Burlingame State Park, 401-322-8910
> **HABITAT TYPE:** marshy, meandering rivers with overhanging
> shrubs and trees
> **EXPECT TO SEE:** beaver, muskrat, waterfowl, marsh birds, osprey,
> turtles, aquatic vegetation, varied shrubs
> **TAKE NOTE:** no development, no motors on rivers; little devel-
> opment on Worden Pond, but watch out for motors and
> treacherous wind; beware of poison ivy and tight curves on
> the Charles River

GETTING THERE

Chipuxet River. From the junction of Routes 1 and 138, go west on Route 138 for 5.2 miles, through the Route 110 intersection, cross the Chipuxet River, and take an immediate left onto Liberty Lane and the parking area for Taylor's Landing.

Charles River. From the junction of Routes 2 and 138, go south on Route 2 for 4.1 miles, then take a shallow left onto an unmarked road to the boat access in 0.1 mile. To reach the Charles River, paddle downstream under the railroad bridge. At the Charles, a left turn leads to Worden Pond.

Worden Pond. From the junction of Routes 110 and 138, take Route 110 south to Tuckertown, and turn right onto Wordens Pond Road. The access is in 0.5 mile on the right.

Worden Pond and its inlet and outlet rivers through the 3,350-acre Great Swamp vie with Wood River as the best paddling in Rhode Island. From the public boat access point at Worden Pond's south end, you can reach all the areas covered in this section. When the wind

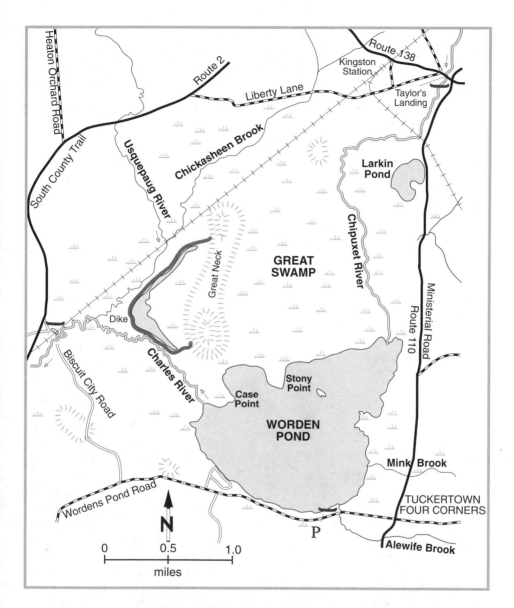

Worden Pond and Great Swamp

blows across Worden Pond, we would put in on either of the rivers. You can also paddle one-way from the Taylor's Landing access down the Chipuxet River, across Worden Pond, and down the Charles River to the Route 2 access, a distance of about 6 miles.

We would only paddle here during times of high water. From Taylor's Landing, paddle upstream into Thirty Acre and Hundred Acre Ponds. You may encounter beaver dams that require portaging. Brush and low water may also block access up the narrow channel. Above the beaver dam, the Chipuxet widens into Thirty Acre Pond—a gorgeous pond rich in wildlife. Woodland and University of Rhode Island agricultural research fields surround the pond—you may notice irrigation pumps along the shore. Only one house occurs on the pond, though you may also see (and hear) a small brick pumphouse near the south end that pumps drinking water from an underground aquifer (beneath the shallow pond) for the town of South Kingstown.

We saw many pied-billed grebes amid the pond's thick vegetation (waterlilies, fanwort, pickerelweed, bur-reed, swamp loosestrife), as well as great blue heron, kingfisher, and painted turtles. An occasional train speeds past the pond's north end. Also at the north end, paddle under the cavernous, arched-stone and concrete railroad bridge and a second

A beaver dam blocks access as we paddle up the Chipuxet River toward Thirty Acre Pond.

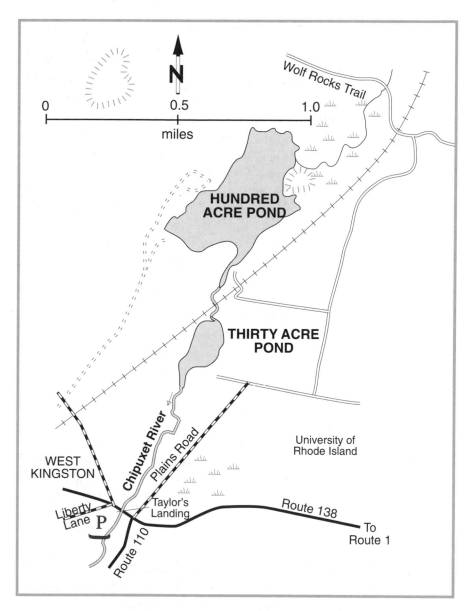

Thirty Acre and Hundred Acre Ponds

much lower bridge to get into Hundred Acre Pond. Though marked by some development, Hundred Acre Pond still offers wonderful paddling on a quiet morning in spring or fall. Along the perimeter, look for black gum whose leaves turn crimson in early fall. Mountain laurel, highbush blueberry, and sweet pepperbush grow thickly along the less developed eastern shore.

Paddle through the pond's marshy northern end, following the winding Chipuxet River on up through the dense swamp of red maple, cedar, alder, and swamp loosestrife, full of songbirds. The channel narrows, and the vegetation converges from the sides until it finally blocks further progress near Wolf Rocks Road. Paddling from Taylor's Landing up to here takes a couple of hours if you allow time for watching birds and investigating the ponds' vegetation.

Chipuxet River. More commonly, people paddle from Taylor's Landing downstream into Worden Pond—a distance of about 3 miles. The narrow river tightly twists through Great Swamp. The current, though noticeable, allows paddling in both directions. Along here, you pass through a red maple swamp, with patches of cattail, bulrush, and *Phragmites* on the oxbow curves, with thick stands of sweetgale, dogwood, winterberry, and sweet pepperbush. Wild rice also grows sparingly along here—look for the tall delicate grass in early fall, when the tasty grain can be shaken from the fruiting heads.

When you reach 1,000-plus-acre Worden Pond, take note of the wind conditions. Strong winds, typically from the south in summer, send up sizable waves across more than a mile of open water. If possible, try to reach Worden Pond before 10 A.M. to improve your chances of avoiding windy conditions.

Because development impinges on the eastern and southern shores and Wordens Pond Road traverses the southern shore, you will likely enjoy the northern shore more. Pass a privately owned island on your left, used as a hunting and fishing camp, and then aptly named Stony Point on the right—which makes a great picnic stop. Large, seemingly out-of-place granite boulders extend out into the pond. On higher ground, beech, white oak, red oak, and sassafras grow, along with more water-tolerant red maple and black gum found throughout Great Swamp.

This natural basin's maximum depth is 7 feet, with an average depth of only 4 feet. Extensive areas of bulrush grow in the shallows. In the cove west of Stony Point, a large seaplane hangar seems oddly alone at the pond's edge. From a sandy point just east of the hangar, you can reach a network of trails that crisscross Great Neck and extend along a dike built to maintain wildlife habitat in the swamp. Great Neck rises to a surprisingly high 182 feet.

It was here on Great Neck in 1675 that the Great Swamp Fight occurred—a battle in King Philip's ill-fated rebellion against the

Large and shallow, Worden Pond is often mirror-smooth in the early morning, but strong winds late in the day can make paddling dangerous.

onslaught of European settlers. When the Pilgrims arrived in New England in 1620, Native Americans befriended and kept them alive, teaching them how to plant corn and live off the New England environment. For several decades, peace reigned. But pressure built as more and more shiploads of settlers arrived in the New World, cleared land, built settlements, and through deeds and treaties pushed the Native Americans onto smaller and smaller corners of remaining wilderness. Chief Massasoit of the Wampanoags had been a friend to settlers, but when he died in 1662, his son Metacom became chief and saw what was happening in a different light. Dubbed King Philip of Pokanoket by the colonists, Metacom convinced the Narragansetts and other tribes in the region to join in resisting the settlers.

In 1675 Metacom led his alliance in a series of offensives—known as King Philip's War—attacking and destroying settlements. As the first heavy snow of December fell on Great Neck, colonial soldiers from Connecticut joined those from the Massachusetts and Plymouth

Colonies and set out on a march inland from the burned-out garrison at Pettaquamscutt. They intended to attack a fortress somewhere in a vast swamp near Kingston. Their "enemy"—a band of about 1,000 Narragansett braves, squaws, and children, plus King Philip's raiders—had gathered with their winter stores inside a freshly built fort. The devastating battle did not end King Philip's War, but it turned the tide.

Charles River. Either put in at the Route 2 access, or continue around the northern shore of Worden Pond from the seaplane hangar, rounding Case Point to reach the Charles River outlet. The Charles—along with the Wood the major source of the Pawtucket—flows through a seemingly denser and more magical part of Great Swamp and twists even more tightly than the Chipuxet. Tall scarlet oak and red maple shade the river, while buttonbush, cinnamon fern, dogwood, swamp rose, swamp loosestrife, and arrowhead claim the shore. Dense canopies of grape, greenbriar, and other vines sweep down to the water's surface. You can almost imagine yourself in a tropical jungle here and expect to see howler monkeys and colorful macaws in the trees. In places, poison ivy drapes over fallen trees so thickly that you have a hard time avoiding brushing against it as you paddle underneath. If you are allergic to poison ivy, be wary and plan your attire appropriately. You may also have to carry your boat over or around an obstruction or two. Because of tight curves along the Charles, you will do much better in a shorter boat.

About a mile from Worden Pond, look for a built-up bank on the right and an obvious spot to pull up your boat by some concrete abutments. This dike creates the Great Swamp Waterfowl Impoundment, a 138-acre wetland providing nesting habitat for numerous waterfowl species. Climb the bank to the trail that extends along the dike and over to Great Neck. Bird watching here is fantastic. On an early-July trip, in a couple of hours we saw and heard perhaps fifty species of waterfowl, warblers, woodpeckers, flycatchers, thrushes, sparrows, and other species. In a mid-October trip we were treated to the rare sight of a peregrine falcon and its nearly successful efforts to catch a teal.

You should see osprey here, diving for fish. Osprey nest atop the power-line poles that cross the swamp. You can actually walk out into the swamp for quite a way on a plank boardwalk. Sections of boardwalk may have deteriorated, so be careful. While you might be tempted to carry your boat over the dike to explore the water on the east side, leave that area to the wildlife.

From the landing by the dike, the tightly twisting river continues west, passing under the power line and then joining with the Usquepaug River, entering from the northeast. You can explore this river for a way—it parallels the railroad tracks for about a mile then turns north, crossing under the railroad bridge. Continuing downstream at the rivers' confluence, you will reach the railroad tracks and the Route 2 access in about 0.75 mile. Paddle along the tracks for a short distance and watch for a fork to the right (look for a sign nailed to a tree indicating Boat Landing). Take this fork and paddle under the railroad tracks to the landing just ahead. If you miss the fork, you will reach shortly the Biscuit City Road bridge followed by the Route 2 bridge. Very aromatic swamp azalea and swamp rose bloom in profusion in late June and early July along the section down to the Route 2 bridge.

60

Wood River and Alton Pond
Hopkinton and Richmond, RI

MAPS: Connecticut and Rhode Island Atlas, Maps 70 and 74
    USGS Quadrangle, Carolina

LENGTH: 6.5 miles

CAMPING: Arcadia Management Area, 401-222-6800;
    Burlingame State Park, 401-322-8910; in Connecticut:
    Pachaug State Forest (Green Falls and Mount Misery Camp-
    grounds), 860-376-4075; reservations: 877-668-2267 or
    www.ReserveAmerica.com

HABITAT TYPE: dammed-up meandering river, shrubby marsh-
    lands, many oxbows

EXPECT TO SEE: muskrat, waterfowl, marsh birds, osprey, great
    horned owl, aquatic vegetation, mountain laurel, swamp rose,
    varied shrubs

TAKE NOTE: little development; no motors

GETTING THERE

Alton Dam. From I-95, Exit 2, go south on Woodville-Alton Road for 3.6 miles to the access on the left.

Woodville Dam. From Alton Dam, go north on Woodville-Alton Road for 1.5 miles (1.5 miles), and turn right at the stop sign onto Woodville Road. Access is on the left in 0.7 mile (2.2 miles), just before the bridge. From I-95, Exit 2, go south on Woodville-Alton Road for 2.1 miles, and turn left at the stop sign onto Woodville Road. Because only one or two cars can park along Woodville Road on the dam's west side, we would not use this as an access.

Hope Valley. From the junction of Route 3 and Mechanic Street in Hope Valley, go south on Mechanic Street for 0.9 mile to the access on the left, at the end of the guardrail just after the I-95 bridge.

The Wood River offers an outstanding paddling resource, certainly one of the most pristine in Rhode Island. The section included here, from Hope Valley to Alton Dam, can occupy you for anywhere from a

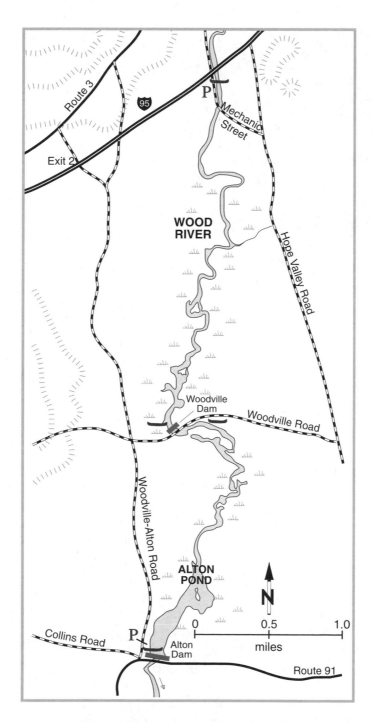

Wood River and Alton Pond

Eastern kingbirds appear often along the shores of New England's rivers and ponds. Note the dark head and back, the white underbelly, and the white-tipped tail.

few hours to a full day or two. We prefer putting in at Alton Dam and paddling upstream, though spring high water could preclude making it all the way to Woodville. With two cars, you could paddle downstream from the Hope Valley access to Alton Dam.

Paddling north from Alton Dam, after passing a few houses, the 39-acre pond narrows to a winding, deep channel, and you seem to leave most fishing activity behind. Along the wild Wood River, numerous oxbows, side channels, eddies, and hidden ponds harbor lots of wildlife. We saw several pairs of wood duck, cormorant, green heron, mallard, kingfisher, and songbirds galore. Osprey wheeled overhead, diving occasionally for fish. Scattered shoreline piles of mussel shells bore evidence of successful raccoon or otter feasting. Paddling along quietly, you should see literally hundreds of painted turtles on a sunny day, basking on floating logs or on tussocks of grass that extend out into the water along the marshy shoreline.

Ancient blueberry bushes, black gum, red maple, and white pine grow along the shore. Where the ground rises steeply from the water, dense, lush stands of mountain laurel bloom spectacularly in June. With the river flowing so slowly, we lost the main channel several times, finding ourselves on one of the oxbow ponds.

A couple of miles upstream, the channel forks. Paddling up the smaller left fork, you quickly come to an old farm, a long-abandoned mill building, and a dead end. The main channel curves right, where you soon reach the Woodville Road bridge over the river and a beautiful dam just beyond. Water was diverted here for the mill. Ruins of a much older stone mill building occur here. Take out on the right bank before the bridge, carry up and over the bridge, and put in on the left side.

Upstream from Woodville Dam, the stream meanders through more marshland, similar to that below the dam, except with less mountain laurel. Large patches of swamp rose make up for the lack of laurel, and arrowhead and pickerelweed line the shores. After about a mile, the marshland and streambed narrow to a shore lined with red maple, gray birch, oaks, ash, and black gum. Painted turtles sun on the numerous snags and overhanging branches. We also enjoyed numerous iridescent green damselflies with black wings that landed on our boats. Two great horned owls eyed us warily from perches above.

Alton and Woodville, part of a string of old textile towns almost hidden along the Wood and Pawcatuck Rivers in southern Rhode Island, formed the economic pillar of this area. Alton Pond formed behind the power-producing dam built by David L. Aldrich in 1860. His mill changed hands over the years but still produces textiles—elastic webbing rather than the cotton and wool of old. And, just like a hundred years ago, fishing remains the favorite activity on the quiet pond.

61

Ninigret Pond
Charlestown, RI

MAPS: Connecticut and Rhode Island Atlas, Map 74
  USGS Quadrangles, Carolina and Quonochotaug
AREA: 1,700 acres
CAMPING: Burlingame State Park, 401-322-8910
INFORMATION: tide charts, www.maineharbors.com
HABITAT TYPE: coastal tidal pond, shrubby marshlands, many
  islands and protected bays
EXPECT TO SEE: waterfowl, marsh birds, rare plants; the most
  pristine dune barrier beach in Rhode Island
TAKE NOTE: development; motors allowed; use caution due to boat
  traffic, wind, and tide; not recommended for novice paddlers

---

GETTING THERE

Charlestown. From Route 1 north, take the Cross Mills/Charlestown Beach exit. Go straight across Route 1A onto Town Dock Road. Access is at the road's end, adjacent to Ocean House Marina.

Charlestown Beach. From Route 1, take the Cross Mills/Charlestown Beach exit, and take an immediate left onto Route 1A, following signs for the Breachway. After 0.7 mile (0.7 mile), turn right at the green sign for the Breachway. Turn right again in 0.4 mile (1.1 miles; small sign for the Breachway). Access is on the right after another 1.3 miles (2.4 miles), just after crossing the causeway bridge.

Breachway. The state maintains an access at the Breachway, about 0.5 mile beyond the previous access, but strong tidal currents recommend against launching here.

Ninigret, Rhode Island's largest coastal pond, though quite developed in places, offers very enjoyable paddling and superb wildlife observation opportunities. However, strong winds, tidal currents, and moderate motor boat traffic during summer weekends can present hazards. Use

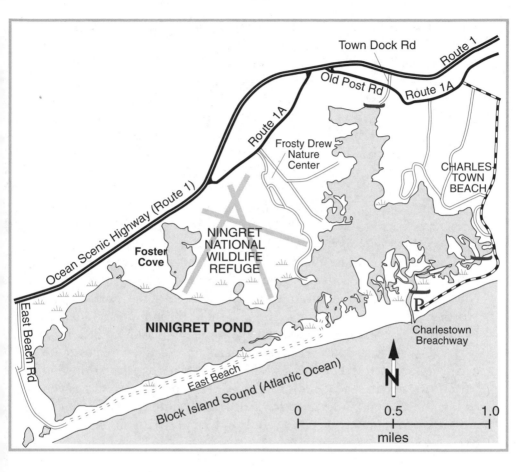

Ninigret Pond

caution, wear your PFD, and paddle the nearby Pawcatuck or Wood Rivers when the wind howls. Novice paddlers should avoid Ninigret.

Away from Charlestown's congestion, the western two-thirds of Ninigret Pond remain relatively wild, with much of it included in Ninigret National Wildlife Refuge. Most of this 400-acre refuge was once a U.S. Navy landing field, which explains the extensive paved areas. Hike around the old airfield to see how nature gradually reclaims miles of runway. More than 250 bird species have been recorded here, with prime birding during spring and fall migrations. But plants provide the real attraction for naturalists. More than half the total number of known plants of yellow fringed orchid (*Platanthera ciliaris*) in New

England occur here, along with at least eighteen other rare or endangered plant species.

The northern and southern shores of Ninigret vary considerably. Vegetation along the northern shore consists primarily of shrubby grassland, along with bayberry, blueberry, beach plum, shadbush, wild cherry, dogwood, cedar, and seaside goldenrod—an ecosystem that provides excellent bird habitat, especially as a stopover for migrating warblers. The marshier tidal coves and inlets sport tall stands of *Phragmites*, with patches of *Spartina* occupying the lower, regularly flooded sections.

Along the pond's southern shore, next to the Ninigret Conservation Area barrier beach, salt marsh grasses—*Spartina patens* and *S. alterniflora*—dominate the vegetation. Sea lavender *(Limonium carolinianum)*, a delicate plant with tiny lavender flowers resembling baby's breath, mixes with the *Spartina*. So much sea lavender has been collected for dried-flower arrangements that in some areas of the Northeast it no longer adds its subtle lavender blush to the salt marsh. Enjoy the plant where it grows, and avoid the temptation to pick it.

The sand here appears almost white, and the water seems quite clean. You will see scallop shells washed up, patches of eelgrass flowing with tidal currents, and clumps of seaweed and sponge on rocks as you paddle the shallows. Anglers here catch lots of winter flounder, as well as bluefish in summer when they enter to feed on young flounder. The pond also harbors commercial quantities of soft-shell clams, quahog, bay scallop, and oysters.

To enjoy crashing waves of the Atlantic, beach your boat, and walk across the dunes to East Beach, accessible only by boat, foot, or four-wheel-drive vehicle. The wildlife refuge section of Ninigret's south shore remains closed to the public to protect nesting least terns and piping plovers—the former threatened and the latter endangered species.

62

Watchaug Pond
Charlestown, RI

MAPS: Connecticut and Rhode Island Atlas, Map 74
USGS Quadrangle, Carolina

AREA: 573 acres

CAMPING: Burlingame State Park, 401-322-8910; Arcadia
Management Area, 401-222-6800

INFORMATION: Kimball Wildlife Refuge: Audubon Society of
Rhode Island, 401-231-6444

HABITAT TYPE: large, open pond

EXPECT TO SEE: gulls, Canada goose, wooded shores,
other boats

TAKE NOTE: motors and water-skiers; personal watercraft
prohibited; limited development

GETTING THERE

Follow signs to Burlingame State Park Picnic Area. From Route 1, turn
north onto Prosser Trail. The Kimball Wildlife Refuge entrance is on the
left in 0.2 mile (0.2 mile). The entrance to the picnic area and Barton C.
Hurley Landing access is on the left in another 0.4 mile (0.6 mile). Veer left
in 0.1 mile (0.7 mile), avoiding the picnic area, to get to the access.

Watchaug Pond, a large body of water located near Rhode Island's
southern tip, sees heavy recreational use but can offer enjoyable paddling, particularly for a family camping at Burlingame State Park. For
others, visit either early or late in the season to avoid the crowds.

While paddling on the pond for the first edition, we encountered
several noisy personal watercraft; the town of Charlestown banned
them in January 2002, however. Heavy use at the southeastern end near
the public boat launch area, along with shoreline development on the
pond's east side, may provide strong incentive to concentrate on the
northern and western sections. The marshy western end feels much

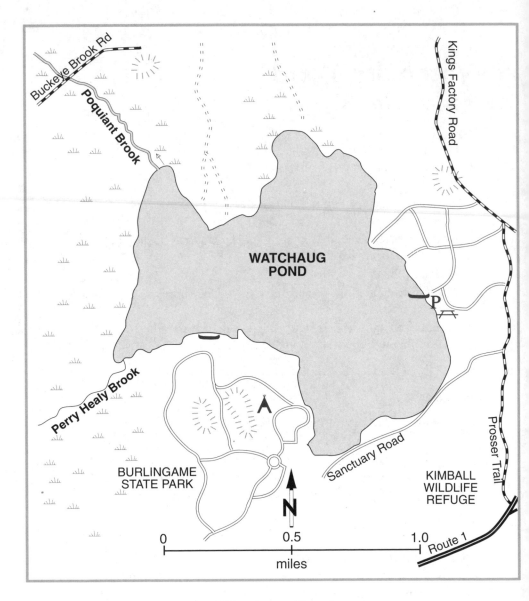

Watchaug Pond

more remote and wild; as dusk approached, we watched an otter near the outlet at the northwestern tip. Even though you rarely see otters in southern New England, if you spend much time paddling around less developed lakes, ponds, and rivers around dawn or dusk, you should see this delightful mammal sooner or later.

The edge of Watchaug Pond just after dawn in early May. The best time to visit this popular pond is in May or after Labor Day.

You can get away from most Watchaug Pond activity by paddling down the outlet, Poquiant Brook, at the pond's northwestern tip. We followed this quiet, meandering brook for at least 0.5 mile through thick marsh. When the wind blows up whitecaps on Watchaug Pond, the brook offers a nice escape into a quiet, secluded area. Look for blueberry bushes, along with cedar, black gum, and a wide assortment of marsh plants. Keep an eye out for elusive wood ducks here.

Kimball Wildlife Refuge, owned and managed by the Audubon Society of Rhode Island, abuts lands near the pond's southern end, with wonderful trails through oak and laurel woodland. With 755 campsites, Burlingame harbors one of the largest camping areas in New England. Nonetheless, the campground often fills to capacity during summer months.

63

Pawcatuck River
Charlestown, Hopkinton, and Westerly, RI

MAPS: Connecticut and Rhode Island Atlas, Map 74
    USGS Quadrangle, Ashaway
LENGTH: 8 miles
CAMPING: Burlingame State Park, 401-322-8910
HABITAT TYPE: wide, undeveloped river, wooded shores
EXPECT TO SEE: osprey, mute swan, beaver, waterfowl, song-
    birds, varied trees
TAKE NOTE: motors allowed

GETTING THERE

Potter Hill. From I-95, Exit 1 in Rhode Island, go south on Route 3 for 1.8 miles
(1.8 miles), and turn right onto Route 216 in Ashaway. Go 0.2 mile (2.0 miles),
and turn left onto River Road (Laurel Street). Go 1.0 mile (3.0 miles) to the
access on the right at the junction with Bridge Street. Park on the left, and
carry down the steep embankment. Please do not use the grassy areas along
River Road for access, as this is private property. There is also access at the
junction of Route 3 and Hiscox Road, with parking for one car.

    Bradford. From Ashaway, take Route 216 south until it joins Route 91. The
access is 0.4 mile south of this junction on the left, just after crossing the bridge.

After the Wood River joins the Pawcatuck (also called Charles above the
Wood) just south of Alton Dam, the combined flow provides a broad,
slow-flowing river between wooded shores. We paddled upstream from
Potter Hill Dam, though with two cars you could paddle this one-way
from Bradford (8 miles; the upstream put-in here), or from Alton Dam
(13 miles), Woodville Dam (15 miles), or Hope Valley (19.5 miles) on
the Wood River (see Trip 60).

    When we paddled here in July, we saw no other boats upstream of
the Route 3 bridge. We loved the sculpted lateral branches, looking like

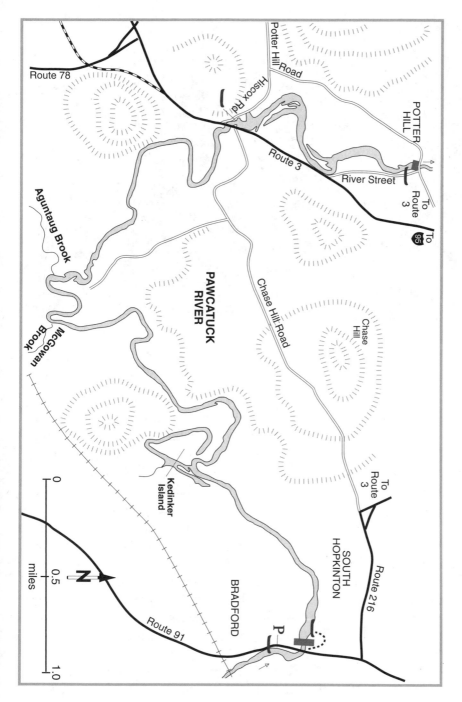

Pawcatuck River

Route 78

Potter Hill Road

Hiscox Rd.

Route 3

POTTER HILL

River Street

To Route 3

To 95

Aguntaug Brook

McGowan Brook

PAWCATUCK RIVER

Chase Hill Road

Chase Hill

Kedinker Island

To Route 3

SOUTH HOPKINTON

Route 216

BRADFORD

Route 91

P

N

0   0.5   1.0
miles

Lacy branches of black gum, Nyssa sylvatica, *extend out over the Pawcatuck River's banks.*

splayed fingers, of the black gum trees *(Nyssa sylvatica)* that cluster along the shores in spots; we wished that we could return in early fall when their leaves turn crimson. Occasional white pines would offer a dark, contrasting green to the fall foliage. Surprisingly, beaver have girdled a lot of the black gums. We often see hemlocks girdled because, presumably, they have resinous bark unpalatable to beaver, but why would they want to kill off deciduous trees? Black gum bark may also be resinous, given that the trees can withstand submersion for decades.

A number of active osprey nests, some on utility poles and some on platforms set up for this purpose, occur along this stretch of the Pawcatuck. We saw several osprey perched or fishing as we paddled along. We also saw and heard many other birds, including great blue heron, green heron, wood duck, Canada goose, mute swan, cardinal, eastern wood-pewee, cedar waxwing, eastern towhee, chickadee, veery, tufted titmouse, catbird, and yellow warbler.

Lots of swamp rose, swamp loosestrife, swamp azalea, and dogwood form an understory beneath the mature canopy of red maple, ash, willow, gray birch, scarlet oak, beech, black gum, and white pine. Occasional marshy areas occur along the normally wooded river course.

Eastern Connecticut

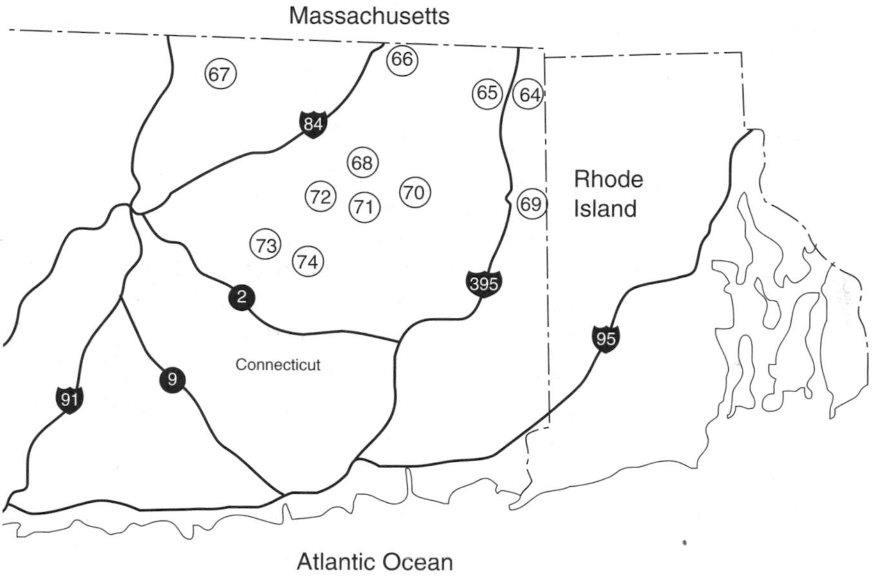

Massachusetts

67

66

84

65 64

68

72 71 70

Rhode
Island

69

73 74

2

395

95

Connecticut

91 9

Atlantic Ocean

64

Quaddick Reservoir and Stump Pond
Thompson, CT

MAPS: Connecticut and Rhode Island Atlas, Map 57
  USGS Quadrangle, Thompson
AREA: Quaddick Reservoir and Stump Pond, 467 acres
CAMPING: Mashamoquet Brook State Park, 860-928-6121;
  reservations: 877-668-2267 or www.ReserveAmerica.com;
  West Thompson Lake, 860-923-2982; in Rhode Island:
  George Washington Camping Area, 401-568-2013
INFORMATION: Thompson Speedway race dates,
  www.thompsonspeedway.com
HABITAT TYPE: marshy reservoir
EXPECT TO SEE: waterfowl, shrubby, wooded shoreline
TAKE NOTE: motors allowed; no development on northern section

---

GETTING THERE
From I-395, Exit 99, go east on Route 200 for 0.7 mile (0.7 mile) to Thompson. Turn left onto Route 193 north, go 1.6 miles (2.3 miles), and turn right onto Brandy Hill Road. After 0.3 mile (2.6 miles), bear left onto Baker Road, and go 1.4 miles (4.0 miles) to the access by the bridge.

Long, narrow Quaddick Reservoir nestles into the extreme northeastern corner of Connecticut, next to the Rhode Island and Massachusetts borders. Those seeking solitude should avoid the two southern sections, especially on sunny summer weekends, because they feature heavy development and teem with motorboats. The reservoir's northern section, described here—one of our favorite paddling spots in northeastern Connecticut—receives much less boat traffic because of abundant aquatic vegetation.

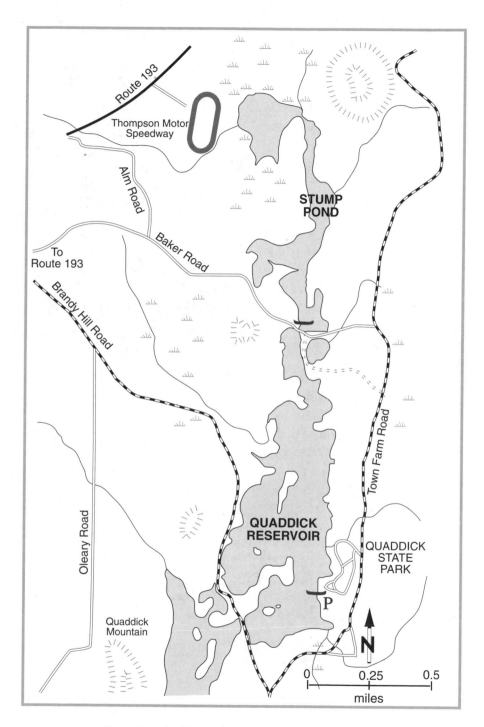

Quaddick Reservoir and Stump Pond

Floating waterlilies and submerged bladderworts, fan-wort, and coontail clog the northern section's clear, shallow water. Water birds abound, especially mallard, black duck, wood duck, and great blue heron. The shallow coves and the far-northern end—known as Stump Pond—provide the richest bird habitat. Thick woods of white pine and mixed deciduous trees surround the northern reservoir, along with sweet pepperbush, highbush blueberry, and sweetgale. Cat-tail, bulrush, and bur-reed embellish the shallow coves and inlets.

When Thompson Speedway is not in use, a paddle on the relatively wild and marshy Stump Pond can be quiet and relaxing.

The only drawback to the northern section—besides the few motorboats that muscle their way in—is the noise that wafts in on a blue haze from Thompson Speedway. The track backs right up to the Stump Pond marsh, filling it with race noises. To avoid the cacophony, check race dates on the speedway's website. Listening to your paddle dip methodically into water while watching wood ducks circle low over the marsh presents a stark contrast between your activity and that of several thousand auto racing buffs who congregate a few hundred yards away. Though a sad commentary that so many more people watch car races than go out to enjoy nature, we would rather have the marsh teem with birds than with paddlers or, worse, motorboats. We wonder what those wood ducks think about our species . . .

65

West Thompson Lake and Quinebaug River
Thompson, CT

MAPS: Connecticut and Rhode Island Atlas, Map 57
  USGS Quadrangle, Putnam
AREA/LENGTH: West Thompson Lake, 239 acres;
  Quinebaug River, 3 miles
CAMPING: West Thompson Lake, 860-923-2982;
  Mashamoquet Brook State Park, 860-928-6121;
  reservations: 877-668-2267 or www.ReserveAmerica.com
HABITAT TYPE: reservoir; wide, shallow river
EXPECT TO SEE: muskrat, snapping and painted turtles;
  wooded shoreline
TAKE NOTE: motors limited to 5 MPH; no development

GETTING THERE

From I-395, Exit 97, go west on Route 44 for 0.7 mile (0.7 mile), and turn right onto Route 12. Go north for 1.9 miles (2.6 miles), and turn left at the light, following signs to West Thompson Lake. After 0.3 mile (2.9 miles), turn right onto Reardon Road, followed by a left after 0.5 mile (3.4 miles) into the West Thompson Lake Recreation Area.

This 200-plus-acre lake, managed by the U.S. Army Corps of Engineers, provides enjoyable paddling and camping opportunities. Indeed, only a few lakes in southern New England—most of them Army Corps facilities—can boast no development along their shorelines. With a 5-mile-per-hour speed limit, you will encounter mostly canoes and kayaks.

The sandy, pebbly shore provides easy access around nearly the entire perimeter, where you can get out for a picnic or foray into the oak-hickory woods in the 2,200-acre recreational area surrounding the lake. The Corps maintains two picnic areas and a campground, which was less than half full on a mid-August Sunday. This lake used to suffer

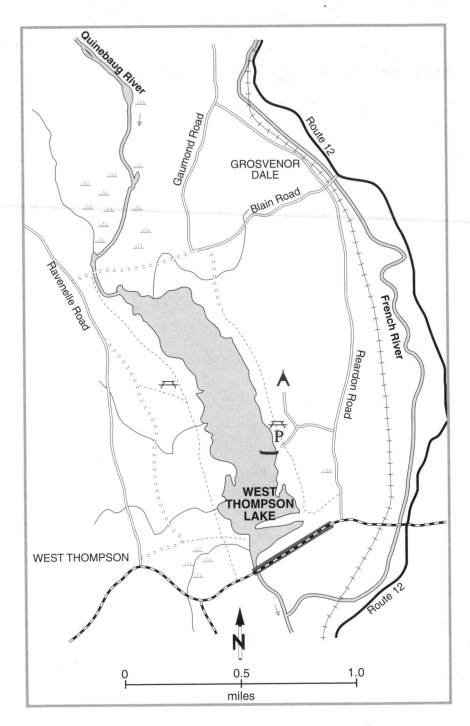

West Thompson Lake and Quinebaug River

from expanses of muddy banks because of fluctuating water levels related to flood control, but since the early 1990s the Corps has raised the pool level, eliminating the band of exposed shoreline.

From the boat ramp on the eastern shore, paddle north and explore the inlets on the east shore and the small islands and rock outcroppings on the west shore. In one inlet that expands into a pickerelweed-choked pool about 125 feet across, we came across a very large snapping turtle hanging lazily near the surface, head pointed downward, searching for its next meal. Paddling north into the Quinebaug River, pretty quickly you pass under an old bridge on a 3.6-mile hiking trail that extends around the lake.

Wild grapevines drape over the wooded shoreline along the river, and a broad marsh opens up just above the footbridge, where we saw great blue and green herons, along with a pair of kingbirds chasing a sharp-shinned hawk. We saw a cuckoo feeding on tent caterpillars, and we spied another large snapping turtle, along with dozens of painted turtles out sunning on logs. Look carefully in the clear water, and you might also see the elusive underwater tire *(Goodyearis submergicus)*; though many of them populate these waters, their bottom-dwelling habits frequently hide them from view. The farther upriver you paddle, the shallower it becomes, and the swifter the current; we paddled nearly 3 miles upstream before a riffle and very shallow water blocked our way.

66

Mashapaug Lake and Bigelow Pond
Union, CT

MAPS: Connecticut and Rhode Island Atlas, Map 56
   USGS Quadrangles, Wales and Westford
AREA: Mashapaug Lake, 297 acres;
   Bigelow Pond, 26 acres
CAMPING: Mashamoquet Brook State Park, 860-928-6121;
   reservations: 877-668-2267 or www.ReserveAmerica.com;
   West Thompson Lake, 860-923-2982
HABITAT TYPE: oligotrophic natural lake, little
   aquatic vegetation
EXPECT TO SEE: osprey; wooded shoreline, scenic hillsides
TAKE NOTE: some development and motors (10 MPH limit) on
   Mashapaug; no motors or development on Bigelow

GETTING THERE

From I-84, Exit 74, go south on Route 171 for 3.7 miles (3.7 miles), and turn left into Bigelow Hollow State Park. Bigelow Pond access is on the left in 0.3 mile (4.0 miles), and Mashapaug Lake access is in another 0.8 mile (4.8 miles), at road's end. Just before the Mashapaug access, you pass the trail to Breakneck Pond on the right.

Mashapaug Lake. This large, natural lake in northeastern Connecticut boasts deep coves, rocky shores, and beautiful surrounding hemlock and white pine woods. Bigelow Hollow State Park, with picnic tables on needle-carpeted ground overlooking the lake's blue water, hugs the southern shore. Trails along here wind among ancient stands of laurel, and the light filtering through the hemlock, pine, and oak canopy seems just right to support a wide array of wildflowers. Most of the lake's eastern shore, with the land rising steeply from the water's edge,

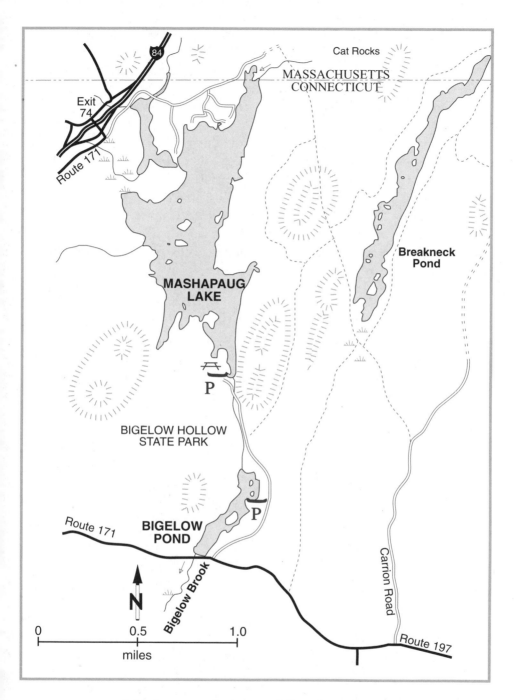

Mashapaug Lake and Bigelow Pond

lies within 8,000-acre Nipmuck State Forest. In some areas huge stone slabs extend down into the water.

While the south end of Mashapaug remains undeveloped except for the picnic area, some limited development fans out along the western and northern shores. Besides the development, road noise from I-84—just 0.5 mile away at the closest point—provides the only other reminder of civilization while you paddle this gorgeous place.

Few aquatic plants grow in these oligotrophic (low-nutrient) waters that boast 20-foot visibility. The state-record largemouth bass (12 pounds, 14 ounces) emerged from Mashapaug in 1961.

Bigelow Pond. On a clear September day we watched an osprey fish the clear water of Bigelow Pond. With only 26 acres, the pond takes little time to explore. It may be better just to picnic here and soak in the pond's scenic beauty.

In contrast with Mashapaug, this quite shallow pond abounds with floating vegetation and sphagnum-moss-covered hillocks where tree stumps have long since rotted away. Look for sundews amid the sphagnum moss in these areas. In early October we saw quite a few nodding ladies' tresses (*Spiranthes cernua*)—a small white orchid occasionally found in boggy areas. Along the shoreline, look for blueberry, sweet pepperbush, and laurel, along with hemlock and white pine growing farther from the water's edge. Fragrant waterlily, yellow pondlily, and water shield grow in the shallows. Beaver occur here at times, and you may see the occasional wood duck.

In Nipmuck State Forest, a mile or so east of Mashapaug Lake, Breakneck Pond offers a wonderful paddling experience in a thick marshland. Intrepid explorers can reach this long, narrow pond only by hiking in—a very long carry with a boat.

～ 67 ～

Somersville Mill Pond and Scantic River
Somers, CT

MAPS: Connecticut and Rhode Island Atlas, Map 54
 USGS Quadrangle, Ellington
AREA/LENGTH: Somersville Mill Pond, 41 acres;
 Scantic River, 3 miles
CAMPING: Mashamoquet Brook State Park, 860-928-6121;
 reservations: 877-668-2267 or www.ReserveAmerica.com
HABITAT TYPE: shallow, marshy pond; narrow, winding
 river through swamp
EXPECT TO SEE: muskrat, Canada goose, wood duck, mallard,
 vines, shrubs
TAKE NOTE: no motors; development near dam

GETTING THERE

From I-91, Exit 47E, go east on Route 190 for 5.3 miles (5.3 miles), and turn right (south) onto School Street (Route 186 goes north here). Access is on the left in 0.3 mile (5.6 miles).

Several small central Massachusetts brooks join to form the slowly meandering Scantic River as it drains extensive wooded marshlands. The section included here backs up behind a dam flanked by gorgeous, old redbrick mills in Somersville. Paddling out from the access, you quickly leave civilization behind. In the river's upper reaches, a golf-driving range's net backs up to the riverbank, and twin high-voltage power lines appear overhead. Neither intrudes too much on the solitude.

Mist drifted off the water as we paddled out early one morning along the wooded shoreline. A kingfisher fled before us as cardinal, catbird, song sparrow, and eastern towhee called from the dense undergrowth and mourning doves sounded their plaintive coos overhead. We noted some big red oaks and very large swamp white oaks hanging out

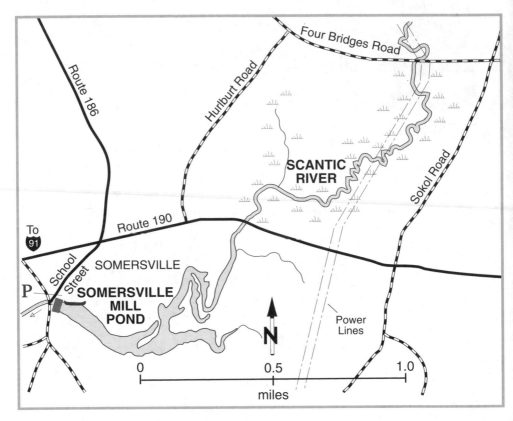

Somersville Mill Pond and Scantic River

over the water. Shoreside shrubs, vines, and flowers stand out most, though, as you paddle up the picturesque Scantic River. Red-willow dogwood, alder, pickerelweed, arrowhead, willow, buttonbush, purple loosestrife, cattail, pondweed, grapes, bur-reed, jewelweed, and water celery line the shallow waterway's banks. We found lots of cardinal flower in bloom and many grapevines draped out over the water.

A beaver lodge just upstream from the Route 195 bridge had so many winter-forage branches surrounding the lodge that we almost couldn't get by. Check out the oxbows and side channels for birds; we saw or heard eastern phoebe, robin, chickadee, tufted titmouse, grackle, great blue heron, spotted sandpiper, crow, goldfinch, flicker, and red-bellied woodpecker.

The Scantic River meanders slowly through scenic marshlands.

Upstream, the channel narrows through tight-twisting turns with no perceptible current. Though plenty of water filled the main channel, we could not make it to Four Bridges Road because of overhanging grapevines and red-willow dogwoods. Maybe someone would be willing to prune back some of the more offending branches.

Knowlton Pond
Ashford and Mansfield, CT

> **MAPS:** Connecticut and Rhode Island Atlas, Map 46
>   USGS Quadrangle, Spring Hill
> **AREA:** 165 acres
> **CAMPING:** Mashamoquet Brook State Park, 860-928-6121;
>   reservations: 877-668-2267 or www.ReserveAmerica.com
> **HABITAT TYPE:** shallow, marshy pond
> **EXPECT TO SEE:** muskrat, wood duck, mallard; swamp-
>   loosestrife-covered islands
> **TAKE NOTE:** cartop access and aquatic vegetation limit motors;
>   no development

GETTING THERE

From I-395, Exit 97, go west on Route 44, through Ashford. After crossing Route 89, go 2.1 miles (2.1 miles), and turn left (south) onto Wormwood Hill Road. Go 1.2 miles (3.3 miles), and park along the roadside on the right.

From I-84, Exit 69, go east on Route 74 to West Ashford. Turn right onto Route 44, go 1.0 mile, and turn left onto Wormwood Hill Road. Follow directions as above.

From the east end of I-384, go east on Route 44, through Mansfield Depot. After crossing Route 195, go 3.6 miles (3.6 miles), and turn right (south) onto Knowlton Hill Road. Go 1.4 miles (5.0 miles), and turn left onto Wormwood Hill Road. Access is on the left in 0.5 mile (5.5 miles).

Don't let the relatively small area of water at the access fool you; most of Knowlton Pond lies to the north, accessible through a shallow, narrow, hidden waterway. Though the area near the access has a lot of open water, aquatic vegetation chokes the pond's northern reaches and surrounds a long north–south string of brushy islands, crowded with swamp loosestrife. Don't paddle here if you crave open water or want to paddle long distances.

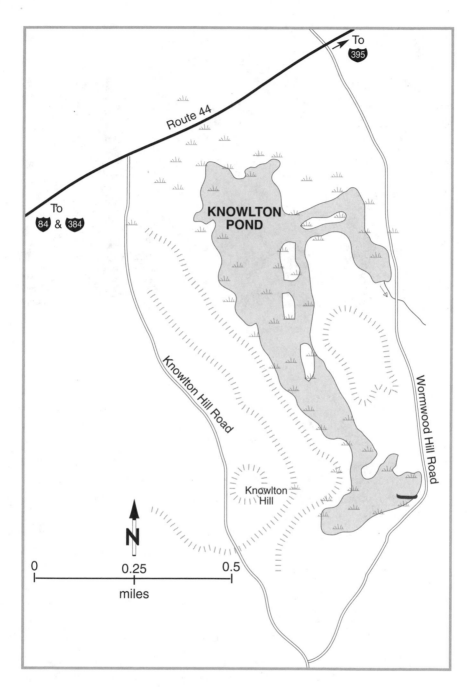

To
395

Route 44

To
84 & 384

**KNOWLTON
POND**

Knowlton Hill Road

Wormwood Hill Road

Knowlton
Hill

N

0   0.25   0.5
miles

Knowlton Pond

Swamp loosestrife stems, with leaves whorled in threes, arch gracefully over New England riverbanks.

As we paddled up the waterway, a flock of tufted titmice called from the oak woods, while eastern kingbirds and barn and tree swallows cruised the water's surface, snatching up abundant insect life that feeds on rafts of aquatic vegetation. We saw some yellow-flowered and large amounts of purple-flowered bladderwort, water celery, yellow pondlily, fragrant waterlily, and water shield. Truly large patches of pondweed (*Potamogeton spp.*), perhaps the most we've seen on any pond, greeted us wherever we paddled.

Mallards and many wood ducks that raise broods here fled before us as we slogged up the waterway. In fall, ducks of several species congregate here during migration.

～69～

Ross Marsh Pond
Killingly and Sterling, CT

MAPS: Connecticut and Rhode Island Atlas, Map 48
   USGS Quadrangle, East Killingly
AREA: 55 acres
CAMPING: Mashamoquet Brook State Park, 860-928-6121;
   reservations: 877-668-2267 or www.ReserveAmerica.com; in
   Rhode Island: George Washington Camping Area,
   401-568-2013
HABITAT TYPE: shallow, marshy pond
EXPECT TO SEE: painted turtle, mallard, wood duck, great
   blue heron, aquatic vegetation
TAKE NOTE: no motors; no development; watch out for stumps

GETTING THERE

From I-395, Exit 91, just east of Danielson, go east on Route 6 for 3.4 miles
(3.4 miles), and turn right (south) onto Sawmill Hill Road. Staying right at the
fork in 0.1 mile (3.5 miles), go 1.7 miles (5.1 miles) to the access on the left.

Wildlife management areas, such as Ross Marsh, often provide outstanding paddling opportunities. Weaving our way north up the winding, open-water channel, we reveled in the solitude as mallards fed on
abundant vegetation and hundreds of painted turtles slid off myriad
stumps and logs into the water as we glided by. When we paddled
here, beaver had dammed up the outlet, maintaining a slightly elevated water level. We startled a couple of fishing great blue herons and
several flocks of wood ducks.

   The diversity of aquatic vegetation and streamside shrubs and
trees impressed us, especially the huge amount of purple-flowered
bladderwort in electric bloom. In most years, a few blooms appear
here and there, but once or twice a decade, the lavender blooms erupt
as though a brilliant carpet had unfolded over the waterway. From late

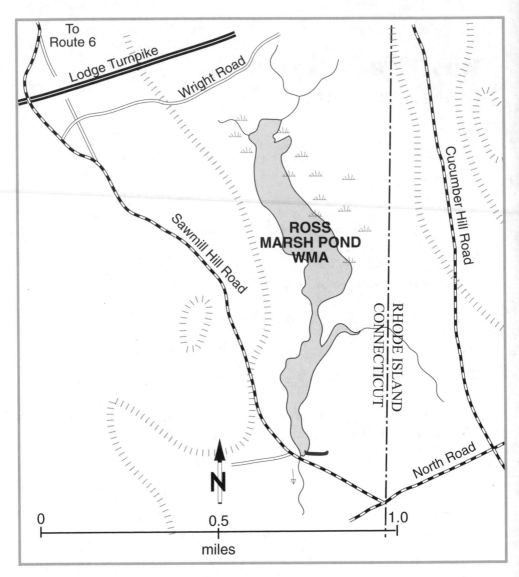

To
Route 6

Lodge Turnpike

Wright Road

Sawmill Hill Road

**ROSS
MARSH POND
WMA**

Cucumber Hill Road

RHODE ISLAND
CONNECTICUT

North Road

N

0   0.5   1.0

miles

Ross Marsh Pond

Crooked stems of bur-reed, with their ball-like flowers, dot the shoreline.

August through early September 2002, we found dozens of ponds awash with color from *Utricularia purpurea* blooms.

On the pond's north end, among the buttonbush and bur-reed, *Phragmites* and cattails fight it out for dominance. You can paddle a couple of hundred yards up the narrow, winding inlet stream through a broad marsh, perhaps having to portage over a beaver dam. Dwarf red maples, streamside alders, and occasional swamp rose line the way. Watch out for stumps here and anywhere else in the pond outside the main channel.

Carnivorous Plants
The Table Is Turned

Carnivorous plants are fascinating—and a common sight as you paddle through the bogs and marshes of New England's lakes and ponds. Specialized adaptations make them one of nature's true wonders and make us wonder how their meat-eating habit evolved.

Carnivory in plants apparently resulted from convergent evolution: the taking on of similar traits among unrelated species. Many different, completely unrelated plant families on nearly every continent have some carnivorous species. These plants have two characteristics in common: almost all live in mineral-poor soils and supplement meager soil nutrients with those from animals, and they use modified leaves to trap food.

Two main capture strategies have evolved: active and passive. Most people recognize the active capture strategy of the Venus's-flytrap, a plant that grows in sandy soils in a narrow band along the coastal border between North Carolina and South Carolina. A few other carnivorous plants have adopted active capture strategies, and one of them grows abundantly— sometimes forming dense mats—in the quiet, shallow marshes and bogs of New England: bladderworts of the genus *Utricularia*. Bladderwort leaves consist of minute bladders that, upon stimulation, inflate and ingest insect larvae and other organisms, to be digested by the plants' enzymes.

Passive capture strategies have taken two main paths among the remaining carnivorous plants. Pitcher plants—*Sarracenia purpurea*—collect rainwater in their funnel-shaped modified leaves. Insects, attracted to nectar secreted around the top of the pitcher, fall in. The plant's stiff, downward-pointing hairs keep most insects from climbing back out. Eventually the insects drown, and a combination of plant and bacterial enzymes reduces the insects to absorbable nutrients.

Another passive-capture plant uses sticky surfaces to ensnare insects. Sundews (genus *Drosera*) form tiny rosettes that protrude from a central root. Stalked glands of two types cover the modified leaf surface. One type secretes a sticky substance that glistens like dew in the sun, giving the plant its name. Entrapped insects, drawn initially by the nectarlike secretions, are digested by enzymes secreted by the second set of glands.

Each of the plants described above—bladderworts, pitcher plants, and sundews—captures its intended victims in a different way, but they all do so because, in nutrient-poor marshes and bogs, absorbing nitrogen and other minerals from insects and other prey gives them a selective advantage over other plants.

Do not be fooled by black, fertile-looking soils of marshes and swamps. Black dirt like this in Iowa means fertile soil, but in bogs it's because of black carbon from undecomposed plants. The tea-colored water, laden with organic acids from decaying vegetation and supplemented by acid rain, effectively washes out the minerals necessary for plant growth. Although two primary nutrients supporting plant growth—carbon dioxide and water—remain plentiful, nitrogen, phosphorus, potassium, and other important elements get leached out or bound up in underlying layers of sphagnum and peat. Carnivorous plants, with their diet of insects and other organisms, supplement the lost nutrients, making them effective competitors in the bog ecosystem.

Bladderworts. Bladderworts grow in quiet, shallow waters or in shoreline muck. Keep an eye out for small yellow or purple snapdragonlike flowers, leading on short stalks to their carnivorous underwater bladders. The vast majority of the plant lives underwater in dense, feathery mats, bearing hundreds of tiny (0.02 to 0.1 inch long), bulbous traps that are the plant's leaves. The bladders have two concave sides and a trapdoor. When an insect larva or other small organism bumps into the door's guard hairs, the bladder's sides pop out, creating suction, the door swings open, and water and the hapless critter get sucked in. All of this occurs in about 1/500 of a second, followed by slow digestion by plant enzymes.

In most ponds mosquito larvae form the bulk of the plant's diet, but it also ingests other larvae, rotifers, protozoans, small crustaceans, and even tiny tadpoles. The digested animal remains are absorbed by plant tissues, causing the trap's sides to go concave again, readying the plant for its next meal. With large prey, such as a tiny tadpole, the door closes around the organism, and part of it gets digested. The next time the hairs get triggered, the plant ingests more of the organism, eventually sucking it all in.

Several species of bladderworts grow in our area, including two with purple flowers, one aquatic and one terrestrial, and as many as ten species with yellow flowers, mostly aquatic but including at least two terrestrials. We usually notice the presence of these plants when we see their snap-dragonlike flowers protruding a few inches above the water's surface. Their dense underwater mats attest to their successful adaptation to nutrient-poor waters. If you lift a mat out of the water slowly and listen carefully, you may hear crackling as the bladders suck in air instead of their intended prey.

Pitcher Plants. Although several other species of *Sarracenia* pitcher plants exist in North America, the northern pitcher plant, *Sarracenia purpurea,* has the widest distribution, growing from British Columbia to Nova Scotia, southward through the Great Lakes region, and down the eastern coastal plain, crossing the Florida panhandle to the Mississippi River. Initially green in spring, the pitcher plant's funnel-shaped leaves turn progressively more purple, becoming deep maroon in fall, and return to green again in spring. During midseason, the red veins of the hood stand in stark contrast to the mostly green pitchers. Flowering occurs in June and July in New England, and single reddish flowers, borne on stout stalks, tower a foot or more above the cluster of pitchers.

In contrast to most other species, the northern pitcher plant does not have a hood to keep rain out. The curved pitchers recline, allowing rain to fall freely into the open hood. Because of dilution of the pitcher's contents, insects drown well before digestion occurs. The stiff, downward-pointing hairs in the plant's throat keep insects from climbing back out, and the rel-atively narrow funnel leaves little room for airborne escape. The upper pitcher walls sport a waxy coating, making for slippery footing. A combina-tion of plant and bacterial enzymes degrades the unlucky insects, and their nutrients pass easily through the unwaxed surface of the lower pitcher.

Amazingly, several different types of organisms can live in the pitch-ers, unharmed by the digestive juices. One genus of mosquito harmless to humans, *Wyeomyia,* lives the aquatic part of its life cycle in the pitcher, and other insects can escape by walking up the waxy cuticle and out over the downward-pointing hairs.

A gorgeous, terrestrial yellow-flowered bladderwort, Utricularia cornuta, *blooms in mid-July.*

Sundews. To find sundews, look for tiny glistening drops at the ends of their traps. Because they are so small—the smallest plants may measure only an inch across—sundews are easily overlooked. Four species occur in our area, and we describe the most common species here: round-leaved sundew *(Drosera rotundifolia).*

This remarkable plant grows mainly in sphagnum bogs, from Alaska to northern California, across the Canadian Rockies and plains, through the Great Lakes, north throughout Labrador, south to the Chesapeake Bay, and down through the Appalachians. The same plant grows in Europe as well; Darwin devoted much of his book *Insectivorous Plants* to this one species. The entire plant averages about 3 inches across and about 1 inch high, with all of its leaves modified into sticky traps. A short leaf stalk ends in a flattened oval pad covered with red, stalked glands. The longer glands secrete a sticky fluid, while the shorter glands secrete digestive enzymes. Insects, attracted to the nectarlike secretions, become trapped. Slowly, imperceptibly, the pad edges roll over slightly, placing the insect in contact with digestive juices.

The usually white but sometimes pink flowers hover well above the plant's leaves, borne on a slender stalk. Although easy to miss, a little careful looking on sphagnum mats will show up many of these reddish rosettes. You should also see several small insects in various stages of digestion. And you, too, can wonder about how these plants developed the incredible ability to supplement the meager amount of nutrients available from the soil with those from insect prey.

70

Pine Acres Lake
Hampton, CT

MAPS: Connecticut and Rhode Island Atlas, Map 47
  USGS Quadrangle, Hampton
AREA: 190 acres
CAMPING: Mashamoquet Brook State Park, 860-928-6121;
  Devil's Hopyard State Park, 860-873-8566;
  reservations: 877-668-2267 or www.ReserveAmerica.com
HABITAT TYPE: shallow, marshy pond
EXPECT TO SEE: beaver, wood duck, great blue heron,
  aquatic vegetation
TAKE NOTE: no motors; no development; watch out for
  underwater stumps

GETTING THERE

From I-395, Exit 92, go west on Route 6 for 11.7 miles, and turn right onto Potter Road (1.4 miles past the junction with Route 97). Parking for the Goodwin Conservation Center is on the right in 0.1 mile; the access road is just past the end of the parking lot.

From the end of I-384, go east on Route 6. Turn left onto Potter Road 2.9 miles past the turn-off for Route 198 north.

Unlike the open water of nearby Mansfield Hollow Lake, an endless sea of aquatic vegetation covers Pine Acres Lake's shallow water (average depth of just 4 feet). Adding to the difficult paddling, some sections teem with leftover stumps from the lake's flooding in 1933. Paddle here in the early morning or late afternoon for some quiet solitude and wildlife observation.

Pine Acres exudes a wild and almost mystical feel. Paddling the northern end, you have to weave your way around literally thousands of stumps and fallen trees. Originally a cedar swamp, the area's Atlantic white cedars were sawn into railroad ties, posts, and shingles long

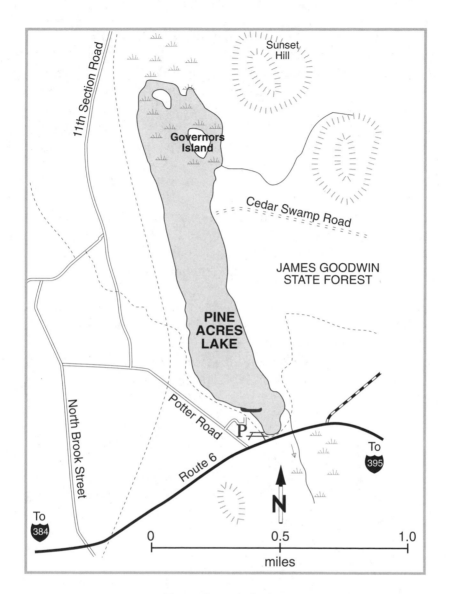

Pine Acres Lake

before the lake's creation. Loggers cut the cedars in winter; horses dragged the boles from the ice. Some small-diameter stumps broken off just beneath the surface seem quite sharp (you probably should avoid paddling your handmade birch-bark canoe here). You almost have to "feel" your way among unseen stumps, periodically rocking your boat off underwater snags. Your slow, methodical pace increases chances of seeing interesting wildlife. A number of beaver lodges ring the pond, and you should see wood duck, great blue heron, and kingfisher. Hiking on the Natchaug Trail that runs along the lake's southern end, or on other nearby trails, you will also see lots of woodland species.

Red maple, the dominant shoreline tree, sets the shoreline ablaze with red in autumn. You will also see white and red pines, spruce, red oak, gray, black, and yellow birches, white ash, sweet pepperbush, blueberry, winterberry, and a few rhododendrons at the southern tip. Aquatic vegetation grows thick: fragrant waterlily, yellow pondlily, and water shield on the surface and thick mats of bladderwort underneath. The farther north you paddle, the more difficult the paddling, as the meager amount of open water gradually merges into swamp. Keep an eye out for acid-loving sundews and cranberry, both found here.

The 1,800-acre James L. Goodwin State Forest, one of Connecticut's first scientifically managed tree farms, surrounds Pine Acres Lake. Goodwin began managing the original farmland for forest productivity in 1913—in a period when others gave little thought to sustainable forestry. He deeded this land to the state in 1964 to demonstrate how wise forest management can serve timber, wildlife, and recreation needs concurrently.

71

Mansfield Hollow Lake
Mansfield and Windham, CT

Maps: Connecticut and Rhode Island Atlas, Map 46
    USGS Quadrangles, Spring Hill and Willimantic

Area: 500 acres

Camping: Mashamoquet Brook State Park, 860-928-6121;
    Devil's Hopyard State Park, 860-873-8566;
    reservations: 877-668-2267 or www.ReserveAmerica.com

Habitat Type: wooded reservoir, deep coves, islands, and
    inlet rivers

Expect to See: beaver, muskrat, mallard, high shrub and
    tree diversity

Take Note: recreational development only; motors limited to
    8 MPH

GETTING THERE

From I-84, Exit 68, go south on Route 195, through Storrs, to Mansfield Center. Go 0.5 mile (0.5 mile) past the Route 89 junction, and turn left onto Bassett Bridge Road at the stoplight and sign for Mansfield Hollow State Park. A picnic area is on the left in 0.9 mile (1.4 miles), and access is on the left in another 0.5 mile (1.9 miles).

From the end of I-384, go east on Route 6 toward Willimantic, and turn left (north) onto Route 195. Go 2.0 miles (2.0 miles), and turn right onto Bassett Bridge Road. Access is on the left in 1.4 miles (3.4 miles).

Its large size, by southern New England standards, makes Mansfield Hollow Lake (or Naubesatuck Lake) a prime recreation destination, particularly for those who crave lots of exercise. Because of an 8-mile-per-hour speed limit, more hand-powered than motor-powered craft ply these waters. It would take at least a day to explore the entire shoreline, every island, and the reservoir's deep coves. You can also paddle up the three inlet rivers, adding greatly to your exploration time.

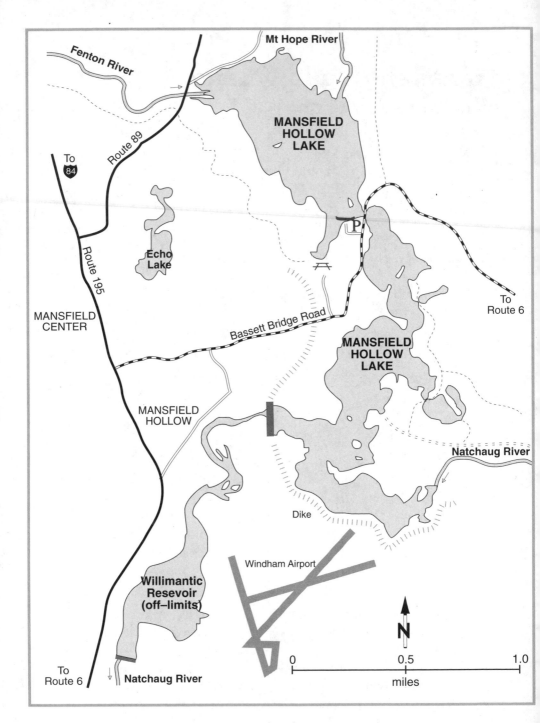

Mansfield Hollow Lake

Bassett Bridge Road causeway divides the waterway roughly in half. The U.S. Army Corps of Engineers, in response to devastating flooding of Willimantic in 1936, created the lake in 1952 with a dam and dikes along the Natchaug River. Like many flood-control reservoirs, Mansfield Hollow's water level fluctuates, though the Corps tries to keep it bank-full in summer. Paddling here after Columbus Day, you may have to contend with an exposed gravelly shoreline.

The narrower southern section of Mansfield Hollow Lake, below Bassett Bridge Road, offers more coves and islands to explore. From the boat access, paddle through one of two large steel culverts into the northeast end of this lower section, where a hidden pond off to the east connects with the main lake by a small channel. This small pond feels very remote and quiet—especially on a windy day. You can carry into another, slightly larger pond farther to the southeast. As you paddle into the southern end, a massive dike looms over the lake like the Great Wall of China. The primary inlet into the lake, the Natchaug River, paddleable for a short distance upriver, flows in at the southeastern tip.

The northern, wider section of the lake, with fewer twisting coves to explore, has a somewhat more natural feel to it, particularly at the north end. Two inlets enter here: Mount Hope River, coming from the north, and Fenton River, coming from the northwest. A few hundred yards up Mount Hope River, a beaver lodge stands sentinel over the rapids and rocks that block your way. You can paddle under Route 89 and up the Fenton River much farther. We've gone about 0.5 mile up here and found the paddling very easy on the slow-moving, meandering channel. Beaver lodges occur along here as well, and numerous muskrats call the banks home; in the late afternoon, you should see both beaver and muskrat.

White pine and red oak dominate the lake's shoreline, along with white oak, shagbark hickory, pitch pine, red maple, gray birch, alder, aspen, elm, willow, and various shrubs, including sweetgale, buttonbush, blueberry, red-osier dogwood, wild grape, swamp azalea, swamp rose, swamp loosestrife, and winterberry. You will also see royal fern and the invasive purple loosestrife. Look for mussels on the sandy bottom and for the round, gelatinous balls of bryozoa colonies clinging to underwater logs. *Phragmites* (common reed) and other grasses populate the few small pockets of marsh. In early October we saw osprey, red-tailed hawk, mallard, black duck, red-breasted merganser, kingfisher, and quite a few eastern bluebirds in migration.

72

Eagleville Pond and Willimantic River
Coventry and Mansfield, CT

MAPS: Connecticut and Rhode Island Atlas, Map 46
   USGS Quadrangle, Coventry

AREA/LENGTH: Eagleville Pond, 80 acres;
   Willimantic River, 1.5 miles

CAMPING: Mashamoquet Brook State Park, 860-928-6121;
   Devil's Hopyard State Park, 860-873-8566;
   reservations: 877-668-2267 or www.ReserveAmerica.com

HABITAT TYPE: shallow, marshy pond; vines and trees
   overhanging river

EXPECT TO SEE: wood duck, Canada goose, great blue heron,
   swamp loosestrife

TAKE NOTE: limited development; cartop access and shallow
   water limit motors; 8 MPH speed limit

GETTING THERE

From Hartford, take I-84 east to Exit 59 onto I-384 east. When I-384 ends, at Routes 6 and 44, go east on Route 44 for 7.8 miles (7.8 miles), and turn right (south) onto Route 32. Go 1.9 miles (9.7 miles), and turn right onto Route 275 (South Eagleville Road) at the boat launch sign. The access is in 0.3 mile (10.0 miles), just across the bridge on the right, off Pine Lake Drive.

Eagleville Pond and the Willimantic River offer hours of wonderful paddling through labyrinthine channels around dozens of low, marshy islands and coves. Swamp loosestrife lines many of these channels, particularly at the pond's north end where the river enters. A railroad track parallels the east shore of the pond, with a gravel pit beyond, and a few houses occur along the pond's southwest shore. Very little development impinges on most of the rest of this gorgeous habitat.

Eagleville Pond and Willimantic River

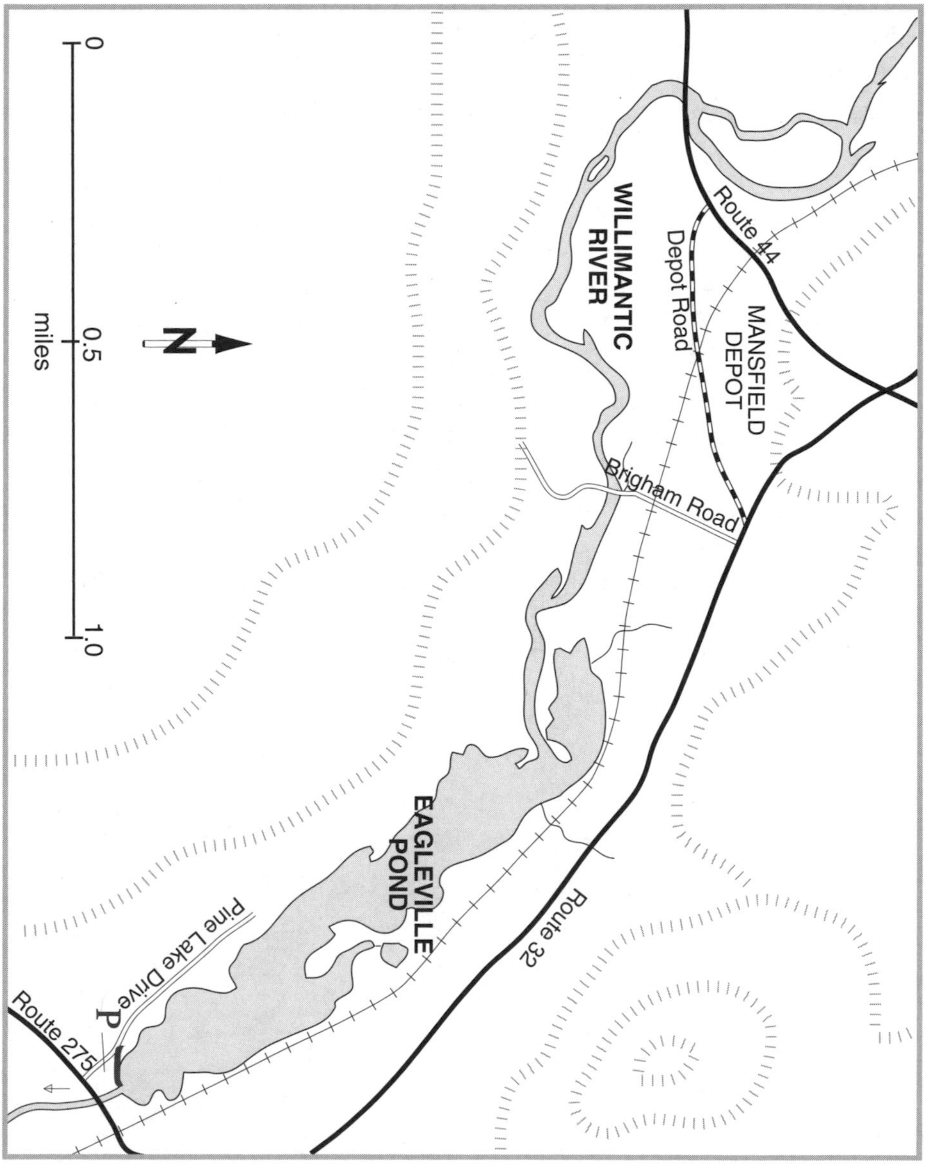
Route 44
Depot Road
MANSFIELD DEPOT
WILLIMANTIC RIVER
Brigham Road
Route 32
EAGLEVILLE POND
Pine Lake Drive
P
Route 275
N
0
0.5
1.0
miles

As we paddled up the pond, wood ducks rose from weed-choked coves, while red-winged blackbirds called from the streambanks. Skulking birds—song sparrow, cardinal, catbird, and common yellowthroat—called from the dense undergrowth. Muskrats harvested pickerelweed along the shore, among the yellow pondlily and water shield. Swamp azalea, jewelweed, joe-pye weed, and lots of alders lined the banks, along with great arbors of grapes overhanging the bankside shrubs. We spied a completely overgrown beaver lodge, noticeable only because of the large array of alders and other branches stuck butt-first into the mud for winter fodder.

Along the river, shagbark hickory, red maple, and basswood formed arching canopies in places, and the occasional gray birch, ash, willow, American hornbeam, black cherry, and black birch (twigs have a wintergreen odor when scratched) joined the ubiquitous red-maple- and red-oak-dominated shoreline. The first part of the river upstream from the pond has no discernible current, but shallow riffles that make paddling difficult start to occur well before the Route 44 bridge.

Paddling back downstream, a red-tailed hawk gave out its piercing cry from the treetops, while a green heron stalked the shoreline. Canada geese tried to look inconspicuous, and a great blue heron stood knee-deep among the lily pads. Amid all this wildlife and beautiful scenery, we hated to leave this beautiful place.

73

Bishop Swamp
Andover, CT

MAPS: Connecticut and Rhode Island Atlas, Map 45
  USGS Quadrangle, Marlborough
AREA: 53 acres
CAMPING: Devils Hopyard State Park, 860-873-8566;
  reservations: 877-668-2267 or www.ReserveAmerica.com
HABITAT TYPE: shallow, marshy pond
EXPECT TO SEE: Canada goose, wood duck, great blue heron;
  rafts of fragrant waterlily and water shield; river otter and
  beaver are possibilities
TAKE NOTE: no development; no motors

GETTING THERE

From I-84, Exit 59, east of Hartford, go east on I-384. When I-384 ends at
Routes 6 and 44, go right (east) onto Route 6. Go 5.7 miles (5.7 miles), and
turn right (south) onto Route 316. Go 0.5 mile (6.2 miles), and turn right
(west) onto Boston Hill Road. Go 1.4 miles (7.6 miles), and turn left (south)
onto Jurovaty Road. Go 0.8 mile (8.4 miles) to the access on the right.

Alternatively, from Route 6, go south on Route 316 for 1.5 miles (7.2 miles),
and turn right (southwest) onto Gilead Road. Go 1.1 miles (8.3 miles), and turn
right onto Jurovaty Road. The access is on the left in 0.5 mile (8.8 miles)

Though beaver maintain channels through the abundant surface vegetation—mostly fragrant waterlily and water shield—you can't escape the
even more abundant Eurasian water-milfoil and fanwort that fill the
water column here. The abundant vegetation, of course, suited the
Canada geese and wood ducks that we saw just fine, and amazingly it did
not seem to affect the family of otters that cavorted on the pond's south
end. Every time they surfaced, either to crunch loudly on fish or to cast
a wary eye in our direction as we watched them through binoculars,
aquatic vegetation clung to their heads and necks—a quite comical scene.

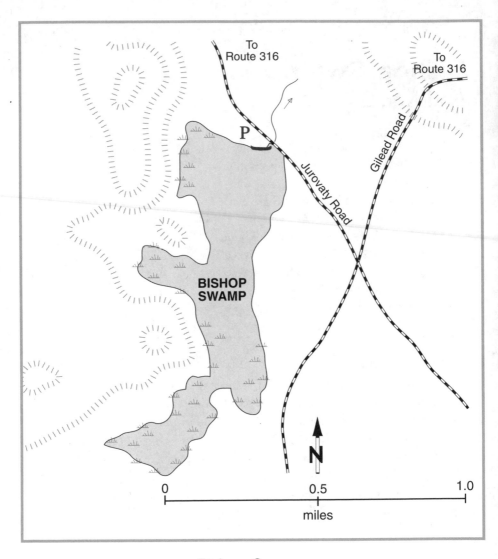

To
Route 316

To
Route 316

Gilead Road

Jurovaty Road

P

BISHOP
SWAMP

N

| 0 | 0.5 | 1.0 |

miles

Bishop Swamp

Though we did not see any beaver in the early morning, we did find several large, jewelweed-encrusted beaver lodges, a couple of them quite close together. We wondered whether the otters had evicted the beaver from one of the lodges, causing them to construct another close by.

A male green frog, Rana clamitans, *peeps out from among the lily pads.*

We saw a lot more in this wildlife paradise, which lies within a stone's throw of (no more than a short commute away from) Hartford. We watched crows mob an owl on an island on the pond's south end. A couple of great blue herons stalked the shoreline, and dozens of tree swallows perched on limbs of dead trees standing in the water of the larger coves. Other birds foraged for food above the water or in the shoreside foliage; we saw robin, goldfinch, mourning dove, red-bellied woodpecker, kingbird, red-winged blackbird, and phoebe. Frogs hopped off the lily pads as we paddled along, trying to avoid the stumps and barely submerged logs.

This idyllic setting suffers, though, from alien invaders. Eurasian water-milfoil and fanwort (not a foreign invader but often introduced from elsewhere) crowd out the yellow- and purple-flowered bladderwort, and purple loosestrife crowds out the native swamp loosestrife, cattail, buttonbush, and joe-pye weed.

74

Mono Pond
Columbia, CT

MAPS: Connecticut and Rhode Island Atlas, Map 46
   USGS Quadrangle, Columbia
AREA: 113 acres
CAMPING: Devil's Hopyard State Park, 860-873-8566;
   reservations: 877-668-2267 or www.ReserveAmerica.com
HABITAT TYPE: shallow, marshy pond
EXPECT TO SEE: wood duck, great blue heron, swamp loosestrife
TAKE NOTE: limited development; small size and aquatic
   vegetation limit motors; 8 MPH speed limit

GETTING THERE

From the junction of Routes 6 and 66 just west of Willimantic, go west on Route 66 for 2.7 miles (2.7 miles), and turn left (south) onto Pine Street at the flashing yellow light. Go 1.0 mile (3.7 miles), and turn right onto Hunt Road. Go 0.2 mile (3.9 miles) to the access on the left.

When we paddled Mono Pond in 2002, it sported a new concrete boat ramp, a huge disappointment for this scenic pond. Though we could detect no fanwort or Eurasian water-milfoil, boat trailers will inevitably bring it in, infecting yet another pond with these invasive, nearly impossible-to-remove species. We fear that the underwater, gelatinous bryozoa colonies will disappear, as they appear to have done in nearby Holbrook Pond, smothered out by dense rafts of fanwort and Eurasian water-milfoil.

Bryozoa had colonized many submerged logs in the pond's north end, and huge rafts of both yellow-flowered and purple-flowered bladderwort filled the water column at the south end. The bladderworts—reputed to suck in and devour mosquito larvae—will become much reduced, if not eliminated, when the fanwort and milfoil take over.

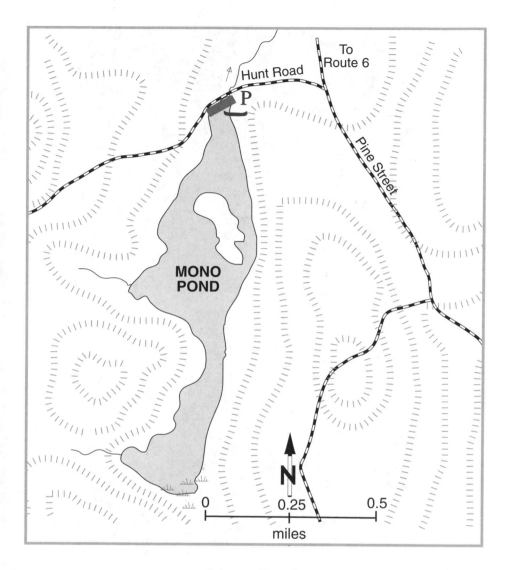

Mono Pond

But the bryozoa will be the real loss, because we see these colonies only rarely. They require pure water, and we assume that choking vegetation causes either stagnation, which compromises water quality or reduced ability for the cilia to sweep the water for the microscopic algae, protozoans, and diatoms that comprise their diet.

A great blue heron takes a break from fishing.

Thick stands of mostly deciduous trees cover the hillsides, hiding some limited development. Sweet pepperbush, highbush blueberry, swamp azalea, buttonbush, and swamp loosestrife line the banks, while seas of water shield and fragrant waterlily cover the water's surface on the south end. By August, paddling through this blanket of vegetation becomes difficult, but our foray into it gave us good looks at many wood ducks and an immature great blue heron as it stalked and ate sunfish along the shore.

Southern Connecticut

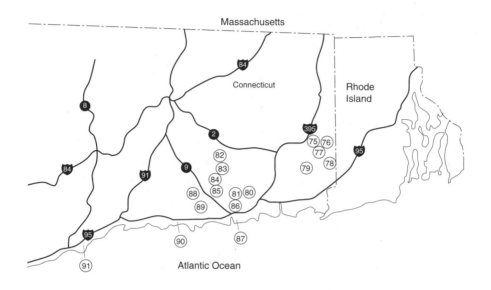

75

Hopeville Pond and Pachaug River
Griswold, CT

MAPS: Connecticut and Rhode Island Atlas, Map 39
USGS Quadrangle, Jewett City
AREA/LENGTH: Hopeville Pond, 150 acres;
Pachaug River, 3.6 miles
CAMPING: Hopeville Pond State Park, 860-376-2920;
Pachaug State Forest (Green Falls and Mount Misery
Campgrounds), 860-376-4075; reservations: 877-668-2267 or
www.ReserveAmerica.com
HABITAT TYPE: dammed-up meandering river
EXPECT TO SEE: waterfowl, varied trees
TAKE NOTE: some development, state campground; motors
limited to 8 MPH

GETTING THERE
From I-395, Exit 86, go east on Route 201 for 1.4 miles to Hopeville Pond
State Park on the right.

Hopeville Pond, a widened 3-mile section of the Pachaug River, offers
very pleasant, relaxing paddling. Its shores include Hopeville Pond
State Park, the site of a former waterpower-driven woolen mill. The
federal government purchased it in 1930, and the Civilian Conservation Corps (CCC) managed it until transferring it to the state in
1959. Today the pond offers fine waterside family camping, hiking,
swimming, and boating. The park adjoins Pauchaug State Forest,
whose 14-mile Nehantic footpath meanders over low hilly terrain,
connecting the northeast side of Hopeville Pond with Green Falls
Pond in Voluntown.

The pond winds through woodland, farmland, and areas with
light cottage development between a dam at the north end close to

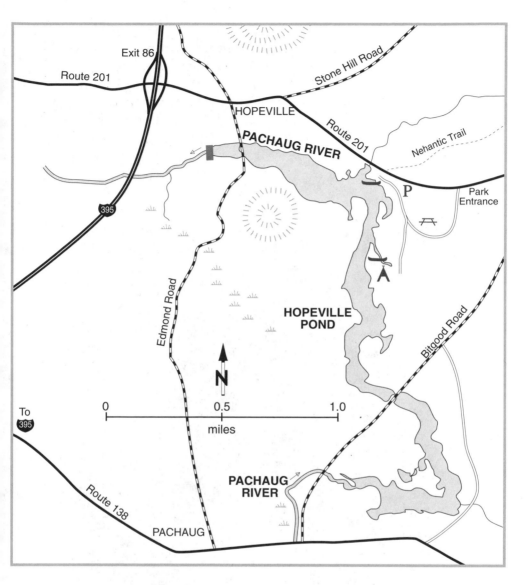

Hopeville Pond and Pachaug River

I-395 and a section of river at the south end, connecting to other ponds farther upstream. To reach larger, more developed Pachaug Pond (831 acres) and much nicer Glasgo Pond (184 acres), continue upstream on the Pachaug River, carrying around the dam.

Like other bodies of water in this part of the state, Hopeville Pond's shallow water carries a deep, reddish brown color caused by natural tannins. You will see lots of painted turtles along here, as well as great blue heron, kingfisher, black duck, mallard, and possibly wood ducks. Several male wood ducks in full breeding plumage landed right in front of our boats near the south end of the pond where we had paused under cover of a tree. Upon seeing us, they immediately took to the air, emitting their high-pitched distress call. We also saw signs of beaver here and a lodge at the south end where the pond narrows to a river channel.

We often see blue flag, Iris versicolor, growing along the banks of marshy ponds.

Eastern Painted Turtle
Quietwater Companion

You won't have to spend much time paddling before spotting your first painted turtle, but getting a really good look may prove a little more difficult. The eastern painted turtle, *Chrysemys picta,* the most visible of our turtle species, may not be the most common. That distinction may belong to the much larger snapping turtle whose bottom-dwelling habit keeps it out of view most of the time. On marshy ponds you may see literally hundreds of painted turtles basking in the sun on stumps, partially submerged logs, rocks, and vegetation—but always within easy reach of underwater safety. Painted turtles remain alert to danger; if you paddle along noisily, they disappear from view long before you draw near.

The painted turtle's carapace—the smooth, fairly flat, gently arched top shell—reaches a length of 7 inches. The colorful, patterned carapace lends the species its name. Narrow lines of yellow separate the dark olive green scutes (interlocking plates evolutionarily adapted from vertebrae to form the shell), and a wider orange band defines the outer edge of the shell (a brownish deposit on the shell may obscure these colors). The head and neck sport distinctive yellow stripes, and dark blotches sometimes mark the yellow plastron (bottom shell).

Painted turtles, found throughout much of the United States, range farther north than any other turtle species. Of the four distinct subspecies of painted turtles, two occur in southern New England. The much more common eastern painted turtle (Chrysemys picta picta) has carapace scutes that line up in rows across the back, while the midland painted turtle (C.p. marginata), found mostly in western parts of the region, has scutes that alternate instead of running straight across. You need to get a really close look to distinguish these subspecies.

Diet consists of both plant and animal material, and you may see them underwater, feeding on submerged vegetation and various crustaceans, tadpoles, snails, and insect larvae. Mostly you will see them basking, a habit attributed to having a body temperature that fluctuates with environmental temperature—emerging from cold water, they absorb solar radiation to raise their body temperature and, therefore, their metabolic rate, helping them grow faster. However, some evidence suggests that they bask to dislodge attached leeches.

Painted turtles mate during spring or summer, usually from late April through mid-June. During courtship, one or more males swim around a stationary female; if she accepts his advances, she dives to the bottom where mating takes place. One to two months later, the female leaves the water to deposit a clutch of usually five to eleven eggs in a nest excavated on open, sloping sand or gravel banks or even lawns not too far from water. She digs the shallow nest with her hind feet and deposits the soft-shell eggs. She may also build several false nests, probably to mislead skunks, raccoons, and other predators that dig up and consume about 90 percent of the turtle's eggs. Incubation temperature determines hatchling gender: males emerge from cool nests (around 75 degrees F) and females from warmer ones (around 85 degrees).

Amazingly, hatchling painted turtles can withstand freezing. In northern parts of their range, the young overwinter in their nests after hatching in fall. With the nest just a few inches deep, temperatures drop well below freezing. The hatchlings' muscle activity, breathing, heartbeat, and blood flow totally stop—yet they usually recover fully when the temperature rises. While most biological functions stop, some minimal brain activity continues, and only about half of their body fluids actually freeze solid. Ice forms in the turtle's extremities and grows inward, but high concentrations of sugars in the blood work like antifreeze to keep the critical core fluids from solidifying,

A painted turtle, a frequent companion of ours in the marsh, suns itself on a rock.

down to 25 degrees F. In years with sparse insulating snow cover, nest temperature drops below 25 degrees, and most hatchlings do not survive. While a few other reptiles and amphibians exhibit similar freezing adaptations, none is as well adapted as the painted turtle hatchling. After the first year, however, painted turtles lose the ability to survive freezing.

In the pond, painted turtles hibernate at above-freezing temperatures in the bottom mud—an area almost devoid of oxygen. Other turtle species also have the ability to hibernate underwater for periods of up to four months without coming up for air. During periods of very low activity, many turtles and frogs absorb oxygen and release carbon dioxide through specialized membranes. But painted turtles, and closely related sliders, survive in totally deoxygenated water for a period of several months. Indeed, these turtles have the greatest known tolerance for oxygen deprivation of any vertebrate in the animal kingdom, with an ability to survive in water totally devoid of oxygen for up to 150 days. Specialized biochemical adaptations make survival possible. They store large reserves of the carbohydrate fuel glycogen, which breaks down to produce energy without using oxygen (a process called glycolysis). Because glycolysis produces lactic acid, another adaptation is required: the release of calcium and magnesium from the turtle's shell to buffer the acid.

And you thought you were looking at just an ordinary pond dweller! Instead, the painted turtle's veritable treasure trove of fascinating and unique biological adaptations enables it to survive the harsh conditions of New England and southern Canada. For more information on turtles, see *The Year of the Turtle: A Natural History,* by David Carroll (Camden House Publishing, Charlotte, VT, 1991), a naturalist's wonderful account of forty years of turtle observation in New Hampshire.

76

Pachaug River and Beachdale Pond
Voluntown, CT

> **MAPS:** Connecticut and Rhode Island Atlas, Map 39
>   USGS Quadrangle, Voluntown
> **AREA/LENGTH:** Beachdale Pond, 46 acres;
>   Pachaug River, 2.5 miles
> **CAMPING:** Hopeville Pond State Park, 860-376-0313;
>   Pachaug State Forest (Green Falls and Mount Misery
>   Campgrounds), 860-376-4075; reservations: 877-668-2267 or
>   www.ReserveAmerica.com
> **HABITAT TYPE:** dammed-up pond, narrow meandering river
>   with dense overhanging shrubs, marshlands
> **EXPECT TO SEE:** osprey, mute swan, waterfowl, marsh birds,
>   aquatic vegetation, varied shrubs
> **TAKE NOTE:** campground but otherwise little development;
>   aquatic vegetation limits motors; 8 MPH speed limit

GETTING THERE

From I-395, Exit 85, go east on Route 138 for about 6.5 miles (6.5 miles), and turn left onto Route 49 north. Access is on the right in 0.7 mile (7.2 miles), just after crossing over the Pachaug River bridge.

   Rhododendron Sanctuary. The Mount Misery camping area and Rhododendron Sanctuary are on the other side of Route 49 from the boat access.

Paddle downstream from the Pachaug River boat access to reach small, shallow Beachdale Pond with its extensive cover of marshy vegetation. Watch for painted turtles and frogs hiding amid the abundant arrowhead, pickerelweed, waterlilies, and grasses. Fanwort, with white flowers and yellow stamens, bloomed when we paddled here in August. We watched an osprey fish, and a pair of mute swans paddled about with four cygnets. To the northwest, you can paddle up Mount

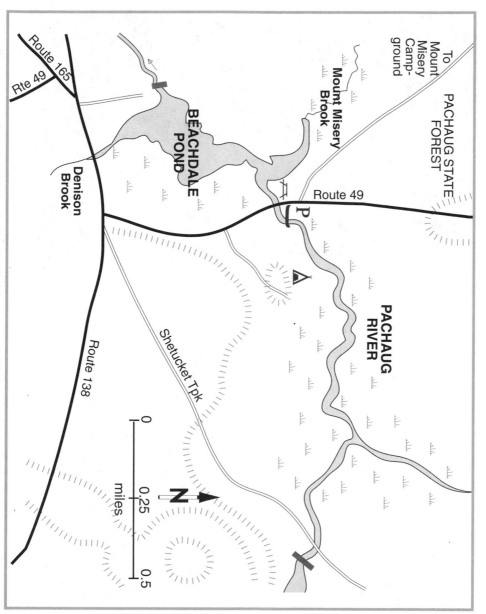

Misery Brook, which winds through the marsh. We paddled upstream for a good 0.5 mile or so before an approaching thunderstorm convinced us to turn around.

Though the pond offers a nice diversion, the Pachaug River upstream from the access offers the real attraction. Once you clear

Mute swans with nearly full-grown cygnets.

Nature's Campsites, a private campground, you enter Pachaug–Great Meadow Swamp, winding your way upstream, dipping your paddle in the yellow-brown water of a pristine swamp on a gradually narrowing waterway. Red maple, grapevine, Virginia creeper, and ubiquitous poison ivy branches overhang the swamp. Eventually these branches block the way, unless some enterprising soul has hacked a path through them. Besides surprising an occasional wood duck brood, we saw many turtles out sunning themselves and reveled in the large patches of bright crimson cardinal flower growing along the banks.

Appropriately, *Pachaug* derives from a Native American word meaning "bend or turn in the river." Pequot, Narragansett, and Mohegan tribes inhabited this area prior to the arrival of Europeans. During the latter half of the seventeenth century, a combined force of colonists and Mohegans defeated the Narragansetts and Pequots, and in 1700 a 6-mile by 6-mile tract of land was granted to the Mohegan war veterans. Eventually the central portion of this tract became "Volunteer's Town," incorporated as Voluntown in 1721.

Numerous hiking and mountain biking trails wend their way through the various sections of the 23,000-acre Pachaug State Forest, the largest state forest in Connecticut. Nearby, a short loop trail traverses a wonderful Rhododendron Sanctuary—a quite unusual isolated stand of ancient rhododendrons and white cedar.

77

Glasgo Pond
Griswold, CT

MAPS: Connecticut and Rhode Island Atlas, Map 39
USGS Quadrangles, Jewett City and Voluntown

AREA: 184 acres

CAMPING: Pachaug State Forest (Green Falls and Mount
Misery Campgrounds), 860-376-4075; Hopeville Pond State
Park, 860-376-0313; reservations: 877-668-2267 or
www.ReserveAmerica.com

HABITAT TYPE: wooded pond

EXPECT TO SEE: wood duck, forested hillsides,
shrubby shoreline

TAKE NOTE: limited development; motors allowed

GETTING THERE

From I-395, Exit 85, go east on Route 138 for 4.0 miles (4.0 miles), and turn right (south) onto Route 201. Go 1.8 miles (5.8 miles), and turn left onto Hillview Heights. Veer right after a short distance, and go 0.3 mile (6.1 miles) to the access.

A grove of sassafras, with very aromatic leaves, greets you at the access. As you paddle out along this narrow, winding pond, many overhanging branches drape out over the water. To get away from the houses and bass-fishing boats, paddle east and squeeze under the Route 165 bridge. Other than the moderate noise from Route 165, the southeastern section feels like a northern wilderness area—you almost expect to hear the wail of a loon, a species absent from Connecticut's inland waterways for many years.

The southeastern section of Glasgo Pond lies mostly within Pachaug State Forest—a sprawling 23,000-acre tract, the largest public land area in southern New England. Red maple, white pine, and scarlet oak ring the shore, along with patches of cedar and tamarack.

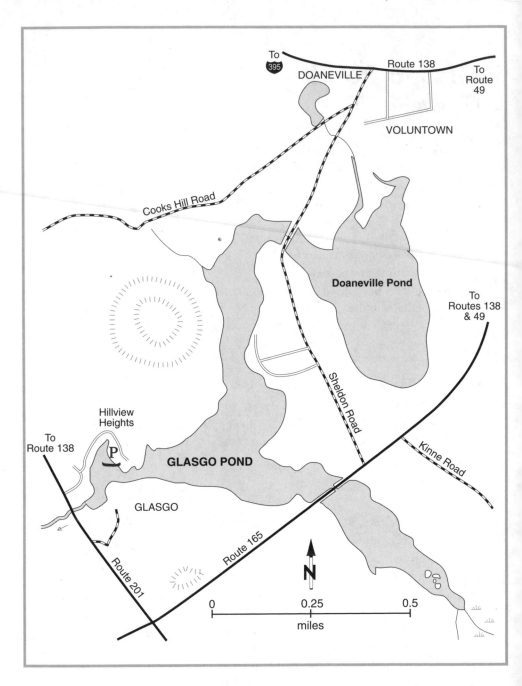

Glasgo Pond

A wide variety of shrubs abound at the shoreline—sweetgale, sweet pepperbush, alder, mountain laurel, blueberry, winterberry. On the sphagnum tussocks, you will find tiny-leaved vines and large fruits of wild cranberry. In early October we also saw nodding ladies' tresses, a late-blooming, white-flowered orchid found in boggy areas. Thick mats of underwater fanwort and bladderwort provide cover for large-mouth bass and pickerel.

Exploring around the small, boggy islands on the pond's far end, you may startle feeding wood ducks. With binoculars, you should get a good look at this very timid cavity-nesting duck, the most striking of our waterfowl. We also saw kingfisher, black duck, and pied-billed grebe here. At the far southeast end the islands seem to merge together, forming a marshy area of bulrush, bur-reed, and grasses. You can hear water gurgling as it flows over a beaver dam here.

Back out on the main pond, you can paddle north, passing houses on both sides, and then under the Sheldon Road bridge into Doaneville Pond. Motorboats can pass under this bridge, making it—for the quietwater paddler—far inferior to the southeast extension. Relatively round Doaneville Pond has quite a bit of development along the heavily wooded shore.

78

Green Falls Pond
Voluntown, CT

MAPS: Connecticut and Rhode Island Atlas, Map 39
    USGS Quadrangle, Voluntown

AREA: 48 acres

CAMPING: Pachaug State Forest (Green Falls and Mount Misery
    Campgrounds), 860-376-4075; Hopeville Pond State Park,
    860-376-0313; reservations: 877-668-2267 or
    www.ReserveAmerica.com

HABITAT TYPE: wooded pond

EXPECT TO SEE: great blue heron, scenic forested hillsides,
    shrubby shoreline

TAKE NOTE: no development; no motors

GETTING THERE

From I-395, Exit 85, go east on Route 138 for 8.5 miles (8.5 miles), and turn
right onto a gravel road at the sign for Green Falls Reservoir, 1.0 mile past
the junction with Route 165 north. Go south for 2.6 miles (11.1 miles) to the
access, passing the picnic area on the right.

Green Falls Pond, one of the most remote bodies of water in this guide,
is a real treasure, ideal for a morning or afternoon of quiet paddling and
a superb spot for family camping. Like Beachdale and Glasgo Ponds,
Green Falls Pond lies within southeastern Connecticut's sprawling
Pachaug State Forest—the largest tract of public land in southern New
England. Well off the beaten path, the state forest generally attracts
only hiking, paddling, or camping enthusiasts.

    The beautiful woods surrounding Green Falls Pond—with a tall
canopy of red, chestnut, and white oaks, sugar maple, yellow birch,
hemlock, sassafras, and shagbark hickory—shade a fairly open, leaf-
carpeted understory of mountain laurel, flowering dogwood, and a
wide variety of spring wildflowers. Blueberry, mountain laurel, and

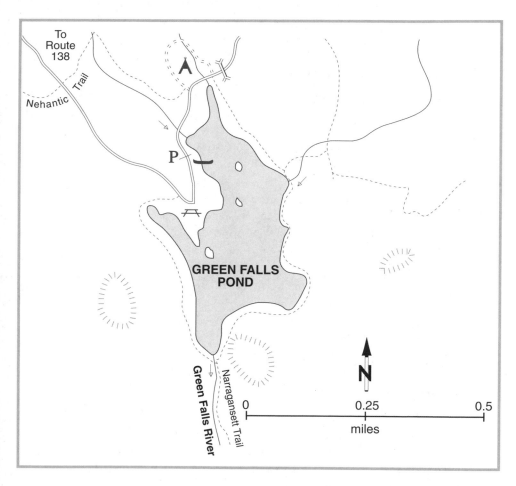

Green Falls Pond

other shrubs line the rocky shoreline, with plenty of places to pull out for a rest, walk in the woods, or picnic. A few islands dot the pond, and several trails weave through Pachaug State Forest, including the Nehantic and Narragansett Trails. From the pond's south end by the dam, you can walk downstream through a deep gorge, with majestic hemlock trees towering well over 100 feet overhead.

Pachaug State Forest permits backpacking, one of the few areas in Connecticut to do so, with special shelters and campsites available along trails for backpackers only (advance registration required).

79

Lake of Isles
North Stonington, CT

MAPS: Connecticut and Rhode Island Atlas, Map 39
USGS Quadrangle, Old Mystic

AREA: 89 acres

CAMPING: Hopeville Pond State Park, 860-376-0313;
Pachaug State Forest (Green Falls and Mount Misery
Campgrounds), 860-376-4075; reservations: 877-668-2267
or www.ReserveAmerica.com

HABITAT TYPE: wooded pond

EXPECT TO SEE: great blue heron, scenic forested hillsides,
shrubby shoreline

TAKE NOTE: former development removed; motors limited by
aquatic vegetation; 8 MPH speed limit

GETTING THERE

From I-395, Exit 79A, go east on Route 2A, making several turns, and turn right (east) onto Route 2. Go 3.5 miles (3.5 miles), and turn left onto Watson Road, 0.7 mile past the Route 164 intersection. Go north on Watson Road for 0.6 mile (4.1 miles), and turn right onto Lake of Isles Road. Access is in 1.2 miles (5.3 miles); at the road's end, take the middle fork.

From I-95, Exit 92, go west on Route 2 to the traffic circle at Route 184. Continue for 8.0 miles, turn right onto Watson Road (1.7 miles after the Route 214 intersection), and follow directions as above.

Lake of Isles, though in the throes of a Eurasian water-milfoil invasion, still provides a wonderful place to paddle, with a highly varied shoreline, clean water, sandy bottom, huge granite boulders along the shore, several attractive islands, and no development—except for a few old Boy Scout structures no longer in use. We hope that the state reclamation program will remove the destroyed docks that dot the shoreline of nearly every cove.

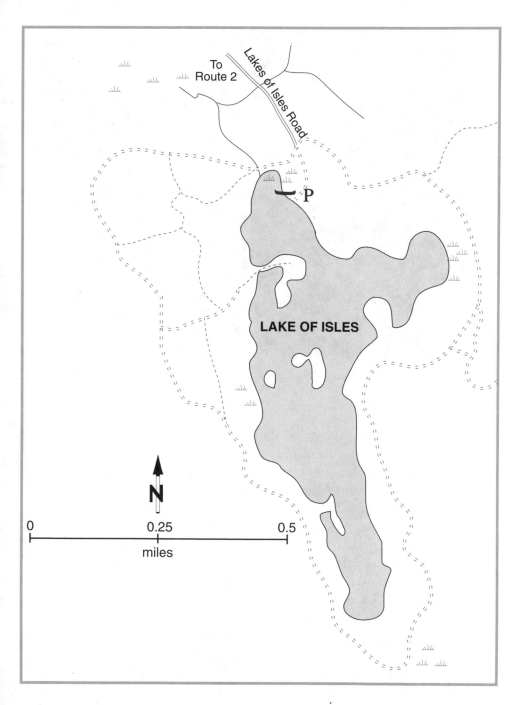

To
Route 2

Lakes of Isles Road

P

LAKE OF ISLES

N

0   0.25   0.5
miles

Lake of Isles

The tiny bladders of carnivorous bladderwort entrap insect larvae and other micro-scopic organisms.

Deciduous trees comprise almost the entirety of the surrounding woodlands, including white and red oaks, red maple, sassafras, yellow and gray birches, elm, American chestnut, white ash, beech, and black gum. The black gum (*Nyssa sylvatica*), with its lacy branches arching nearly straight out with just a slight downcurve, had turned scarlet in early September, at least a month ahead of the other deciduous trees. Lots of blueberry bushes, swamp honeysuckle, alder, and other shrubs grow thickly along the shore. Floating pond vegetation covers the inshore waters and the marshy easternmost cove.

Instead of Lake of Isles—there are only two islands—we should call it Lake of Deep Coves; it takes quite some time to paddle the lake's entire shoreline, weaving in and out of myriad coves. In one we came upon a great blue heron that had just speared a sunfish with its stiletto-like beak. The Eurasian water-milfoil had not yet crowded out the abundant purple-flowered bladderwort on the lake's southern end, but inevitably it will, given the dramatic change we experienced between 1992 and 2002.

80

Powers Lake
East Lyme, CT

MAPS: Connecticut and Rhode Island Atlas, Map 28
USGS Quadrangles, Hamburg and Montville
AREA: 153 acres
CAMPING: Rocky Neck State Park, 860-739-5471;
Hammonasset Beach State Park, 203-245-2785;
Devils Hopyard State Park, 860-873-8566;
reservations: 877-668-2267 or www.ReserveAmerica.com
HABITAT TYPE: wooded pond
EXPECT TO SEE: turtles, scenic forested hillsides, shrubby shoreline
TAKE NOTE: limited development; motors limited to 8 MPH

GETTING THERE

From I-95, Exit 74, go north on Route 161 for 0.5 mile (0.5 mile), and turn left (south) onto Route 1 (Post Road). Go 0.5 mile (1.0 mile), and turn right onto Lower Pattagansett Road. It becomes Upper Pattagansett Road. Go 2.7 miles (3.7 miles), and turn right onto Whistletown Road by the entrance to the Yale University Outdoor Education Center. Go 0.6 mile (4.3 miles), and turn right onto the marked access road.

Except for the state-owned boat access, Yale University owns the entire surrounding area (some 2,000 acres) here. Yale students, faculty, and associated groups use the recreation area at the lake's southwest end for retreats, picnics, and outdoor recreation. The paddling is great, the woodland flora varied, and the wildlife abundant. A surprising diversity of deciduous trees grows along the shoreline: four different species of oaks (red, white, scarlet, and chestnut), American chestnut, sassafras, yellow birch, red maple, tulip tree, hickory, black gum, beech, and Atlantic white cedar. Mountain laurel, blueberry, alder, and other shrubs form thick stands along the shore, making landing difficult, but some protruding granite slabs provide access to shore for a picnic lunch or a break from paddling.

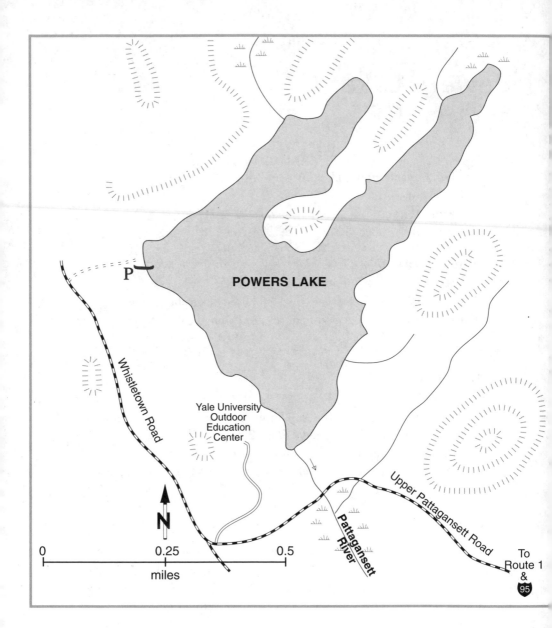

P

POWERS LAKE

Whistletown Road

Yale University
Outdoor
Education
Center

N

0   0.25   0.5
miles

Upper Pattagansett Road

Pattagansett River

To
Route 1
&
95

Powers Lake

Two long fingers of this horseshoe-shaped lake make it seem larger than 153 acres. The longer finger frames a beautiful marshy area, though various waterlilies pretty well block access to the northernmost section by midsummer. In this part of the lake, look for tiny, delicate sundews on hummocks of grass and sphagnum moss. You should find two different species of this unusual plant—round-leaved sundew, *Drosera rotundifolia*, and spatulate-leaved sundew, *D. intermedia*—that gains sustenance from insects caught by sticky hairs on its leaves. Most exciting, however, was the reptile life around the lake. We saw a number of northern water snakes, lots of painted turtles, a stinkpot turtle, and a quite rare spotted turtle *(Clemmys guttata)*.

While close to major population centers, Powers Lake remains undeveloped. Vegetation covers the surface of the northeastern end.

81

Uncas Pond
Lyme, CT

MAPS: Connecticut and Rhode Island Atlas, Map 28
USGS Quadrangles, Hamburg and Old Lyme
AREA: 69 acres
CAMPING: Rocky Neck State Park, 860-739-5471;
Hammonasset Beach State Park, 203-245-2785;
Devils Hopyard State Park, 860-873-8566;
reservations: 877-668-2267 or www.ReserveAmerica.com
HABITAT TYPE: small, elongated, wooded pond
EXPECT TO SEE: forested hillsides, shrubby shoreline,
mountain laurel
TAKE NOTE: limited development; no motors

GETTING THERE

From I-95, Exit 70, go north on Route 156 for 3.8 miles (3.8 miles), and turn right at the access sign for Nehantic State Forest onto rough paved Keeny Road. Go 1.2 miles (5.0 miles) to the fork, and stay right (left goes to the picnic area) to the access in 0.3 mile (5.3 miles). An alternate access is at the picnic area.

Located in Nehantic State Forest, Uncas Pond offers a wonderful paddling experience. Though small and with some development, the forested hillsides, clear water, and absence of motors beckon paddlers. The pond bears the name of Chief Uncas of the Pequot Nation. *Uncas*, which means "fox," recalls different images, depending upon your viewpoint. James Fenimore Cooper's *Last of the Mohicans* transplanted this chief into the forests of upper New York. To his Native rivals—the Niantics and Narragansetts—and even to his adopted Pequot Nation, his name conjured up a circling forager who would strike when opportunity came, and indeed he did. The son of Mohegan Chief Owenoco, Uncas joined the more powerful Pequots after marrying a daughter of their Chief Sassacus, but rebelled several times against his father-in-law's rule. Banished to the Narragansetts, he later subdued them.

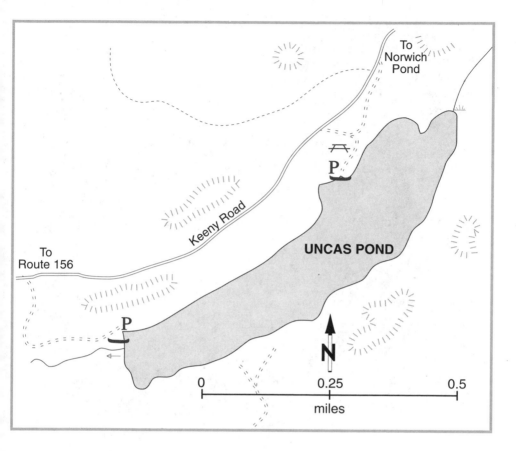

Uncas Pond

Uncas sided in each fight with English settlers and in their successful war against King Philip's coalition of Indian nations in 1675. A monument to Uncas in nearby Norwich honors this friendship.

Uncas Pond's environs sport a tremendous diversity of trees and shrubs, almost all deciduous, including white, red, and scarlet oaks, black gum, red and sugar maples, beech, gray and yellow birches, sassafras, tulip tree, American chestnut (sprouts from blight-killed trees), a few hemlock, alder, mountain laurel, and swamp azalea. Around most of the pond, the land rises steeply from the water's edge. Laurel, in particular, grows densely along the shore. In some areas you can't even see the actual shoreline, much less get out and walk along the bank. A narrow band of aquatic vegetation—pickerelweed, fragrant waterlily, water shield, pondweed, and yellow pondlily—protects the shoreline. At the

Uncas Pond nestles into the hills of Nehantic State Forest and offers a very pleasant morning or afternoon of paddling—without motors.

northeast end, floating vegetation grows thicker in a small marshy area. We also found pipewort *(Eriocaulon aquaticum)*, with its buttonlike flower heads, poking up out of the shallow water. Look for freshwater mussels along the sandy bottom.

Nehantic State Forest offers pleasant hiking and a nice picnic area near the pond's north end. From the access, a trail extends along the north side of the pond through a beautiful area of huge boulders, thick carpets of ferns, huge mountain laurel, and feathery flowering dogwoods.

82

Babcock Pond
Colchester, CT

MAPS: Connecticut and Rhode Island Atlas, Map 36
USGS Quadrangle, Moodus
AREA: 147 acres
CAMPING: Devils Hopyard State Park, 860-873-8566;
reservations: 877-668-2267 or www.ReserveAmerica.com
HABITAT TYPE: shallow, marshy pond
EXPECT TO SEE: wood duck; rafts of fragrant waterlily
and water shield
TAKE NOTE: no development; cartop access and shallow, weedy
pond limit motors; 8 MPH speed limit

GETTING THERE

From Route 2, Exit 16, go south on Route 149 for 3.3 miles (3.3 miles), and turn left at the stoplight onto Route 16. Go east for 1.0 mile (4.3 miles) to the access on the right.

From Route 2, Exit 18, go west on Route 16 for 3.3 miles to the access on the left.

Babcock Pond, though small, offers superb marshland paddling. This shallow pond, lying within the Babcock Pond Wildlife Management Area, sports huge, unbroken rafts of fragrant waterlily, along with other abundant aquatic vegetation, including pickerelweed, water shield, yellow pondlily, and at least two species of bladderworts—yellow- and purple-flowered. Because of the aquatic vegetation, paddling here can present a challenge, especially late in the season, and works best with the goal of a leisurely visit to study the plants.

If other paddlers have not beaten you to the water, also expect to see wood ducks, a few other waterfowl, and the occasional muskrat. The undeveloped wooded shoreline consists primarily of deciduous

Babcock Pond

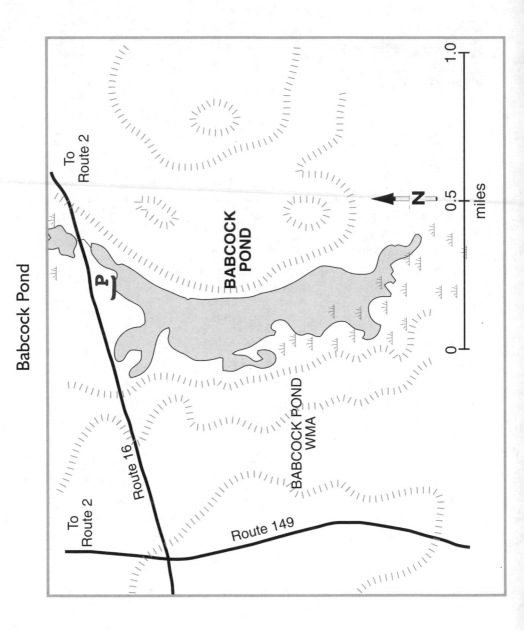

To Route 2

P

BABCOCK POND

BABCOCK POND WMA

Route 16

To Route 2

Route 149

N

0   0.5   1.0

miles

A muskrat, unconcerned by our presence, munches on vegetation.

trees, with red maple seeming to be most abundant, along with a shrubby understory.

If you paddle under Route 16 onto the small pond north of the road on sunny days, expect to see lots of painted turtles sunning themselves in a pond literally ringed with swamp loosestrife. We spent quite some time trying to photograph pollinators on the purple axillary flowers of the loosestrife.

83

Moodus Reservoir
East Haddam, CT

> **MAPS:** Connecticut and Rhode Island Atlas, Map 36
>   USGS Quadrangles, Deep River and Moodus
> **AREA:** 486 acres
> **CAMPING:** Devils Hopyard State Park, 860-873-8566;
>   reservations: 877-668-2267 or www.ReserveAmerica.com
> **HABITAT TYPE:** shallow, marshy pond, deep coves
> **EXPECT TO SEE:** wood duck, flowering shrubs, water shield,
>   yellow-flowered bladderwort, fanwort
> **TAKE NOTE:** limited development; motors allowed

GETTING THERE:

From Route 9. From Route 9, Exit 7, go east on Route 82 for 4.9 miles (4.9 miles), and turn left (north) onto Route 151. Go 1.2 miles (6.1 miles), and turn right onto East Haddam–Colchester Turnpike. Go 2.6 miles (8.7 miles), and turn right onto Launching Area Road at the access sign. Go 0.2 mile (8.9 miles) to the access.

From Route 2. From Route 2, Exit 18, go west on Route 16 for 4.3 miles (4.3 miles), and turn left onto Route 149. Go south for 1.7 miles (6.0 miles), and go straight onto Eli Chapman Road as Route 149 veers right. Go 0.4 mile (6.4 miles), and turn left onto Mott Lane. Go 0.8 mile (7.2 miles), and at the T turn right onto East Haddam–Colchester Turnpike. Go 0.6 mile (7.8 miles), crossing the reservoir causeway, and turn left onto Launching Area Road at the access sign. Go 0.2 mile (8.0 miles) to the access.

From Route 2, Exit 16, go south on Route 149 for 3.3 miles to the junction with Route 16, and continue as above.

Moodus comes from the Pequot Indian word *machimoodus*, meaning "land of noises." The area's loud booms have mystified residents for hundreds or even thousands of years. A deep fault line may cause these booms, which a resident says sound like sonic booms and which generally cannot be felt—only heard. These tremors should have no impact

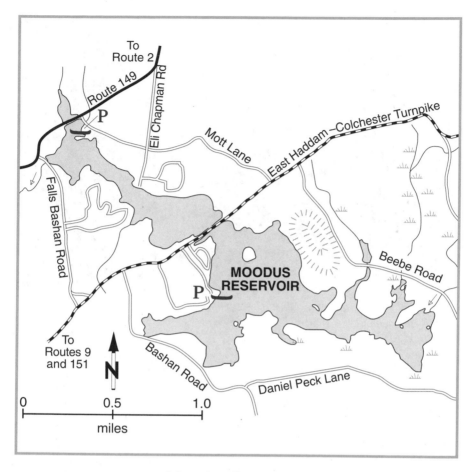

Moodus Reservoir

on your paddling (although neither the authors nor AMC can guarantee that a huge chasm won't suddenly open up—emptying the reservoir and swallowing you and your boat).

The reservoir provides excellent paddling, particularly on a calm spring day when the shorelines come alive with nesting songbirds and spectacular wood ducks try to hide in the marshy coves. You could easily spend a day on this shallow reservoir, exploring the many long sinewy coves and watching for painted turtles amid the floating pond vegetation. We recommend that you paddle early or late in the day and avoid busy summer weekends; we paddled here early on a Sunday in July and found plenty of solitude.

Tree swallows nest in standing dead trees at the shallow, marshy east end of Moodus Reservoir.

Don't bother exploring the reservoir's smaller section, northwest of the East Haddam–Colchester Turnpike causeway; detractions include a much more developed shoreline, more water-skiers, and bigger boats than southeast of the causeway. The development that does occur on the larger, southeastern section clusters near the access.

In the marshy coves keep an eye out for wood duck, green heron, great blue heron, and painted turtles. You may also see hundreds of tree swallows, which inhabit the standing dead trees in the eastern end of the reservoir and feed on flying insects above the water's surface. In the ten years since this book's first edition, many of those trees have fallen, leaving fewer nesting cavities for swallows. Typical trees surround the reservoir: red, scarlet, and white oaks, sassafras, yellow and gray birches, red maple, beech, and a few white pine. Along the shores, look for mountain laurel, highbush blueberry, and large patches of swamp azalea, with long, sticky white flowers that bloom in late June.

When we paddled here in July, huge rafts of water shield, with its relatively inconspicuous red flower and gelatinous underwater sheath, filled the deeper coves, covering the surface so densely that we could see no water. In more open areas, the small, white fanwort flowers and yellow-flowered bladderwort put on a nice display.

～ 84 ～

Salmon River
East Haddam and Haddam, CT

MAPS: Connecticut and Rhode Island Atlas, Map 36
  USGS Quadrangles, Deep River and Moodus
LENGTH: 4 miles
CAMPING: Devils Hopyard State Park, 860-873-8566;
  reservations: 877-668-2267 or www.ReserveAmerica.com
INFORMATION: Goodspeed Opera House, 860-873-8668
HABITAT TYPE: shallow, marshy, tidal Connecticut
  River estuary
EXPECT TO SEE: mute swan, Canada goose, red-tailed hawk,
  swamp rose, hemlock-clad hillsides
TAKE NOTE: some development upstream; motors in
  lower stretches

GETTING THERE

From Route 9. From Route 9, Exit 7, go east on Route 82 for 3.5 miles (3.5 miles),
and turn left (north) onto Route 149. Go 1.0 mile (4.5 miles) to the marked
access on the left. Along the way, you will pass the Goodspeed Opera House.

From Route 2. From Route 2, Exit 18, go west on Route 16 for 4.3 miles
(4.3 miles), and turn left (south) onto Route 149. Go 7.2 miles (11.5 miles) to
the marked access on the right.

From Route 2, Exit 16, go south on Route 149 for 10.5 miles to the
marked access on the right.

The Salmon River, popular with canoers and kayakers—we encountered several dozen on a Sunday in July—provides outstanding bird-
watching opportunities. A red-tailed hawk soared overhead as we
watched a pair of osprey hover above the clear water, looking for a
meal. Later, we watched an osprey feed on a silvery fish. We paddled
through an unconcerned pod of forty-six mute swans—an invasive
species that competes with native birds—and listened to the songs of

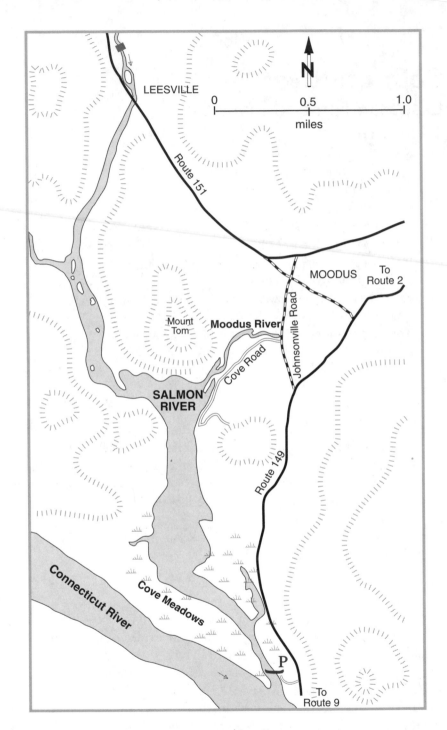

Salmon River

many streamside and woodland birds: red-winged blackbird, grackle, common yellowthroat, yellow warbler, white-throated sparrow, goldfinch, ovenbird, tufted titmouse, robin, catbird, veery, phoebe, great crested flycatcher, brown thrasher, kingfisher, and tree and barn swallows.

The marshy lower section near the access, including the cove immediately on the right, has a much different feel from that of the wooded sections upstream near Leesville Dam and its fish ladder. Look for gorgeous patches of swamp rose, particularly in the cove on the right, which also sports vigorous patches of wild rice. Upstream, some gorgeous stands of hemlock grace the hillsides; mountain laurel and other shrubs fill the shoreline in places, backed up on hillsides clad in a rich diversity of woodland tree species. Though some development occurs upstream, including a small resort, the shallow water limits motorboat access. We found it well worth the paddle up to Leesville Dam.

If you arrive here from Route 9, you will pass the historic Goodspeed Opera House, which hosted national premiers of musicals such as *Annie* and *Man of La Mancha*. It continues to put on renowned musical theater.

Abundant waterfowl, including Canada geese, use the Salmon River as both a breeding ground and a stopover during migration.

85

Selden Creek and Whalebone Creek
Lyme, CT

MAPS: Connecticut and Rhode Island Atlas, Map 27
USGS Quadrangle, Deep River

LENGTH: Selden Creek, 2.7 miles;
Whalebone Creek, 1 mile

CAMPING: Primitive camping on Selden Neck,
203-526-2336; Rocky Neck State Park, 860-739-5471;
Hammonasset Beach State Park, 203-245-2785;
reservations: 877-668-2267 or www.ReserveAmerica.com

INFORMATION: tide charts, www.maineharbors.com

HABITAT TYPE: Connecticut River estuaries, marshlands,
protected coves

EXPECT TO SEE: waterfowl, mute swan, herons and egrets, osprey

TAKE NOTE: no development; motors allowed; use extreme caution off Selden Neck cliffs—novice paddlers should avoid this area; wear your PFD

GETTING THERE

From Route 9, Exit 6, go east on Route 148 for 2.7 miles, cross the Connecticut on the Chester–Hadlyme Ferry, and park immediately on the left. If the ferry is not operating, go north on Route 154, cross over the Connecticut on Route 82, go south to Route 148, and go right to the parking area by the ferry.

From I-95, Exit 70, go north on Route 156, and go left onto Route 82. When Route 82 goes right, go straight onto Route 148. Park on the right at the ferry.

Whalebone Creek. Just downriver from the access, the inlet to Whalebone Creek provides entry to one of the most pristine tidal freshwater marshes in Connecticut. How can it be tidal and freshwater at the same time? The incoming tidal rush raises Connecticut River

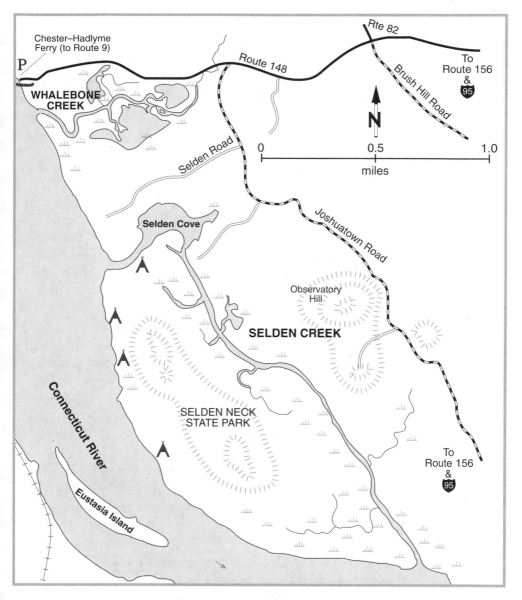

Selden Creek and Whalebone Creek

water levels as far north as Hartford, but strong river currents keep salt water from coming much more than about 10 miles upstream. Just to the south of Whalebone Creek, fresh and salt water mix to create brackish water conditions; not until Great Island do salt marsh ecosystems dominate.

Two signal lights guard the entrance to Whalebone Creek. Entering, you pass a tall, granite cliff on the left, festooned with wild grape and other vines—a preferred habitat for hard-to-see white-eyed vireos. In the early-morning light we watched a raccoon scurry up the rock face, peering down with obvious annoyance. Heavily wooded hillsides occur on the left, but marsh dominates the right, dotted here and there with trees and shrubs adapted to the ever-changing water level.

Farther in, wild rice (*Zizania aquatica*), which reaches 10 feet or more in height, dominates the marsh. Its round, jointed, hollow stems grow up to an inch in diameter at the base. Long, wide leaves up to 4 feet long and as much as 2 inches wide emanate from the stalk, whose top bears flowers and seeds in a form called panicles. Paddling here in late summer, you get a feel for how Native Americans in Minnesota harvest grain from a closely related species (*Z. palustris*)—carefully bend over one of the tall stems and shake it to release the sheathed seeds. In the thick wild rice marshes of Minnesota, Native Americans literally fill their canoes as they harvest the grain.

Along with wild rice, look for bulrush, buttonbush, cattail, pickerelweed, blue iris, and a host of other marsh plants. Birdlife abounds. Even in early autumn, the place seemed alive with red-winged blackbird, marsh wren, swallows, kingfisher, black duck, wood duck, great blue heron, Canada goose, and mute swan. At high tide—the preferred time to paddle here—you can explore quite far into Whalebone Creek, with winding channels and pools of open water.

Selden Creek. About 0.75 mile south of the access, Selden Creek extends left around a tall island hill known as Selden Neck. It returns to the Connecticut nearly 3 miles south, forming one of southern New England's true paddling and camping gems. A 6-mile-per-hour speed limit on Selden Creek keeps down the motorboat traffic, but we would avoid busy summer weekends.

Paddling in one of the small side creeks accessible at high tide, we watched schools of small, silvery alewives or herring skip along the water's surface, using their strong tails in an apparently defensive response to our disturbance. In some cases a fish overthrust and flopped back and forth, getting nowhere, but most seemed to skip along for a foot or two at a time.

When you get to the southern access onto the Connecticut River, we strongly recommend that you turn around and paddle back up Selden Creek. Wakes reflecting off the outer Selden Neck cliffs cause

We watched this snowy egret fish for several minutes before it took flight.

huge waves that can swamp an open boat. As you paddle downriver from the ferry and any other time you paddle the river, we strongly recommend wearing your PFD. Novice paddlers should avoid this area.

The state permits primitive camping on Selden Neck. Of the four campsites, you reach one from Selden Creek, the others from the Connecticut River. Our favorite remains Quarry Knob—the farthest south—where you camp on a knoll overlooking the river and have easy access to the 226-foot rocky peak of Selden Neck. You may stay for one night after registering and paying a fee. Book your site early.

While in the area, you might want to take a side trip to Gillette Castle, a fascinating stone mansion built between 1914 and 1919 by the eccentric stage actor William Gillette, who became famous for his portrayal of Sherlock Holmes. The state purchased the property in 1943 to become Gillette Castle State Park.

86

Lord Cove
Lyme and Old Lyme, CT

MAPS: Connecticut and Rhode Island Atlas, Maps 27 and 28
USGS Quadrangle, Old Lyme

AREA: Wildlife management area, 265 acres;
estuary length, 4 miles

CAMPING: Rocky Neck State Park, 860-739-5471;
Hammonasset Beach State Park, 203-245-2785;
reservations: 877-668-2267 or www.ReserveAmerica.com

INFORMATION: tide charts, www.maineharbors.com

HABITAT TYPE: Connecticut River estuary, brackish marshland,
many islands and protected coves

EXPECT TO SEE: waterfowl, mute swan, herons and egrets,
osprey, marsh wren, muskrat

TAKE NOTE: little development; shallow water limits motors

GETTING THERE

From I-95, Exit 70, go north on Route 156 for 0.7 mile to the access on Pilgrims Landing Road on the left, a few feet in. Parking restrictions: three hours maximum, Friday through Sunday, May 15 through September 19. For longer stays, leave someone with the boats at the landing, park at the Exit 70 commuter lot, and hoof it back to the access.

Lord Cove offers splendid paddling, particularly during shorebird and waterfowl migrations. Brackish marshes dotted with low, grassy islands take at least a half a day to explore fully. Though you won't see as many shorebirds, we recommend paddling here around high tide to avoid exposed mudflats. To access more northern reaches, you have to paddle over a large, shallow, open-water expanse. When winds from the south whip up whitecaps, paddle nearby Uncas Pond (Trip 81) or Powers Lake (Trip 80).

We saw ducks and laughing gulls, along with many snowy egrets on Lord Cove. Look for marsh wren nests in, and muskrats harvesting,

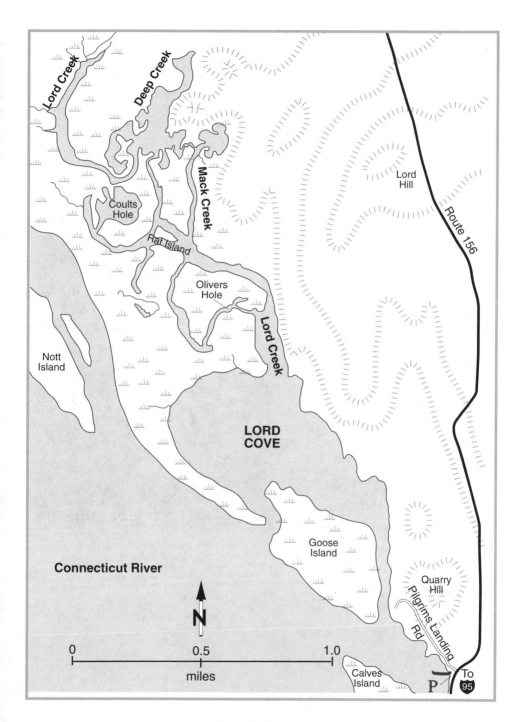

Lord Cove

narrow-leaved cattails. You can paddle way back into the marsh, twisting and turning among the many islands. We sat still and watched an osprey hover over the marsh, eventually diving talons-first on a fish, submerging completely beneath the surface. Popping up, it beat its wings furiously, first against the water's surface, then against the sky, straining to gain altitude with a heavy-bodied, silvery fish, fully as long as the osprey, clutched in its talons. We watched the two sail out of sight, gulls in hot pursuit, hoping to make it drop its prized possession.

Osprey are common in Lord Cove, and we watched this one dive and catch a large, silvery fish.

～ 87 ～

Great Island Estuary and Wildlife Management Area
Old Lyme, CT

MAPS: Connecticut and Rhode Island Atlas, Map 28
   USGS Quadrangle, Old Lyme

AREA/LENGTH: Wildlife management area, 504 acres;
   Lieutenant River, 3.5 miles

CAMPING: Rocky Neck State Park, 860-739-5471;
   Hammonasset Beach State Park, 203-245-2785;
   reservations: 877-668-2267 or www.ReserveAmerica.com

INFORMATION: tide charts, www.maineharbors.com

HABITAT TYPE: shallow saltwater estuary, grassy marshlands,
   many islands and protected bays

EXPECT TO SEE: waterfowl, mute swans, herons and egrets,
   shorebirds, osprey

TAKE NOTE: little development; motors allowed

GETTING THERE

Lieutenant River. From I-95 north, Exit 70, go south on Route 156 for 0.4 mile to the access on the right, just before the bridge. From I-95 south, Exit 70, go west on Route 1, and turn left onto Route 156 south. Access is in 0.5 mile on the right.

   Smiths Neck. Continue south on Route 156 from the Lieutenant River for 1.4 miles (1.4 miles), and turn right onto Smith Neck Road, which dead-ends at the access in 0.9 mile (2.3 miles).

This shallow saltwater estuary draws large groups of sea kayakers on summer weekends. Paddling here on a Sunday in late August, we saw more kayaks than we have seen anywhere else in the Northeast. You can get away from the crowds, however, by paddling into the twisting channels of Great Island Wildlife Management Area. Griswold Point, a sand spit owned by The Nature Conservancy that provides some wind protection and a buffer from Long Island Sound, offers a great

Southern Connecticut   295

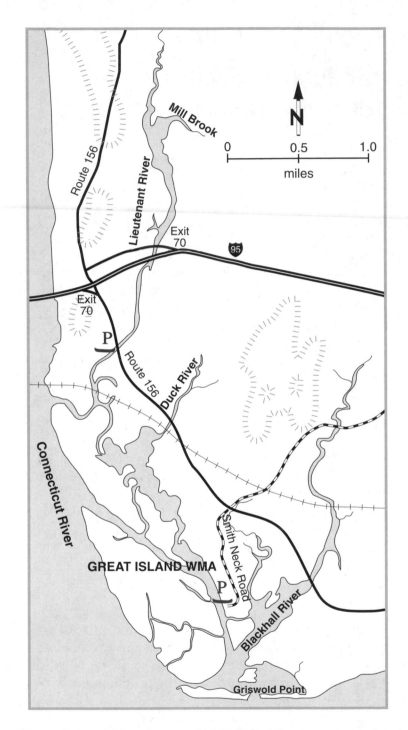

Great Island Estuary and Wildlife Management Area

place to picnic and a refuge for nesting piping plovers (endangered species) and least terns (threatened species). Please obey warning signs.

With fall shorebird migration in full swing, we saw hundreds of sandpipers and plovers, including least and semipalmated sandpipers, black-bellied and semipalmated plovers, greater and lesser yellowlegs. Soras (a type of rail) and saltmarsh sharp-tailed and seaside sparrows skulked in the dense stands of *Spartina* and *Phragmites*. We also noted a large number of mute swans.

Here in the 1960s, scientists discovered osprey eggshell thinning caused by DDT, which led to a lawsuit that ultimately led to the banning of DDT. Having exhibited a remarkable recovery, twenty or more pairs of osprey now nest in the refuge, and we watched them hover and dive for fish.

The Blackhall, a beautiful marshy river, provides wonderful paddling. Red, scarlet, and white oaks line the banks, along with sassafras, black gum, cedar, blueberry, and the occasional mountain laurel. *Phragmites*, which gives way to narrow-leaved cattails upstream, creeps out from the shore. Look for marsh wren nests in the cattails. We saw green heron, snowy and great egrets, osprey, and cormorant here.

Up on the Lieutenant River, we watched barn swallows snatch insects on the wing, while listening to numerous catbirds and cardinals call from the dense shoreline vegetation. Kingfishers fled before us up the river, while flocks of ducks took wing or fled into high grass. A fish ladder installed on a tributary, Mill Brook, provides spawning access for alewives to a series of small ponds and, someday with another ladder, to Rogers Lake.

Salt Marsh
Where River and Sea Meet

The unusual salt marsh ecosystem enjoys tremendous biological productivity yet stresses its inhabitants—plants especially—so severely that few species can prosper. The stress comes from constant change. Incoming tides flood the marsh, saturating the peaty soil with water. As tides recede, the exposed surface may actually dry out on a hot, breezy day.

The water's changing salinity, even more than the fluctuating water level, determines what can survive. As seawater surges into the marsh, salinity increases, reaching a peak at high tide. As the tide drops, so does the salinity, reaching a minimum at low tide when incoming fresh water from the river or inlet streams flushes out or dilutes the seawater. Salinity conditions often vary markedly in different portions of a salt marsh—from nearly pure fresh water at one end to salinity nearly matching that of the ocean at the opening to the sea. Salinity-controlling agents include the volume of fresh water flowing into the marsh, the tidal differential along that section of coastline, and the size and configuration of the connection to the sea.

Periodic flooding and salinity fluctuations impact plants tremendously. Such specialized conditions allow just two species of grass—*Spartina alterniflora* (saltwater cordgrass) and *S. patens* (saltmeadow grass)—to dominate this ecosystem. The *Spartinas* comprise a rare natural monoculture for as far as the eye can see in the largest salt marshes. The instability inherent in monocultures has apparently not affected the *Spartina* marshes, which have exhibited little evidence of disease or significant tidal die-off over many thousands of years.

Spartina alterniflora occupies the lower ground, where twice-daily flooding inundates it with salt water. In ideal conditions *S. alterniflora* reaches 10 feet in height, though more commonly it reaches less than half that. *S. patens*, which grows to 2 feet, dominates the high marsh—the firmer land flooded only irregularly, at spring tides and during storms. Generations of coastal New England farmers harvested this species as feed for their livestock (an acre of salt marsh produces twice as much hay as the best dryland hayfields). You can recognize *S. patens* by the broad "cowlicks" that form on the marsh as swaths of the grass get matted down. A lower, flexible stem section defends against wave forces and strong current.

Glasswort (genus *Salicornia*), a succulent species able to withstand salt marsh rigors, grows upright with swollen, jointed stems. Its name may derive from its onetime use in making glass (the ash is very high in sodium carbonate, an ingredient in glass). Amid the *S. patens* you may also see the delicate flowers of sea lavender *(Limonium carolinianum),* a plant long collected for dried-flower arrangements. Pressure from collectors has reduced sea lavender abundance considerably; please enjoy it from your boat. Look for other specialists here—seaside goldenrod with thick fleshy leaves, sea aster, sea plantain, and sea purslane among them.

Complex mechanisms allow plants to adapt to high and constantly changing salinity levels. Living organisms maintain a fairly precise balance of fluid and dissolved substances in their cells. When concentrations of dissolved compounds vary across cell membranes, water tends to flow from the less concentrated to the more concentrated to equalize the "osmotic gradient." Water in plant cells that is more dilute than seawater—the case with most plants—flows out through the cell membrane, drying and killing the plant cells. This drying is why most plants cannot survive life in the salt marsh. *Spartina* can survive through a complex series of evolutionary adaptations. For an excellent discussion of these adaptations, see *Life and Death of the Saltmarsh,* by John and Mildred Teal (Ballantine Books, 1969).

In the less saline extensions of many salt marshes, you may see wild rice and other less salt-tolerant species. On tidal rivers, seawater can only

Along with the more common Spartina alterniflora *and* S. patens, *you may see the more dramatic* S. cynosuroides, *or big cordgrass, along tidal rivers.*

penetrate upriver a short distance before fresh water dilutes it to such an extent that freshwater plants and animals can survive. Paddling up these rivers, you can watch the progression of species—and species diversity—as you progress inland. On a large-volume river such as the Connecticut, salt water cannot penetrate far upstream. The tidal rush, however, slows the river's flow and raises the water level for many miles upstream without increasing its salinity.

Most animals, unlike plants, can move about to counter changing water levels. Most mollusks and invertebrates either bury themselves deep in the muck or swim in the current, like the fish that live or spawn here. Mussels and barnacles attach tightly to rocks, pilings, or other solid objects and so cannot move about. To survive the twice-daily drying at low tide, these mollusks close up tightly. Some of the fish that inhabit the salt marsh can regulate the osmotic balance of their bodily fluids to adjust to the changing salinity of the water. Some lower invertebrates actually bloat up in lower-salinity water, then shrink as the salinity increases.

The fiddler crab (so called for the very large size differential between its claws) has several adaptations to salt marsh life. Like all crabs, it has gills, but it also has a primitive lung, enabling it to breathe air as long as it keeps the lung moist. It can also survive without oxygen for long periods when it tunnels down into the oxygen-deficient mud. The fiddler crab also enjoys a remarkable salt-and-water regulation system that enables it to maintain constant osmotic equilibrium both in diluted seawater and in water more concentrated than seawater, as found in briny tidal ponds that have evaporated over a period of days or weeks.

The rich, salt marsh birdlife needs to adapt less to the environment. At low tide dozens of wading birds feed on insect larvae and crustaceans in the exposed mud flats. Clapper rails and marsh wrens nest amid the *Spartina*. Harriers weave back and forth low over the marsh in search of mice, and osprey scan the deeper water for fish. Snowy and great egrets, little green and great blue herons patrol the marsh for small fish and other prey. During spring and fall migrations, many waterfowl species stop over in salt marshes before winging southward. Early-morning paddlers may see raccoons and an occasional river otter.

Insects also play an important role in the salt marsh, and efforts to control them—chiefly mosquitoes—have caused some of the most significant human impact on this ecosystem. In the 1930s the Civilian Conservation Corps drained vast areas of salt marsh. Evidence of this only modestly successful effort to eliminate standing water can still be seen clearly today throughout the salt marshes. After fifty years, you can still paddle a short way into some of these long, straight, mosquito-control ditches at high tide.

Many commercially important fish and shellfish species depend on the salt marsh ecosystem. A full two-thirds of the eastern U.S. commercial fish and shellfish catch—including oysters, scallops, clams, blue crabs, shrimp, bluefish, flounder, and striped bass—depend on the salt marsh for at least some phase of their life cycle.

Sustaining nutrients, borne on incoming rivers and streams, support this productivity. The inflowing fresh water spreads out and deposits its sediment, rich with minerals and nutrients. Unfortunately, this same water carries pollutants, as well. All too often we see signs warning of polluted water off-limits to shellfishing. But the salt marsh plays a vitally important role in breaking down many of these pollutants. Like a giant sewage treatment plant, it purifies water and extracts toxins—but the organisms that help purify the water become toxic in the process. The long-lasting pesticide DDT, used from the late 1940s until the early 1970s, concentrated in salt marsh organisms, from crustaceans and fish, up the food chain to osprey and other predators. By the time of DDT's banning, the osprey had almost vanished from New England's salt marshes.

Hundreds of thousands of acres of coastal salt marsh, though vitally important to us economically and biologically, have been lost to development during the past hundred years. The relatively small remnants of these once vast stretches are still threatened by development and pollution. Feeling the tidal current under a boat while watching *Spartina* wave in the breeze and osprey fish overhead helps us appreciate the importance of these resources.

Those of us who value the salt marsh's unique beauty and who understand this ecosystem's fragile nature must guarantee that additional salt marsh acreage will not be lost to development and pollution. Learn about the salt marsh environments in your area, and talk to local planning officials to find out how you can help protect these wonderful places.

88

Pattaconk Reservoir
Chester, CT

MAPS: Connecticut and Rhode Island Atlas, Map 27
   USGS Quadrangle, Haddam
AREA: 56 acres
CAMPING: Rocky Neck State Park, 860-739-5471;
   Hammonasset Beach State Park, 203-245-2785;
   reservations: 877-668-2267 or www.ReserveAmerica.com
HABITAT TYPE: shallow, marshy pond
EXPECT TO SEE: forested hillsides, shrubby shoreline
TAKE NOTE: no development; no motors

GETTING THERE

From Route 9, Exit 6, go west on Route 148 for 1.5 miles (1.5 miles), and turn right (north) onto Cedar Lake Road. Go 1.6 miles (3.1 miles) to the Pattaconk Lake State Recreation Area on the left. The large parking area is another 0.4 mile (3.5 miles) on the right. Carry your boat about 75 yards down to the water from the back of the parking lot.

Hidden away in Cockaponset State Forest in south-central Connecticut, Pattaconk Reservoir, a small but stunning undeveloped body of water, provides wonderful paddling. In a part of the state known more for tidal river paddling, Pattaconk offers a refreshing alternative with a real mountain pond feel to it. If you visit here in summer, you will see dozens of other people paddling, swimming, hiking, and off-road bicycling. If you prefer more solitude, paddle similar, but larger, nearby Messerschmidt Pond.

   Deciduous trees dominate the surrounding woods, including four different oak species (red, white, chestnut, and scarlet), three birch species (gray, black, and yellow), red maple, sassafras, beech, shagbark hickory, black gum, American chestnut, and tulip tree. Mountain laurel,

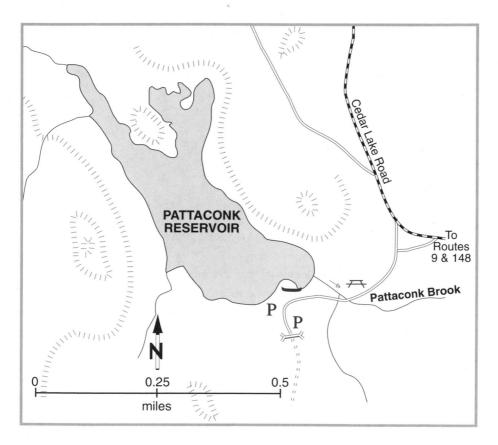

Pattaconk Reservoir

highbush blueberry, and sweet pepperbush grow densely along the shore, overhanging the water in many places, making the shoreline mostly inaccessible. Where you can get onto the shore, the open woods beyond offer great hiking.

Some vegetation floats on the water (fragrant waterlily, pondweed, water shield, yellow pondlily). When we paddled here in 1992, very little vegetation appeared underwater. When we returned ten years later, an infestation of Eurasian water-milfoil had begun to fill the void, literally. The clean water with sandy bottom supports freshwater mussels and patches of what we think are small, nodding white orchids in the shallows. Occasional boulders dot the shoreline of this beautiful pond.

89

Messerschmidt Pond
Deep River and Westbrook, CT

MAPS: Connecticut and Rhode Island Atlas, Map 27
   USGS Quadrangle, Essex
AREA: 73 acres
CAMPING: Hammonasset Beach State Park, 203-245-2785;
   Rocky Neck State Park, 860-739-5471;
   reservations: 877-668-2267 or www.ReserveAmerica.com
HABITAT TYPE: shallow, marshy pond
EXPECT TO SEE: floating heart, fragrant waterlily, water shield
TAKE NOTE: no development; no motors

GETTING THERE

From Route 9, Exit 5, go west on Route 80 for 3.7 miles (3.7 miles), and turn left (south) onto Route 145 (Stevenstown Road). Go 1.3 miles (5.0 miles) to the marked access on the left.

From I-95, Exit 84, go north on Route 145 for 3.0 miles to the marked access on the right.

Though small, Messerschmidt Pond offers an opportunity for a wonderful morning of paddling. Lying wholly within Messerschmidt Wildlife Management Area, the pond's low earthen dam at the south end and a couple of groves of Norway spruce provide the only evidence of human presence. Paddling the entire shoreline takes much more time than the pond's acreage would suggest because of undulating deep coves, peninsulas, and a couple of very large wooded islands.

Shrubs line the shore, leading to hillsides covered with deciduous trees, many of them oaks. A large patch of buttonbush, its fluffy ball-like flowers festooned with bees in mid-July, covered the backside of one island, while stands of swamp azalea and mountain laurel—both of which put on showy displays in June—dominated stretches of

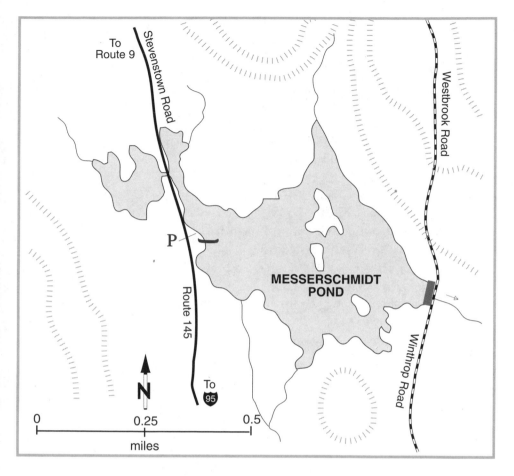

Messerschmidt Pond

shoreline. Though fragrant waterlily and water shield rule the surface, yellow-flowered bladderwort and fanwort fill much of the underwater volume. Surprisingly, we also found some fairly large patches of floating heart *(Nymphoides cordata)*, an uncommon aquatic plant, in bloom in mid-July.

As we paddled into the northern cove, eastern kingbirds chased a red-tailed hawk, while catbirds, cardinals, and hermit thrushes called from the undergrowth. We had a very relaxing paddle here, away from the motorboats and development that characterize most bodies of water in the area.

90

East River
Guilford and Madison, CT

MAPS: Connecticut and Rhode Island Atlas, Map 26
USGS Quadrangle, Guilford
LENGTH: 6 miles
CAMPING: Hammonasset Beach State Park, 203-245-2785;
reservations: 877-668-2267 or www.ReserveAmerica.com
INFORMATION: tide charts, www.maineharbors.com
HABITAT TYPE: salt marsh estuary
EXPECT TO SEE: waterfowl, egrets, osprey, fiddler crabs, *Spartina*
TAKE NOTE: limited development with areas protected by CT
Audubon Society; motors allowed; plan your paddle around
wind and tides

GETTING THERE

From I-95, Exit 59, go east on Route 1 for 1.6 miles (1.6 miles), and turn right onto Neck Road. Bear right after a few hundred yards, then continue southwest for 2.1 miles (3.7 miles), following Boat Launch signs.

You can also launch from Route 1 where it crosses the river. Park in the large lot on the northeast side.

The East River—the boundary between Guilford and Madison—provides superb tidal salt marsh paddling. From the access on Grass Island, the river extends about 6 miles inland in a fairly wide, gently winding channel, with lots of small tributary streams to explore. Near the boat launch, the Neck River bears off to the right but heads into a more populated area. You could easily spend a full day exploring this area, observing the many changes caused by rising and falling tides.

At high tide you can look out over the broad expanses of *Spartina* (salt marsh grass). As the tide falls, the horizon disappears behind high sod banks clad with mussels and alive with fiddler crabs and other generally hidden salt marsh creatures. Look for herons and egrets hunting

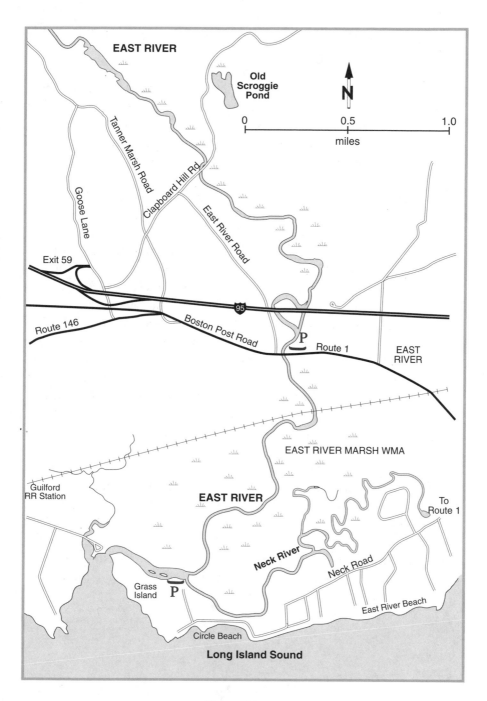

East River

small crabs and fish in the network of water-filled drainage ditches that extend through the marsh.

In the 1930s and 1940s drainage ditches were dug throughout coastal salt marshes in an effort to eliminate mosquito-breeding stagnant water pools. Though only marginally successful, the effort put hundreds of people to work during the Great Depression. At high tide you can squeeze your boat into some of these long, straight ditches, getting away from the main tidal river current and permitting close examination of salt marsh flora and fauna.

You pass under a number of bridges, including one for Amtrak on the heavily traveled Northeast Corridor, about 1.5 miles upstream. A quarter mile past that, you can stop at the Route 1 bridge to visit one of the stores along the highway—on an incoming tide, make sure to tie your boat securely. The I-95 bridge follows just after the Route 1 bridge, and highway noise here can detract somewhat from this wonderful stretch of river, but it gradually fades as you paddle upriver.

A short distance north of I-95, the Connecticut Audubon Society protects land known as the Guilford Salt Meadow Sanctuary on both sides of the river. At high tide you can explore numerous small inlet streams teeming with birdlife, including osprey, northern harrier, herons, and egrets. Red and white oaks, sassafras, sumac, cedar, flowering dogwood, and a few black gum trees grow along the high ground. Watch out for poison ivy and Lyme-disease-carrying deer ticks if you decide to explore on foot.

By timing your visit, you can paddle upriver from the boat access on an incoming tide, enjoy paddling around the salt marsh at high tide, then paddle back after the tide turns. Several miles up East River, high tide occurs quite a bit later than at the coast, which is about twenty minutes before Bridgeport. The wind, however, may cause more difficulty than the modest current. By visiting in early morning or early evening, you might be able to avoid the typical afternoon wind.

Housatonic River and the Charles E. Wheeler Wildlife Management Area
Milford, CT

MAPS: Connecticut and Rhode Island Atlas, Map 21
   USGS Quadrangle, Milford
AREA: Wildlife management area, 812 acres
CAMPING: Kettletown State Park, 203-264-5169;
   Hammonasset Beach State Park, 203-245-2785;
   reservations: 877-668-2267 or www.ReserveAmerica.com
INFORMATION: Connecticut Audubon Coastal Center at Milford
   Point, 203-878-7440; tide charts, www.maineharbors.com
HABITAT TYPE: Housatonic River estuary, brackish marshland,
   many protected waterways
EXPECT TO SEE: waterfowl, mute swan, shorebirds, herons and
   egrets, osprey
TAKE NOTE: little development; motors limited to 5 MPH and by
   shallow water; winds, tides, and wakes can be dangerous—
   novice paddlers should avoid this area

GETTING THERE

From I-95, Exit 34, go south on Route 1 (Bridgeport Avenue) for 0.5 mile (0.5 mile), and turn right onto Naugatuck Avenue at the stoplight. Go north for 0.3 mile (0.8 mile), and turn left onto the access road, just before the I-95 overpass far above.

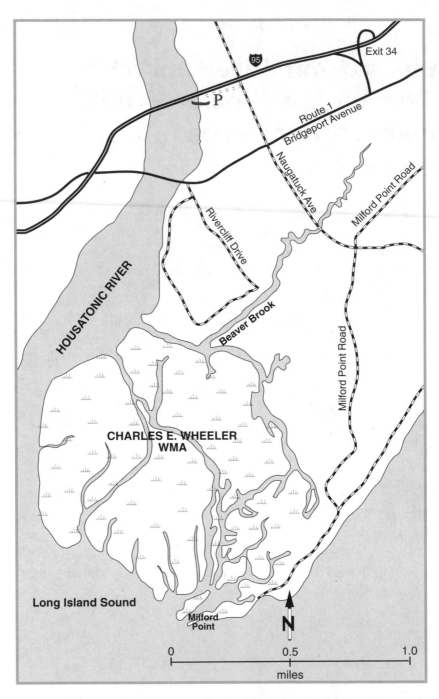

Housatonic River and the Charles E. Wheeler
Wildlife Management Area

A clapper rail, normally very secretive, strolled out into plain view as we paddled by.

The Charles E. Wheeler Wildlife Management Area's protected waters harbor a wide array of interesting bird species. Getting to these waters, however, presents a challenge, one best left to experienced paddlers. Though wind affects the salt marsh's interior only modestly, to get there you have to paddle a mile down the Housatonic River. Strong winds, tidal currents, and motorboat wakes can wash water over your gunnels, potentially swamping your boat. Within the marsh, a 5-mile-per-hour speed limit helps, but we found personal watercraft zooming about, scaring the birds and causing massive bank erosion. Because policing the waterways would be a full-time job for someone, we strongly recommend that personal watercraft be banned from the wildlife management area.

A number of long, wide passageways, each with several side channels, penetrate the heart of the marsh, which extends a little over a mile in both the north–south and east–west directions. If you can, paddle here in August during peak shorebird migration. As we explored the *Spartina*-lined waterways, we saw herring, great black-backed and ring-billed gulls, double-crested cormorant, great blue heron, snowy and common egrets, semipalmated and piping plovers, short-billed dowitcher, lesser and greater yellowlegs, unidentified peeps (probably semipalmated sandpiper and possibly others), black duck, mute swan, Canada goose, cardinal, kingfisher, osprey, red-winged blackbird, and swamp, song, and saltmarsh sharp-tailed sparrows. Two rather tame clapper rails—normally very elusive—stepped out into plain view, begging to be photographed, as we lingered nearby.

Western Connecticut

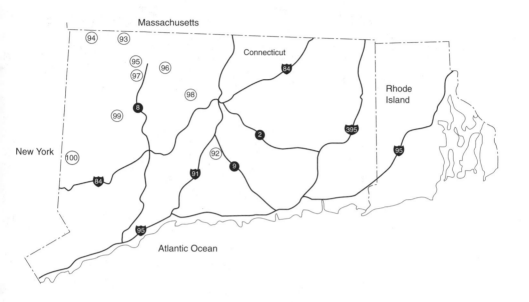

Massachusetts

Connecticut

New York

Rhode Island

Atlantic Ocean

92

Mattabesset River, Coginchaug River, and the Cromwell Meadows Wildlife Management Area
Cromwell and Middletown, CT

MAPS: Connecticut and Rhode Island Atlas, Map 35
   USGS Quadrangle, Middletown

LENGTH: Mattabesset River, 5 miles;
   Coginchaug River, 2 miles

HABITAT TYPE: river through extensive marshland, many bays
   and side channels

EXPECT TO SEE: muskrat, waterfowl, marsh birds, aquatic
   vegetation, varied shrubs

TAKE NOTE: no development; motors allowed; because of wind,
   waves, and wakes, wear your PFD; novice paddlers should
   avoid this area

GETTING THERE

From downtown Middletown, go south on Main Street. Turn left onto Union Street at the stoplight. In 0.1 mile, pass under Route 9, and veer left for 100 feet. Take an immediate right into the Harbor Park parking area.

Though some road noise emanates from numerous four-lane divided highways that ring Middletown, the Cromwell Meadows Wildlife Management Area still represents an extraordinary paddling resource, all the more so because of its metropolitan location. Huge numbers of nesting and migrating waterfowl congregate here, and nowhere else in our exploration of Connecticut have we seen so much wild rice (*Zizania aquatica*).

   Paddle north from the Connecticut River Harbor Park access, nominally upstream—the tides travel this far upriver, and you may have to paddle against the current in either direction. The current presents little problem, however, compared with motorboat wakes and

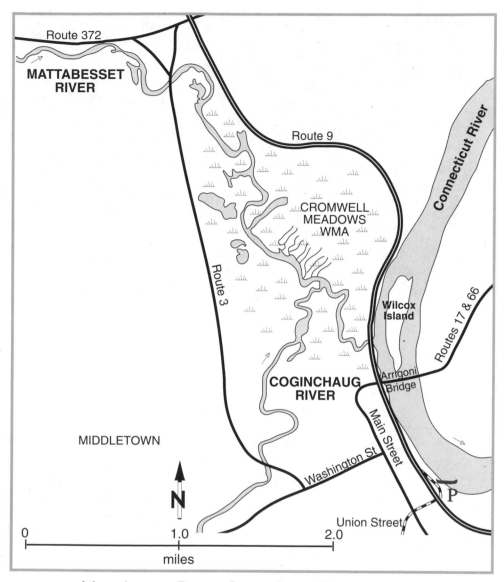

Mattabesset River, Coginchaug River, and the
Cromwell Meadows Wildlife Management Area

wind-driven waves that pile up over a couple of miles of open water. Because the Connecticut bends and bows, the winds cause less havoc here than on straighter stretches of river. Under windy conditions, we strongly recommend that you wear your PFD or, better yet, paddle elsewhere. Novice paddlers should avoid the Connecticut River.

The dainty flowers of floating heart, Nymphoides cordata, *grace the shallows.*

As we paddled on a late-August afternoon under the Route 9 bridge and into the Mattabesset River, a big surprise unfolded before us: the vast, wild, Cromwell marshlands, full of wood ducks, kingfishers, and cardinals. The area teems with wildlife and interesting plants. Chimney swifts and barn swallows darted over the water's surface, while spotted sandpipers and great blue herons stalked the shores. The rich, golden tops of wild rice, backlit in the setting sun, swayed in the light breeze. Deer came down for an evening drink, and muskrats swam by, towing grasses destined for winter stores. We sat just watching, reluctant to leave this enchanted place. We and the waterfowl will return to watch the spring unfold.

93

Wood Creek Pond
Norfolk, CT

MAPS: Connecticut and Rhode Island Atlas, Map 50
USGS Quadrangle, South Sandisfield
AREA: 151 acres
CAMPING: American Legion State Forest, 860-379-2469;
Burr Pond State Park, 860-482-1817;
reservations: 877-668-2267 or www.ReserveAmerica.com
HABITAT TYPE: marshy pond
EXPECT TO SEE: Canada goose, turtles, scenic forested hillsides,
shrubby shoreline
TAKE NOTE: no development; vegetation and shallowness
limit motors

GETTING THERE

From Route 44 in Norfolk, go north on Route 272 for 1.5 miles (1.5 miles), and turn right (east) onto Ashpohtag Road at the Wood Creek Pond launch sign. Go 0.4 mile (1.9 miles) to the marked access road on the left.

Located in an out-of-the-way setting near the northwest tip of Connecticut, Wood Creek Pond offers a very pleasant morning or afternoon of paddling in a shallow, marshy, heavily vegetated pond about a mile long. Near the south end, you may see nesting Canada geese. As you approach, if the geese have young, notice the adults' defensive posturing, ruffling their neck feathers to look more forbidding to would-be aggressors.

As you paddle north, hillsides rise steeply from the shore, heavily wooded with mountain laurel, red maple, and other deciduous trees interspersed with hemlock and white pine. The pond's surface vegetation of fragrant waterlily, water shield, pondweed, and yellow pondlily can get quite thick; coontail and yellow-flowered bladderwort hang in large masses beneath the surface. Take a few minutes to look at the

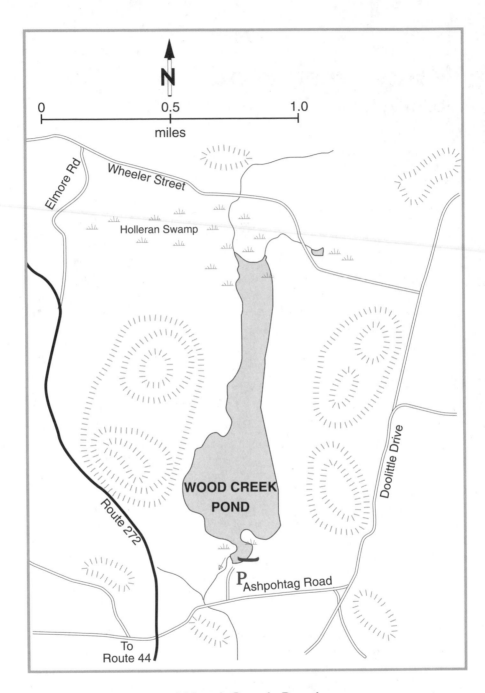

Wood Creek Pond

Very shallow and thick with vegetation, Wood Creek Pond provides hours of exploration and discovery for the quietwater paddler.

yellow pondlily flowers. The waxy yellow "petals" are actually sepals; the smaller true petals look more like stamens. A wide pistil with yellow cap and reddish sides covers the middle of the flower.

The shallow north end can be almost impenetrable, with thick soupy muck a few inches beneath the surface made up of decades-old, partially decomposed vegetation on its way to becoming peat. Methane, hydrogen sulfide, and other gases bubble out with the distinctive odor of anaerobic digestion. Wend your way carefully around stumps and submerged logs camouflaged by the soupy water.

Look for the shallow, bowl-shaped depressions that pumpkinseed sunfish make for depositing eggs in the sandy bottom. The aggressive male stands guard over the eggs until they hatch, fanning them with his tail, and then defending them until they're large enough to survive on their own. The males show such perseverance that you can hover right over them, watching them from inches away.

94

Housatonic River
Canaan, North Canaan, and Salisbury, CT
Sheffield, MA

MAPS: Connecticut and Rhode Island Atlas, Maps 49 and 50
  Massachusetts Atlas, Map 44
  USGS Quadrangles, Ashley Falls and South Canaan
LENGTH: 11.5 miles
CAMPING: In CT: Housatonic Meadows State Park and
  Macedonia Brook State Park, 860-927-4100;
  reservations: 877-668-2267 or www.ReserveAmerica.com.
  In MA: Beartown State Forest, 413-528-0904;
  reservations: 877-422-6762 or www.ReserveAmerica.com
INFORMATION: Bartholomew's Cobble: The Trustees of
  Reservations, 413-298-3239 or www.thetrustees.org
HABITAT TYPE: broad, tree-lined river
EXPECT TO SEE: tree-lined shores, varied shrubs, large patches of
  arrowhead, wildflowers, warblers, and other treetop species
TAKE NOTE: little development; few motors

GETTING THERE

Falls Village, CT. From Canaan, go south on Route 7. Turn right onto Route 126 (Main Street) toward Falls Village. In 0.3 mile (0.3 mile), fork right onto Brewster Road/Route 126. In 0.3 mile (0.6 mile), when Route 126 goes right at the T, go left, and take an immediate right onto Water Street. Go straight downhill for 0.5 mile (1.1 miles), under the railroad overpass, and just after crossing the iron bridge, turn right onto Housatonic River Road. Access is in 0.5 mile (1.6 miles) on the right at the dam.

Ashley Falls, MA. From Ashley Falls at the junction of Route 7A and Rannapo Road, go 0.8 mile west on Rannapo Road to the access at the bridge. From the north, when Routes 7 and 7A split, take Route 7A south for 0.6 mile (0.6 mile), and turn right onto Rannapo Road. Go 1.6 miles (2.2 miles) to the access on the left, just before the bridge.

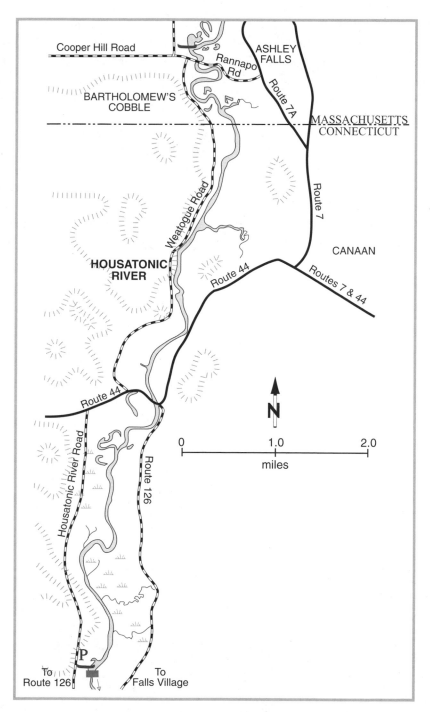

Cooper Hill Road

ASHLEY FALLS

Rannapo Rd

Route 7A

BARTHOLOMEW'S COBBLE

MASSACHUSETTS
CONNECTICUT

Route 7

Weatogue Road

HOUSATONIC RIVER

CANAAN

Route 44

Routes 7 & 44

Route 44

N

0   1.0   2.0
miles

Housatonic River Road

Route 126

P

To Route 126

To Falls Village

Housatonic River

When we paddled here on an August weekend, dozens of canoes floated by us as we paddled upstream through the lazy current. If you crave solitude, stay away from this section of the Housatonic River on summer weekends. Little development marks the river's shores, but for one short section of a little more than a mile, busy Route 44 parallels the river.

Though we did not see large amounts of wildlife because of boat traffic, tree-species diversity along the river impressed us; we quit identifying species after fifteen. Basswood and silver maple appeared in profusion. This section of the Housatonic Valley harbors hundreds of rare native plants, drawing scores of naturalists. The northern section of the Housatonic River included here, just over the border in Massachusetts, flows along Bartholomew's Cobble, arguably the most important plant preserve in the Northeast.

Bartholomew's Cobble

The 329 acres of Bartholomew's Cobble—a National Natural Land-mark—harbor an extraordinary number of rare plant species. Several trails wind through the woods, along the Housatonic River, and up over limestone and marble outcroppings. Because you must stay on trails, binoc-ulars may be advantageous if you'll be scanning the cliffs for rare ferns.

More than fifty species of ferns and fern allies grow here, along with 800 plant species from nearly a hundred families. You will need a plant guide, available at the visitor center, if you hope to distinguish purple-stemmed cliffbrake from maidenhair spleenwort. For anyone with strong interests in plants, Bartholomew's Cobble represents an unparalleled northeastern resource.

GETTING THERE

From Ashley Falls, the turn-off from Rannapo Road is 0.1 mile west of the Ash-ley Falls access. From the north, it is 0.1 mile before the access at the bridge.

Maidenhair spleenwort, Asplenium trichomanes, *is one of many fern species that grow at Bartholomew's Cobble.*

95

Lake Winchester
Winchester, CT

MAPS: Connecticut and Rhode Island Atlas, Map 50
USGS Quadrangle, Norfolk

AREA: 246 acres

CAMPING: Burr Pond State Park, 860-482-1817; American
Legion State Forest, 860-379-2469;
reservations: 877-668-2267 or www.ReserveAmerica.com

HABITAT TYPE: shallow reservoir, shrubby marshlands,
protected bays

EXPECT TO SEE: beaver, woodland birds, spring wildflowers,
mountain laurel, aquatic vegetation

TAKE NOTE: no development; motors limited to 8 MPH; watch
out for submerged rocks and tree stumps

GETTING THERE

From Winsted, go west on Route 44, and turn left (west) onto Route 263 at the edge of town (1.2 miles from the northern terminus of Route 8). Go 4.5 miles (4.5 miles), through Winchester Center, and as Route 263 curves left, go straight onto West Road at the Winchester Lake sign. Go 0.6 mile (5.1 miles) to the access on the right.

Lake Winchester's beautiful setting, coupled with little development, makes it one of our favorite destinations in northwestern Connecticut. You could easily spend half a day exploring this small lake's highly varied shoreline and rocky coves. We prefer paddling here in spring when the abundant mountain laurel blooms, and in summer when the highbush blueberries ripen. Also look for pink lady's slipper, trillium, Solomon's seal, and other spring wildflowers. By midsummer, water shield and waterlilies begin to cover the surface in shallower areas.

Paddling here in the evening, expect to see beaver swimming about, especially in the coves. The clean water supports freshwater mussels and good fishing. We also enjoyed the abundant birdlife in the

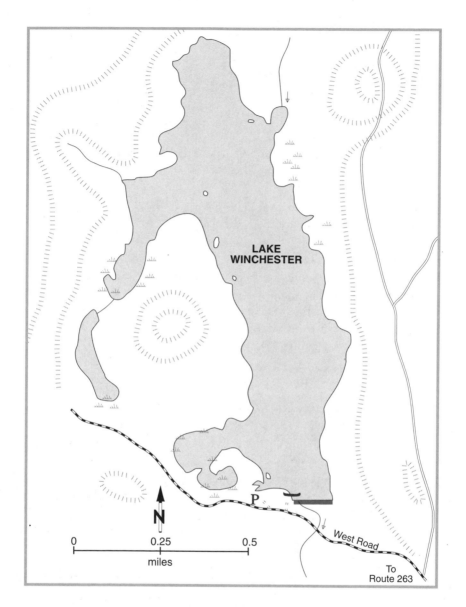

**LAKE
WINCHESTER**

N

| 0 | 0.25 | 0.5 |

miles

P

West Road

To
Route 263

Lake Winchester

lake's more hidden reaches. Look for red maple, beech, red oak, and
black and gray birches among the large pines and hemlocks along the
shore. As you paddle along, watch out for rocks lurking just below the
water's surface, along with old stumps from trees cut off at ice level
after the reservoir's formation.

96

Lake McDonough
Barkhamsted, CT

MAPS: Connecticut and Rhode Island Atlas, Map 51
　　USGS Quadrangle, New Hartford

AREA: 391 acres

CAMPING: American Legion State Forest, 860-379-2469;
　　Burr Pond State Park, 860-482-1817;
　　reservations: 877-668-2267 or www.ReserveAmerica.com

HABITAT TYPE: forested pond

EXPECT TO SEE: scenic, forested hillsides, shrubby shoreline

TAKE NOTE: development limited to park facilities; 10 MPH
　　speed limit; northwest arm off-limits to motors; $4 entrance
　　fee and $4 per boat in 2002

GETTING THERE

From Route 8 in Winsted, go east on Route 44 for 3.2 miles (3.2 miles), and turn left (east) onto Route 318. Go 3.0 miles (6.2 miles), and turn right (south) onto Route 219. Go 0.6 mile (6.8 miles) to the Lake McDonough Recreation Area on the right.

　　From I-91, Exit 40, go west on Route 20 for 12.7 miles (12.7 miles), and turn left (south) onto Route 219. Go 6.9 miles (19.6 miles) to the access on the right, 0.6 mile past the junction with Route 318.

Lake McDonough lies just to the south of enormous Barkhamsted Reservoir, which supplies drinking water to the Hartford area. The Hartford Metropolitan District maintains both reservoirs, though Lake McDonough does not supply drinking water. Even though you have to pay to get in and to launch a boat, anglers and recreational boaters flock to the waters of this beautiful place on sunny summer weekends. You can get a real workout here, paddling on open water along gorgeous forested hillsides.

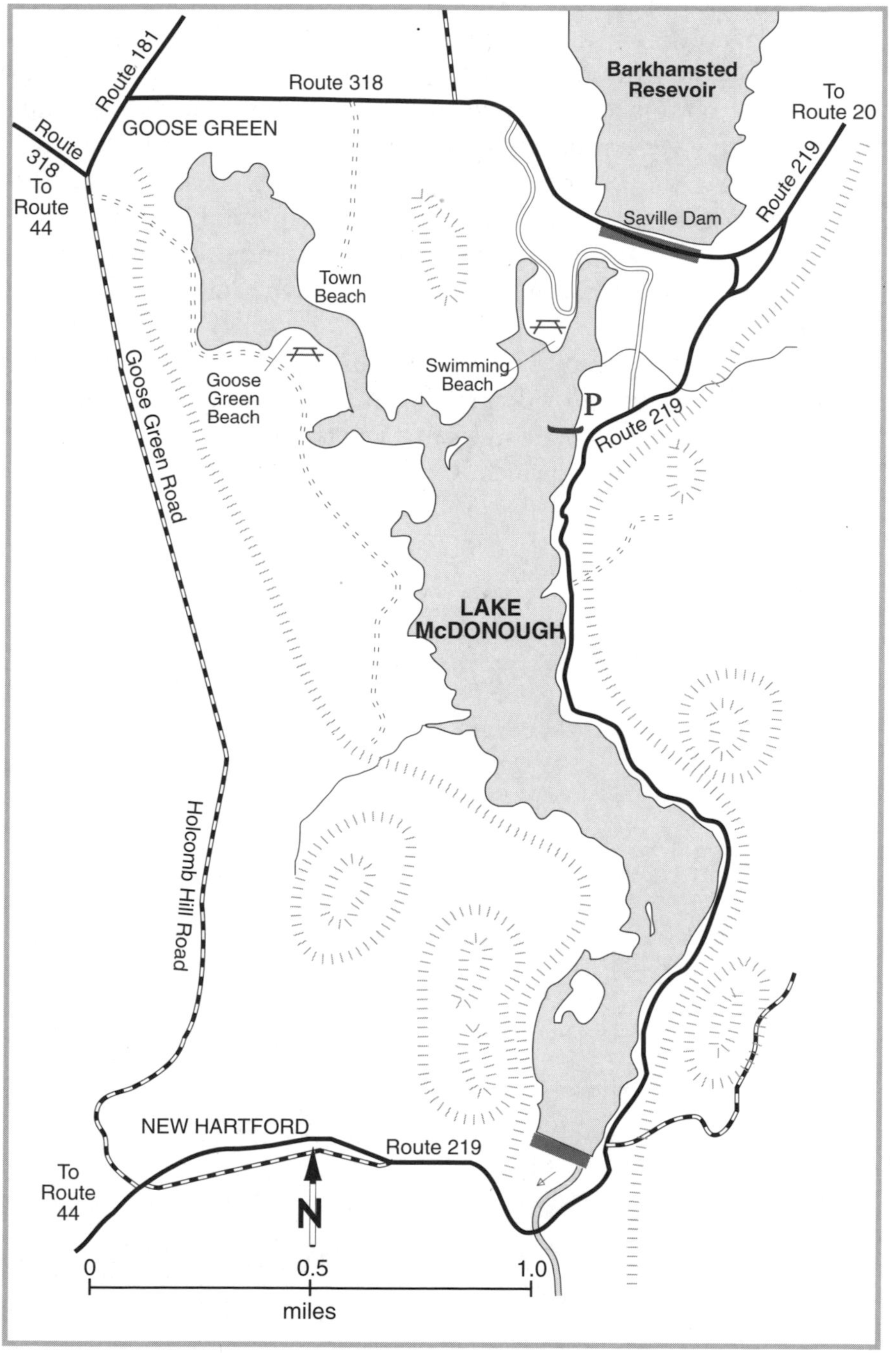
Route 181
Route 318
GOOSE GREEN
Route 318 To Route 44
Barkhamsted Resevoir
To Route 20
Route 219
Saville Dam
Town Beach
Swimming Beach
Goose Green Beach
Goose Green Road
P
Route 219
LAKE McDONOUGH
Holcomb Hill Road
NEW HARTFORD
Route 219
To Route 44
N
0
0.5
1.0
miles

Lake McDonough

Make sure to paddle the northwest arm, the nicest section because of a ban on motors and greater distance from Route 219, which extends along the lake's north–south axis. Grassy shores, clear water, and a generally sandy bottom characterize this section. Surprisingly, we could find no floating vegetation anywhere on the lake; the metropolitan district may lower the water level each fall, which would discourage vegetation from getting established. With so little natural vegetation, the lake seems somewhat sterile. We saw no turtles and only a few birds— including a family of Canada geese. The one beaver lodge appeared old and long abandoned.

The larger portion of the lake extending to the south sports a few attractive islands that provide great picnic spots. We found the west shore—with its many coves and small inlets—a lot more interesting than the east shore, along which Route 219 passes.

Burr Pond
Torrington, CT

MAPS: Connecticut and Rhode Island Atlas, Map 51
USGS Quadrangle, Torrington
AREA: 88 acres
CAMPING: American Legion State Forest, 860-379-2469;
Burr Pond State Park, 860-482-1817;
reservations: 877-668-2267 or www.ReserveAmerica.com
HABITAT TYPE: forested pond
EXPECT TO SEE: scenic forested hillsides, shrubby shoreline
TAKE NOTE: development limited to park facilities; motors
limited to 8 MPH; watch out for submerged boulders

GETTING THERE

From Route 8, Exit 46, go right (west) for 0.2 mile (0.2 mile) on Pinewoods
Road, and turn left (south) at the stoplight onto Winsted Road, following the
signs for Burr Pond State Park. Go 1.0 mile (1.2 miles), and turn right onto
Burr Mountain Road at the flashing yellow light. The entrance to Burr Pond
State Park is on the left in 0.5 mile (1.7 miles), and the access is on the left in
another 0.2 mile (1.9 miles).

Families come here to paddle, to hike or bike, or to enjoy the beach at
Burr Pond State Park. Paddling south along the eastern shore, you will
pass the park facilities, including picnic tables nestled in the woods, a
sandy swimming beach, restrooms, and a concession stand. Many boulders lurk just beneath the surface, waiting to add to their accumulated
layers of paint. Large slabs of rock extend out into the water in places,
providing sunny picnic or rest spots. A couple of very nice islands beg
to be explored. Except on sunny weekends, you should be able to get
away from most of the activity, especially early in the morning.

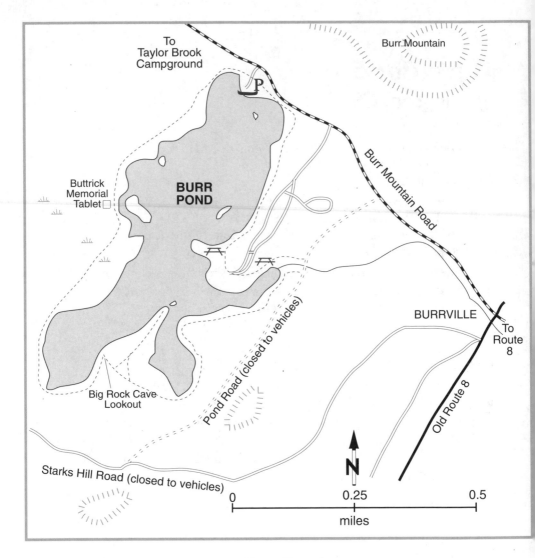

Burr Pond

Deciduous trees predominate—red and white oaks, beech, red maple, white, black, and gray birches, alder, and a few tulip trees—along with white pine and hemlock. During late July and August, laden blueberry bushes may seriously slow the paddling. At the extreme southern tip, the spreading root systems of waterlogged stumps remaining from the pond's creation almost 150 years ago provide protective cover for fish.

A beautiful trail extends around the pond, at the south end passing a lookout point at Big Rock Cave. On the west shore, near the large island that you can just barely squeeze a boat around, you may see the Buttrick Memorial Tablet. Philip Buttrick, secretary of Connecticut's Forest and Park Service from 1924 to 1929, helped to preserve this and two other unspoiled areas—immediately west and north—as state forest reserves, but he chose this point for the spreading of his ashes.

Near the pond's outlet, just outside the park, another plaque marks the location of the first condensed-milk factory, built a few years after Milo Burr constructed a dam across the confluence of several mountain streams to create Burr Pond. Gail Borden discovered the process of milk preservation by evaporation and here set up the first plant in 1857. In 1861 the company relocated to Wassaic, New York, to serve an expanding market, including Union troops at the outbreak of the Civil War. Fire destroyed the original plant in 1877.

Farmington River and Pequabuck River
Avon, Farmington, and Simsbury, CT

MAPS: Connecticut and Rhode Island Atlas, Map 43
USGS Quadrangles, Avon and New Britain

LENGTH: Farmington River, 11 miles;
Pequabuck River, 2 miles

CAMPING: American Legion State Forest, 860-379-2469;
Burr Pond State Park, 860-482-1817; Black Rock State Park,
860-677-1819; reservations: 877-668-2267 or
www.ReserveAmerica.com

HABITAT TYPE: slow-flowing, tree-lined river

EXPECT TO SEE: waterfowl, riverine birds, varied shrubs and trees

TAKE NOTE: little development; few motors because of shallow
water; watch out for poison ivy near the Farmington River
downstream parking area and boat launch; challenging paddling
on the Pequabuck

FARMINGTON RIVER
GETTING THERE

Downstream Access. From I-91, Exit 36, go west on Route 178 for 6.2 miles
(6.2 miles), and turn right onto Route 185. Go 2.5 miles (8.7 miles) to the
access on the right, at the stoplight just before the bridge. Note the huge
sycamore in the parking area.

Upstream Access. From the junction of Routes 4 and 10 in Farmington,
go west on Route 4. Immediately after crossing the bridge in 0.2 mile, turn
into the unmarked access on the left.

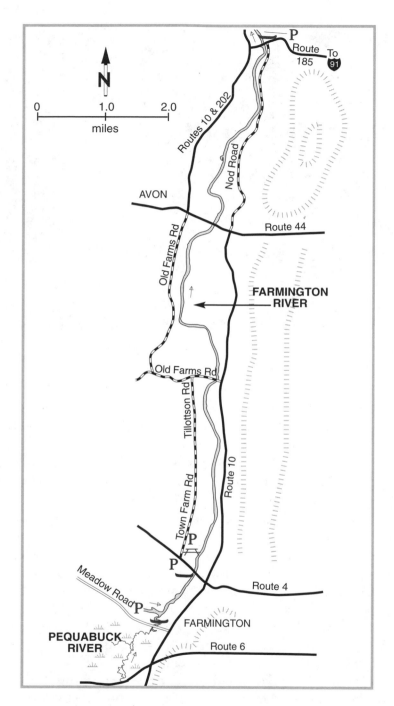

N

0   1.0   2.0
miles

Routes 10 & 202

Route 185

To 91

Nod Road

AVON

Route 44

Old Farms Rd

FARMINGTON RIVER

Old Farms Rd

Tillottson Rd

Town Farm Rd

Route 10

P
P

Route 4

Meadow Road

P

FARMINGTON

PEQUABUCK RIVER

Route 6

Farmington River and Pequabuck River

A red-breasted merganser prepares to dive for fish on the Farmington River.

We would save the Farmington River for those summer months when other rivers get too scratchy for enjoyable paddling. In the middle of a dry summer, our boats floated in plenty of water. Even at low water levels, however, the Farmington does flow along. Paddling here in spring or other times of high water would have to be a one-way trip.

On our way up the river from the Route 185 access, we encountered a few minor riffles; by staying near shore in faster water, we had no problem getting by. Because of the current, it took us half as much time to go upstream, compared with the same distance downstream. Along the way we met a few rowing crews and many groups of canoers. You may hear firearms from the Connecticut State Police Training Area about a mile upstream from the access, and you may see a golf cart or two cross over the river on a narrow bridge, but otherwise the Farmington River flows through surprisingly undeveloped land, given its close proximity to large population centers.

We watched a family of red-breasted mergansers dive for fish and saw black duck, kingfisher, spotted sandpiper, many treetop species, and a pair of red-tailed hawks soar overhead. We noticed substantial diversity of deciduous tree species, including silver maple, basswood, ash, hickory, red and white oaks, catalpa, elm, sycamore, and paper birch. Shiny leaves of lushly growing poison ivy appeared everywhere. Watch for poison ivy surrounding the boat launch and, indeed, around the entire parking area.

PEQUABUCK RIVER
GETTING THERE

From the junction of Routes 4 and 10 in Farmington, go south on Route 10 for 1.0 mile (1.0 mile), and turn right onto Meadow Road at the stoplight. Go 0.3 mile (1.3 miles) to the access on the right, just over the bridge.

The Pequabuck flows into the Farmington River just downstream from the access on Meadow Road. Paddling the Pequabuck upstream into the current as the river twists and turns through Shade Swamp can provide quite a challenge. We recommend paddling here in shorter boats. The insides of turns consist of shallow water over sand, so you have to make wide turns. In doing so, however, the onrushing current pushes your boat's front end into the bank that curves back toward you. Overhanging branches make paddling even more difficult. So why paddle here?

Because of the wildness within a stone's throw of metropolitan Connecticut, because of the swamp's beauty, because of the challenge, because of the opportunity to hone your paddling skills, or because of the lack of other paddlers. We loved paddling here for the nearly two hours it took to go up to Route 6 and back. We saw evidence of beaver activity and lots of painted turtles, along with cedar waxwing, goldfinch, yellow-rumped and yellow warblers, and several other species.

99

Bantam River, Bantam Lake, and Little Pond
Litchfield and Morris, CT

MAPS: Connecticut and Rhode Island Atlas, Map 41
USGS Quadrangle, Litchfield

AREA/LENGTH: Bantam Lake, 933 acres;
Bantam River, 2 miles

CAMPING: White Memorial Foundation (two campgrounds),
860-567-0857 or www.whitememorialcc.org; Black Rock
State Park, 860-677-1819; reservations: 877-668-2267 or
www.ReserveAmerica.com

HABITAT TYPE: large natural lake; meandering river,
shrubby marshlands

EXPECT TO SEE: osprey, mute swan, ducks, marsh birds, aquatic
vegetation, varied shrubs

TAKE NOTE: development and motors on lake; no development
or motors on river

GETTING THERE

From Litchfield, go west on Route 202. From the Constitution Way stoplight, continue for 1.4 miles (1.4 miles), and turn left onto Bissell Road. Go 0.7 mile (2.1 miles), veer right onto Whites Wood Road, and go 0.2 mile (2.3 miles) to the access on the right, just over the bridge.

At 933 acres—the largest natural body of water in Connecticut— Bantam Lake draws many motorboaters, especially on weekends. We much prefer the north end of the lake and the motor-free Bantam River inlet that flows through a marshland owned by the White Memorial Foundation. Though you will not paddle alone on Bantam River, especially on weekends, it offers one of the premier paddling destinations in western Connecticut.

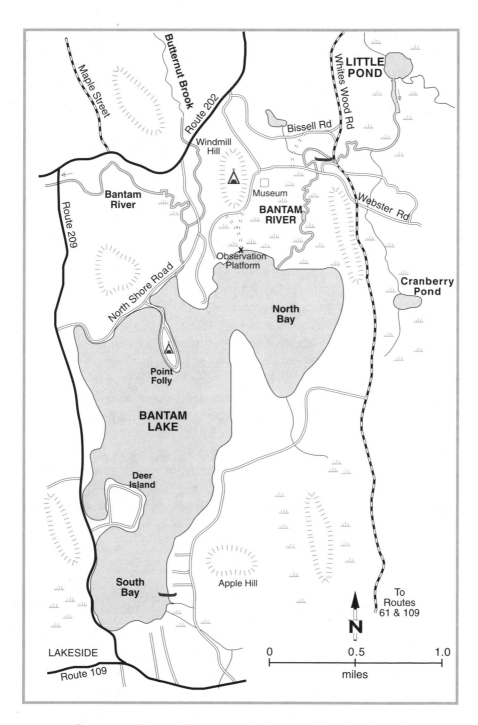

Bantam River, Bantam Lake, and Little Pond

The White Memorial Foundation, founded in 1913, protects one of southern New England's finest wildlife sanctuaries. The 4,000-acre tract includes upland hardwood forests, fields, marshlands, and open water. The foundation manages some land for forest production or wildlife habitat but leaves some untouched for research on natural succession. More than 35 miles of trails crisscross the area, including 1,700 feet of elevated boardwalk around Little Pond. The foundation stocks many natural history publications on the area.

On the winding Bantam River you can expect to see osprey, kingfisher, great blue heron, and many other bird species. Look for beaver near dusk; each time we paddled here, we had to portage over small beaver dams. We watched many basking painted turtles splash into the water as we cruised by. The barely noticeable current does not impede upstream paddling as this wonderful river passes through a sparse red maple swamp, the shores festooned with alder, willow, viburnum, dogwood, buttonbush, winterberry, cattail, bulrush, bur-reed, pickerelweed, and grasses galore.

Few places in Connecticut boast as much bird diversity as found here, with nearly 250 recorded species (115 nesting here). Highlights for us included an osprey perched in a dead tree over the river, feeding on a fish clutched in its talons, and a normally secretive swamp sparrow, with its bright rufous cap and prominent white throat patch, hopping around in plain view.

Paddling around to the right as you enter North Bay from the river, note the old concrete piers left over from a railroad spur used to cart away blocks of ice sawn from the frozen lake. Some of the piers now hold a bird observation platform. Farther down the lake, Point Folly houses a White Memorial Foundation campground, complete with another bird observation platform.

100

Squantz Pond
New Fairfield, CT

MAPS: Connecticut and Rhode Island Atlas, Map 31
USGS Quadrangle, New Milford

AREA: 288 acres

CAMPING: Kettletown State Park, 203-264-5169;
Macedonia Brook State Park, 860-927-3238;
reservations: 877-668-2267 or www.ReserveAmerica.com

INFORMATION: Squantz Pond State Park, 203-797-4165

HABITAT TYPE: deep lake, massive granite boulders

EXPECT TO SEE: Canada goose, wood duck, painted turtles,
scenic forested hillsides

TAKE NOTE: road and development on east side; motors allowed
(7.5 HP limit at state access)

GETTING THERE

From I-84, Exit 6, go north on Route 37 for 4.5 miles (4.5 miles), and turn right onto Route 39. Go northeast for 3.9 miles (8.4 miles) to Squantz Pond State Park on the left. After entering the park, access is on the right in 0.1 mile (8.5 miles).

Though Squantz Pond appears to be an extension of Candlewood Lake—Connecticut's largest at 5,420 acres, with 72 miles of shoreline—Route 39 separates the two. In fact, Squantz Pond already existed at the time of Candlewood Lake's creation in the 1930s. While to some, Squantz Pond will seem built up and crowded with motorboats, it does not hold a candle to Candlewood Lake's congestion. Other than the Charles E. Wheeler Wildlife Management Area in Milford, Squantz offers about the best paddling in southwestern Connecticut. Indeed, if you can avoid busy summer weekends and stick to the western shore—instead of the heavily developed eastern side with its Route 39 road noise—you can have a quite nice paddle here.

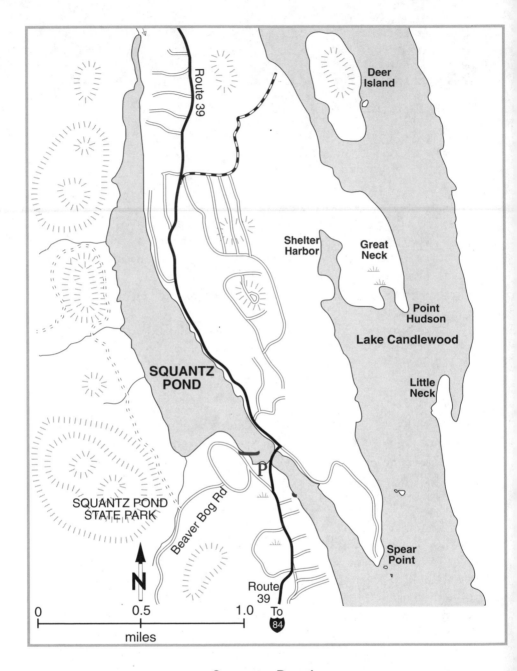

Route 39

Deer
Island

Shelter
Harbor

Great
Neck

Point
Hudson

Lake Candlewood

SQUANTZ
POND

Little
Neck

P

SQUANTZ POND
STATE PARK

Beaver Bog Rd

N

Route
39
To
84

0   0.5   1.0

miles

Spear
Point

Squantz Pond

Massive granite boulders line the undeveloped western shore. Hemlocks sweep down over the water, mountain laurel nestles amid the granite boulders—some covered with polypody fern—and tall oaks and hickories march up the slope, providing a deep, shady woodland. Pull out almost anywhere along here for a picnic lunch or to enjoy a walk in the woods—an informal, leaf-carpeted trail extends along most of the shoreline, rising above the steep rock faces. If you swim from the shore here, beware of the many hidden boulders lurking in the murky water that could cause serious injury to divers.

In contrast to the deep waters of most of the pond, the shallow northern tip harbors dozens of painted turtles and other marsh denizens in a small protected inlet. We also saw mallards and a handful of wood ducks amid some small patches of reeds and cattails. This very small pocket of marsh lies not very far from houses, docks, and motorboats. If you enjoy paddling marshy areas, see Bantam River, Bantam Lake, and Little Pond (Trip 99) and Housatonic River and the Charles E. Wheeler Wildlife Management Area (Trip 91), which teem with wildlife.

Alphabetical Listing of Lakes Ponds, Reservoirs, and Rivers

MASSACHUSETTS

RHODE ISLAND

CONNECTICUT

Leave No Trace

The Appalachian Mountain Club (AMC) is a national educational partner of Leave No Trace, Inc., a nonprofit organization dedicated to promoting and inspiring responsible outdoor recreation through education, research, and partnerships. The Leave No Trace program seeks to develop wildland ethics—ways in which you can act in the outdoors to minimize your impact on the areas you visit and to protect our natural resources for future enjoyment.

By practicing and passing along these seven principles, you can help protect the special places you love:

- Plan ahead and prepare
- Travel and camp on durable surfaces
- Dispose of waste properly
- Leave what you find
- Minimize campfire impacts
- Respect wildlife
- Be considerate of other visitors

If you would like to learn more about how you can help promote these simple principles, consider the Leave No Trace Master Educator Course. This five-day course is designed especially for outdoor professionals and land managers. The AMC has joined the National Outdoor Leadership School (NOLS) as the sole providers of the Leave No Trace Master Educator course through 2004. The AMC offers this course at locations throughout the Northeast.

For more information or to join Leave No Trace, please contact:

Leave No Trace, Inc.
P.O. Box 997
Boulder, CO 80306
800-332-4100
www.LNT.org

About the Author

ALEX WILSON is a writer in Brattleboro, Vermont. He is an avid canoeist and naturalist and has cowritten three other canoe guides with John Hayes: *AMC Quiet Water New Hampshire and Vermont, AMC Quiet Water Canoe Guide: Maine,* and *AMC Quiet Water Canoe Guide: New York.* He is the publisher of *Environmental Building News* and is a widely published freelance writer on energy, building technology, and environmental issues for such magazines as *Architecture, Progressive Architecture, Fine Homebuilding, Popular Science, Home,* and *Consumers Digest.*

JOHN HAYES is a former professor of biochemistry and environmental science at Marlboro College in Marlboro, Vermont. He has canoed and kayaked in Minnesota's Boundary Waters Canoe Area, in Georgia's Okefenokee Swamp, and in Florida's Everglades, as well as throughout the Northeast. When he is not in the classroom, he often leads natural history field trips to Central America, Africa, Borneo, the Southwest deserts, the Rockies, and the Everglades. He is coauthor with Alex Wilson of three other canoe guides for the Appalachian Mountain Club.

About the AMC

Since 1876, the Appalachian Mountain Club and its members have worked to promote the protection, enjoyment, and wise use of the mountains, rivers, and trails of the Northeast. We encourage people to enjoy and appreciate the natural world because we believe that successful conservation depends on this experience.

Join us!

Hiking, paddling, biking, skiing—from backyard nature walks to week-long wilderness explorations, the AMC offers activities for all kinds of outdoor adventurers. Join the AMC and connect with new people, learn new skills, and feel good knowing you're helping to protect the natural world you love. In addition to hundreds of activities offered every month through your local AMC chapter, you can also enjoy discounts on AMC workshops, lodging, and books.

Outdoor Adventures and Workshops

Develop your outdoor skills and knowledge through the AMC programs! From beginner backpacking and family canoeing to guided backcountry trips, you'll find something for any age or interest.

Lodging

AMC's huts, lodges, camps, and campsites—located throughout the Northeast—offer unique outdoor adventures. Perfect for every kind of mountain traveler.

Books and Maps

AMC's hiking, biking, and paddling guides lead you to the most spectacular destinations in the Northeast. We're also your definitive source for how-to guides, trail maps, and adventure tales.

For more information about the Appalachian Mountain Club, call 617-523-0636 or visit us online at www.outdoors.org.

Appalachian Mountain Club
5 Joy Street
Boston, MA 02108
www.outdoors.org